Dreams Are Unfinished Thoughts

by Brian Paone

Editor: Dan Ezra Golden
Copy Editor: Denise Barker
Proofreaders: Katrina KinCannon & Teresa Evans
Artwork: Jeff Cavanaugh
Photographer: Cameron Kline

All lyrics used with permission
Published by Scout Media
Copyright 2014
ISBN: 9780991309122

Written:
January 29, 2006 – October 12, 2007
(Lynn, MA / St. Marys, GA / Kingsland, GA)

Second Edition Edited & Revised:
February 2013 – August 2014
(Yokosuka, Japan)

For more information on my music and books:
www.BrianPaone.com

For more information on God Lives Underwater & David Reilly:
www.DavidReillyGLU.com

MANTIS ONE

*"What do you think you mean to me? /
How important you must seem."*
God Lives Underwater: "Waste of Time" - GLU

The year that I got married was the first year since 1995 that I would be without one of my best friends, David Fitzgerald Reilly. My emotions were pulled back and forth, right and left, as I realized that David wouldn't be at my wedding. David always had a talent for making our friendship so trying, tribulating, and rewarding all at the same time.

June 21, 1995, was probably the date when our story started, even though I didn't meet David until the next night on June 22. It's funny how almost every major life-changing moment never really just happens; it develops. I often try to trace why and how David and I met in the first place. To bring it to the absolute moment that would allow me to know that he even existed.

I have to take it all the way back to the third concert I ever attended. Lollapalooza '92 at Great Woods in Mansfield, Massachusetts, with my high school friend Bill. He eventually became very fundamental in shaping the music I listened to in my mid-to-late teens.

When I entered Bishop Fenwick High School in Peabody, Massachusetts, back in 1990, I was listening to what would be considered classic rock: Pink Floyd, Electric Light Orchestra, Genesis, The Who, Queen, Yes, Rush, Jethro Tull, The Monkees, Private Lightning, Cat Stevens, and Neil Diamond.

My first concert ever was Yes in the summer of 1989. They were touring on the *Anderson Bruford Wakeman Howe* album. My second concert was Jethro Tull in the fall of 1989. They were touring on the *Rock Island* album.

By the time 1992 had rolled around, I had also gotten into a diversity of modern artists like REM, Depeche Mode, Jesus Jones, EMF, Big Audio Dynamite, Tesla, Midnight Oil, INXS, Ned's Atomic Dustbin, Edie Brickell & New Bohemians, Duran Duran, Public Enemy, Digital Underground, 3rd Bass, Faith No More, Nirvana, Live, and Guns N' Roses.

Even though I somehow completely skipped over the 1980s' hair band movement, my guilty pleasure had quickly included some of those producer-based bands, such as The KLF, Enigma, C+C Music Factory, Snap, Blackbox, Shakespeare's Sister, Pete Bardens, and Milli Vanilli.

Bill talked me into going to Lollapalooza with him, since he had no one to go with. The festival had Pearl Jam touring on the *Ten* album, Red Hot Chili Peppers touring on the *Blood Sugar Sex Magik* album, and Soundgarden touring on the *Badmotorfinger* album. All on the same bill. Even if I had just gotten into those particular bands, I had to go.

That was the tour where a certain band called Ministry was also coheadlining. I had actually never heard of Ministry. Honestly, I just wanted to get through their set to hear the

Red Hot Chili Peppers.

As I sat in the first row of Section 8 next to Bill at Great Woods, I was ultimately led down the path of who I am now. Ministry came out and opened with "N.W.O." from *Psalm 69*. It was like a whole new undiscovered world had opened up in front of me.

Prior to that moment, I had no idea what industrial music really was. It was angry. It was raw. It was militant. It was pounding but still empathetic. And it didn't care if you listened or not, because it was going to be loud! I had never felt a merger of such a human emotion with such a mechanical sound before. I bought *Psalm 69* the very next day. I haven't looked back since.

During my junior year of high school, my eyes opened even further to a larger world of industrial music. As I approached my high school friend Jim during lunch break one day, he had his headphones on. I asked him what he was listening to.

"A band called Nine Inch Nails," he answered. "Their new album came out this week."

I had heard of Nine Inch Nails, but I had never actually heard them. He didn't even ask me if I wanted to hear their music. He ordered me to.

"You need to listen to this song," he said.

I put on the headphones, and he pressed Play. My introduction into a more commercial industrial genre began with the opening drums to the song "Wish" off the album *Broken*. I listened to that three-and-a-half minute song and realized it was exactly what I had been looking for emotionally in music.

That Friday night I went and bought *Broken*. I also picked up Nine Inch Nails' first album, *Pretty Hate Machine*. I spent the rest of that weekend dissecting them, note by note, lyric by lyric.

Through my obsession with Ministry and Nine Inch Nails I then discovered, with much love, Front 242. Jim and I went to see Front 242 in Rhode Island in 1993. They were touring on the *06:21:03:11 Up Evil* album.

I had finally found my niche in music. I wanted to know, own, and memorize every industrial band out there.

One day during the summer before my senior year, the local radio station played a song by a brand-new band called Stabbing Westward. Upon hearing that song, I realized that industrial and rock could live together.

I had been completely bitten by the bug. I needed to become an industrial-music-elitist, also known as a Rivethead. Any musical suggestions anyone gave me or if a review of a band even remotely mentioned the word *industrial* somehow, I bought the album. As a rabid fan of the genre, I couldn't get enough.

At the time I was in a thrash metal band called Vertical Smile. We had only played one show. We also had only written two songs. I quit Vertical Smile to start my own industrial band.

I had a few friends in high school who had become Rivetheads like me, who also had the motivation to be in an industrial project. My first real band, called Yellow #1, was born. Yellow #1 only made me hungrier for anything under the industrial umbrella that I could get my hands on.

The afternoon of June 21, 1995, was already warm enough in Massachusetts for swimming. My high school friend Dave, also a member of my band Yellow #1, asked his dad to open the pool.

Dave was infamously otherwise known as Dogboy, because

of a particular hairstyle that he wore to high school one day. It resembled the character Dogboy from the MTV show *Liquid Television*.

For these outdoor summer events, often we brought out one of those small boom boxes. We would listen to 104.1 WBCN while we took turns beating each other in the pool with pool noodles.

On that particular day the WBCN deejays were between songs and had mentioned a contest for 104 people to see two bands—Maids of Gravity and God Lives Underwater—the very next night at the Paradise club in Boston.

Oddly enough I was a subscriber to a new monthly magazine at the time, called *huH*. It focused primarily on new and upcoming alternative bands. Unfortunately, it didn't run for too long. They had just featured a two-page story on God Lives Underwater that included a full-page photo of the band.

With each edition the magazine came with a free sampler disc of new bands. God Lives Underwater wasn't on the sampler, but Maids of Gravity were. I really liked their song "Only Dreaming." I was also very interested in God Lives Underwater, due to the write-up they had received in the magazine. The article had compared them to Nine Inch Nails and Stabbing Westward.

I don't remember exactly if Dogboy's portable phone was already outside. Maybe he had to run inside and get it. Nevertheless one of us said to the other, "We should call. I'm not doing anything tomorrow night. Are you?" And the other replied, "No."

This was a win-only show. Tickets couldn't be purchased. WBCN was giving away a pair every thirty minutes until they had reached their quota of 104–the station's frequency was 104.1.

I know it was me who called the station. I don't think we were the exact caller on our first try. But eventually I made the correct call.

"Yes!" the deejay exclaimed. "You are the sixth caller! You just won two tickets to tomorrow night's show!"

What should I have done after just winning two tickets to see a band that I had put in the back of my mind to check out, based purely on a review in a magazine? I had to leave immediately, find my nearest music store, and buy the debut album!

We had to go to Soundwaves in Danvers to find the God Lives Underwater album *GLU*. That store has long since gone out of business, thanks to Newbury Comics and Best Buy. At the time, however, it was owned and operated by the drummer of the 1970s megaband Boston.

They only had one copy of *GLU*. Dogboy suggested that I buy it instead of him, since I had been the one who called and won the tickets. I wasn't going to disagree with that! I put down my eight dollars, and we went back to his house.

While we returned to our pool-shenanigans, we put *GLU* into the boom box. That was the first time I had ever heard David's voice.

Over the next twenty-four hours, up until we left for the show, I must have listened to that album at least ten times. I embedded the *GLU* album into my head so well that I felt confident I could sing along to every word on every song.

I was determined to get there early. I even studied their photo from the *huH* article, so I would recognize them, in case we accidentally bumped into any of them before the show.

Dogboy and I got there maybe a little too early. We were the first ones in line outside the venue's front doors on Commonwealth Avenue in Boston. We sat with our backs to the bricks on the sidewalk. We listened to the low-end thumping of a soundcheck that came from inside. The volume was still too low to distinguish which band it came from. We looked out over the congested street. The buildings were so close together that they almost touched each other.

The infamous MBTA Green Line sliced down the middle of the street. The train bumped along its tracks in the middle of the traffic. It filled the air with the high-pitched screech of its brakes at every stop.

After some time waiting, the front door finally opened. The members of God Lives Underwater came out: David Reilly, Jeff Turzo, Andrew McGee, Adam Kary, and their roadie/guitar tech, Tim Turzo.

Despite my diligent studying of the photo from the *huH* article, the only reason I recognized them, and in particular David, was because of his nose ring. David's nose ring looked like a stereotypical silver ring that a cartoon bull would wear in its nose. That ring gave David the illusion that he was the front man. He was the leader, the important one.

"I think that's God Lives Underwater. That guy is David Reilly, the singer," I said to Dogboy.

"If you think it is, go say something," Dogboy replied.

Even if that was David, his hair had grown considerably since the picture from the article. There we were with the guy who was so obviously the lead singer of God Lives Underwater, but I completely doubted myself. I realized that I was basing everything off a picture in a magazine.

As the man began to walk away down Commonwealth

Avenue, I thought, *That's obviously him. He's walking away. Are you going to miss the only chance that you might have all night to say hello, because you're too afraid to make a fool of yourself to a stranger?*

I had to get over any illusion that I would be like a lost puppy meeting a wise and elder wolf. I moved off the wall. I did a fast trot to catch up with the band. I opened my mouth and asked, "Excuse me. Are you David from God Lives Underwater?"

He looked at me.

It may have taken him only a second to reply, but it was almost a second too long. It made me want to apologize. I almost wanted to go back to the wall.

"Yes, I am," he finally answered.

I felt like I needed to justify bothering him. "We are here for the show tonight. Absolutely love your album." *Blah, blah, blah.*

I would have a better time remembering what I ate for lunch every day of the second grade than to remember what else I said at that moment. What I do recall was that he told me that they were going to get something to eat. The guys in Maids of Gravity were in the poster store across the street, if we wanted to say hi to them too.

I said something short of a thank-you and *can't wait for the show.*

They walked away.

What struck me at that particular moment was his demeanor when he spoke. I was surprised at how soft-spoken he was. It might have been the way his lips formed the words around his teeth. I noticed, almost immediately, how thin his top lip was. It caused his front teeth to show more than normal when he spoke. It also gave the slight illusion that he had buckteeth. The bull ring that hung down from his nose almost rested right on his thin top lip. That probably didn't help the illusion either.

His speaking voice was a little higher than his singing voice. It was almost nasal with a subtle lisp. It had a hidden charm. It was very non-threatening. His tone of voice practically matched his posture and body size. David was average height, yet lanky, with a very small frame. He had an authoritative presence, but he also gave the impression of being meek and frail.

I walked back to Dogboy, who had never moved off the brick wall of the club. I told him that Maids of Gravity were in the poster store across the street. We decided to stop looking like two teenagers at a Michael Jackson concert. We moved away from the line that only consisted of us and went to the poster store.

Sure enough Ed Ruscha of Maids of Gravity was inside. We spent some time speaking with him. We commented on all the old movie posters together. After that we went back to claim our spot in front of the club. We were still the only two people in line.

After another long and uneventful period of waiting, the God Lives Underwater guys returned to the club. Three of them, and the roadie Tim, went inside, but David came to us. He told me that God Lives Underwater had a new album coming out in September called *Empty*. They were going to perform a handful of those new songs to fill up the headlining slot time.

I told David that my favorite song off *GLU* was "Nothing." David said that I wasn't being fair to the other songs on the album. Just when I thought he was being serious, he told me that his favorite song was "Lonely Again." I remember this remained his favorite song until their third album.

I was wearing a *Rocky Horror Picture Show* baseball hat, and David inquired about it. He asked if I had liked the play. I told him that I was an avid attendee of the show in Harvard Square.

From that moment on he called me Rocky, or sometimes just Rock, because of my hat. He told me that he was terrible at remembering names. It would help him remember who I was.

I noticed how the sun shone off the rings on David's fingers. It seemed that every finger on both hands was decorated with some sort of silver ring, all different in sizes and designs. I always thought that this added to the mechanical illusion of the band's sound.

David then proceeded to ask us if we wanted to go inside the club with him, so we wouldn't have to keep waiting outside.

I was so startled by his offer that I almost didn't know what to say.

David turned to the security guard who was working the door. "They're with me."

The doorman gave him a nod of understanding as we went inside.

We were welcomed by a long and skinny hallway. At first it felt like we had entered the Bat Cave. We passed the coat check and the merchandise counter. Although the hallway was dimly lit, it was brightly covered in old posters of bands that had played here before.

Just when we thought that the hallway wasn't going to end

or that there wasn't a club at all, the hallway grew even darker and smaller. As we turned the corner, the hallway opened up into a large room. I didn't want to lose David, but I also wanted to look around.

The stage was enormous. It was only about two feet off the ground and had no barriers. I couldn't miss the big white pole in the middle of the floor. It was directly in front of the stage. That pole was so large, nobody could get their arms around it. If that wasn't enough, it was in the most undesirable place right in front of where the singer would most likely be. There was only enough room for maybe five rows of fans. Beyond that point, there was a possibility that the view of the stage would be obstructed.

The Paradise had a very open feel. There was a balcony that went all the way around the club. There were booths on platforms for people who wanted to sit at a table. David took us backstage, past the booths, and into the dressing room.

We were able to stay with the guys in God Lives Underwater and Maids of Gravity until it was time for Maids of Gravity's set, hours after we had been brought backstage to hang out.

Dogboy and I stayed to the side of the stage while Maids of Gravity played. They were touring to promote their self-titled debut album. Since the club held at least six hundred, it seemed very empty with only 104 people attending the show.

God Lives Underwater were onstage next. It felt so comfortable for me to see them there. I already felt like I knew all of them. They weren't just the-band-we-came-to-see anymore.

Dogboy and I pushed our way right up front. We were almost directly underneath David's microphone stand. I made sure I sang along to every song they played off *GLU*. I listened intently to the new songs off *Empty*.

If I remember correctly, they only played "Fool," "All Wrong," "23," and "Empty" from the upcoming album. They also played every single song off *GLU* except "Drag Me Down." I later found out that "Drag Me Down" was never played live, due to the click track being too fast.

During "Waste of Time," David lowered the microphone just enough so my voice was actually picked up in the speakers during the chorus. I had to push my body halfway on the stage to get my mouth closer to the microphone.

During the second chorus, a bouncer didn't know what I was doing. He didn't understand that David was letting me sing along with him. The bouncer ran over and pushed me so hard off the stage that my head hit the big pole. *The Crow* T-shirt that I was wearing got ripped by the force of his push as his fingers let go of my neck. I'll never forget that moment.

David had a very unique stage presence for their type of music. Industrial rock generally commanded a sense of anger and chaos, but David stood still between the dual keyboards that he and Jeff played. A guitar dangled around his neck. A microphone eagerly waited to be sung into. It was amazing how much the whole band emanated energy in such subtle movements.

It wouldn't be until later that I would realize that his stage presence reflected his personality. It was always intense, yet always subtle.

His blonde hair was in twisty, but not dirty, dreads. Both hands gripped the microphone when he sang. His silver rings overshadowed the pattern he strummed on the guitar strings.

He would look at the ground when there were no vocals and shake his head to the beat.

David rarely moved side to side onstage. He just didn't need to. It was his command presence, along with his black praying mantis tattoo that engulfed his entire right forearm, that let everyone know exactly who he was.

As God Lives Underwater ended their set, David motioned for us to meet him by the side door. Dogboy and I made our way through the emptying crowd, and I knocked.

"C'mon!" David said as he opened the door.

Dogboy and I were brought backstage again. The bands had a load-out time of 1:00 a.m. to leave for the next show. We had about two hours to spend with them backstage.

The back room of the Paradise was filled with couches and chairs. The members from Maids of Gravity were also there. A case of beer had been brought in.

When David offered both Dogboy and I a drink, I told him that I didn't drink. Then I realized that Dogboy and I were the only two people that were invited backstage.

Where were the girls? I wondered. *The groupies? The stripper pole in the middle of the room?*

Okay, maybe I had never expected a stripper pole. But as an eighteen-year-old, and it was my first time backstage, my knowledge only came from what I had seen in Mötley Crüe documentaries. This was completely different. It was just me, Dogboy, and all of the band members from both bands.

At first David was shocked that I didn't drink. He didn't necessarily grill me about it, but he simply wanted to know why. I told him that I never had the urge to. I didn't care if other people did. It just wasn't something that I was interested in.

There were a few solid moments, at this point, where all I wanted to do was impress him. This was David Reilly, the man who had opened the door for me to hang out with him. He didn't need to do any of that. He could have sent us on our way. He could have traded us in for strippers! I wanted to meet him at his level. I wanted to be able to even catch a glimpse of his coolness.

I waited for the shoe to drop. I waited for him to realize that there was no reason, nor any fun, in hanging out with us anymore. He was the one who needed to be impressed and entertained, not me.

Probably because I had just turned down a free beer, he seemed intrigued about what my limits were.

"Do you smoke dope?"

Thoughts flashed through my head. If I said no, he would deem me totally uncool. The bouncers would be called to take us away. I *really* would never be able to see the strippers then.

Since David had been so hospitable to us, my immediate reaction was to just be honest. "No."

He didn't grill me any further on that answer thankfully. I could tell that he was still a little surprised. I proceeded to tell him that I had never even had a cigarette before. I realized I looked completely uncool to everyone in God Lives Underwater and Maids of Gravity. Even Dogboy shook his head. He mentally waved with his eyes, NO, NO, NO! Nonetheless everyone seemed to respect my answer. Even David looked right at me and told me how much he respected my choices, as well as not being afraid to stand firm with them.

Dogboy and I sat on a couch that was on the right side of the room. David sat next to us in a chair. The guys from Maids of Gravity left the room to either go get food or drinks or to figure out where the heck those strippers were. Jeff, Adam, and Drew were either back in the club schmoozing it up with the radio people or out getting food themselves.

The door to the backstage area closed. David was left alone with just us. I was shocked that the singer of the headlining band would rather hang out with two eighteen-year-old kids than get food.

David and I always had a very different relationship than everyone else, and I think it had started at this very moment. David took the initiative to blur the lines between some fan who had showed up at his band's show and had harassed him outside to something more personal. A friendship that would last a lifetime.

The significance of that moment still didn't stifle the feeling that he had the upper hand. He could kick us out at any time. I wanted so much to prove myself to him. There was no real reason why he should even have kept our company. I held in my breath, which exhausted me. It would be a while before I could finally let it out.

"I have a story about why you should never be a junkie," David softly said, innocently, with a twinge of sadness.

I paused for a moment. I forgot where I was. I forgot that, just a few hours earlier, I had just met him. I forgot that I was backstage at a club. I had gotten lost in his world. I sat next to a man who I didn't know much about, other than his name and a handful of lyrics.

When he spoke again, none of that mattered. All of that went away. David always had a very high wall of privacy. Maybe it was because I didn't even accept a beer from him that he dropped that wall to a complete stranger.

"Almost everyone I have met has believed that all my songs

are about girls or relationships," David began. "If you really listen to the lyrics on both *GLU* and the upcoming album, they're about heroin."

I didn't even know what heroin looked like. I had never seen it in my life. I gave him my best poker face so he would keep talking.

"Take 'No More Love.' That song is very specifically about my ex-girlfriend Heather. It's based on a fight about drug use that we had in her kitchen. *I can feel your heavy stare. / I run my fingers through my hair.* Those lyrics are very specific. During the fight, all I could do was play with my dreads."

As straight-faced as I could keep my expression, I nodded like I knew what he was talking about. I was intrigued about the rest of the story. I also didn't want him to think that I had no comprehension of what he was saying.

"Heather was a junkie. We started using together. After a while she got clean, but I couldn't. She told me that she would leave me if I didn't get clean too. She wound up leaving me, and I realized I had to get clean. We kept in touch, but nothing serious. She recently met a new guy. They're engaged. The twist here is that this new guy is a junkie too. She started to use again because of him. Here I am, clean because she left me for being an addict. There she is, with someone new who got her using again. That's pretty much what the new album is about."

At that moment I felt, at least from a human perspective, that I had "big brother" emotions. Not just in response to his story, but in response to David as a person as well. I didn't know how to respond or even act. I could sympathize with the betrayal he felt, but I couldn't empathize.

I would later realize that it wasn't sympathy David was

looking for. He was just looking for someone who he could tell his situation to. Someone who didn't know any of the parties involved. Someone who could see it from an outside angle.

The majority of his band's emotional lyrics were actually based on those few sentences that he had just told me. At the time I never thought about it. Now I realize how significant it had been that David had opened up so much to me right from the beginning.

As it got even later, we discussed more surface stuff, like movies and bands. At about one o'clock, the bouncer finally told David that the gear had to be loaded soon. All of their equipment still remained onstage.

It was very surreal and quiet in the club when the other band members returned. Dogboy and I helped Adam carry out all of his drums. We loaded them into their white van parked in the alley.

David gave me his email address, and I told him that I would contact him soon. I promised to be at every show, every time they came. He told me that it didn't look like they would be touring again, at least not to Boston, until after September when *Empty* would be released.

Before they left, David said something to me along the lines of "You seemed to be the only person here tonight who really cared about the band. If we don't get in touch with each other before the next show, I'll make sure your name will be on the guest list."

Adam came back and gave each of us a cassette sampler of three God Lives Underwater songs for helping him load his drums. It included two songs that were going to be on *Empty*: "All Wrong" and "Fool," and also "Nothing" from *GLU*. The tape was in a blue cardboard sleeve that had the mantis logo on the front and just the three song titles on the back.

I ripped off the Paradise wall a poster of the band, which was advertising the *GLU* album. All of the band members, except for Drew who wasn't around, signed it. David signed it, *Thank You.*

"See ya later, Rock," he said.

Although I had to wait four months to see David again, it would only be another three months before the new album came out.

MANTIS TWO

"What does the next life bring? / I just want to feel okay."
God Lives Underwater: "23" - Empty

Dogboy and I listened to that three-song sampler in our cars over and over for the next three months straight. We got to know "Fool" and "All Wrong" even better than we knew our own Yellow #1 songs.

I remember one particular time when Dogboy and I were in his car at a red light in Danvers Square. As we listened to the three-song cassette, we had a riveting conversation about how "All Wrong" and "Fool" just sounded like how God Lives Underwater was meant to sound.

God Lives Underwater had successfully introduced their fans to their signature sound on their very first album, *GLU*. These new songs were exactly in the same vein and style that the band had since perfected. We decided that God Lives Underwater definitely had their own unique atmosphere that was a direct result of their keyboard and synthesizer lines in their music.

The second God Lives Underwater album, *Empty*, was released on September 12, 1995, and I bought it the day it came out. I rushed home and immediately put on my headphones. I opened up the lyrics book and pressed Play. I was ready to read along with the album.

"All Wrong" and "Fool" were the second and third songs on the album. I had already listened to those songs for three months nonstop on the cassette sampler that Adam had given me. This didn't make the opening of the album all that exciting for me. Except, of course, for the first track on the album, "Still." Even so I had the lyrics in front of me, and they were different than what I had thought David had sung on the sampler.

As I read along with the song "Still," I noticed that some lyrics printed in the insert were inconsistent with the actual song on the album itself. These were lyrics that had been printed in the booklet, but were never sung by David at all.

I made a mental note to ask him about these lyrical discrepancies the next time we got to hang out. I was certain that there was going to be a next time.

My friend Matt and I were discussing our opinions about *Empty* as we stood in line for a David Bowie and Nine Inch Nails show at Great Woods. David Bowie was touring on the *Outside* album. Nine Inch Nails were still promoting *The Downward Spiral* album. It was a very special coheadlining show. That was also the week *Empty* came out. Matt told me that he thought it needed to grow on him. He didn't warm up to it as quickly as he did with the first album, *GLU*.

I took this personally, like he had told me that he didn't like something I had written myself. Maybe it was the fact that I could understand where so many of the album's emotions came from. I felt like I had known David much longer than just that one night. I knew about his problems with his ex-girlfriend Heather. She had become more than a name. She had provoked emotions in me that I didn't even deserve to have.

David and Jeff had been interviewed on MTV by veejay Kennedy the same week that *Empty* was released. One question that she had asked really stuck out. It was answered in a great way to exemplify their sound. Dogboy and I had been trying to come up a way to describe how God Lives Underwater sounded to other people who had never heard them. And here it was

> *MTV (Kennedy):* As David and Jeff tell us, they feel their songs are traditional rock songs. They like to use the latest technology, but they're not a techno band!
>
> *Jeff:* I think that the only reason people would perceive us as techno is because we spend time programming. We try and be creative with the way our record sounds, but that doesn't necessarily mean that it's techno. We just happen to get into our gear as much as people who make techno do.
>
> *David:* But if you were to take out the guitars and vocals, it would sound like techno sometimes. But that's why we're not a techno band, because we like guitars and vocals.

I had digested *Empty* for almost a month when my weekly copy of the *Boston Phoenix*, a local newspaper, featured an ad for a God Lives Underwater, KMFDM, and Life of Agony show at the Avalon on October 17, 1995. KMFDM was touring on the *Nihil* album. Life of Agony was touring on the *Ugly* album.

My immediate reaction was to take the show personally. Who did these people think they were to advertise my friend's show without my permission? My next reaction was more subtle. I needed to go!

Of course I also doubted that David even remembered me. Our night at the Paradise had been embedded in my head so strongly that I was afraid that I viewed David completely differently than how he saw me. Could he really remember me? It was unlikely that he would.

That was where a lot of my nervousness came from. David was still on a pedestal in my head. What if I faded into just another fan? I had already put so much emotional weight into our friendship that I thought we were above that status. What if my perception was much bigger than the truth?

I decided that it would be best if I went to the God Lives Underwater show as early as I could, hoping to grab anyone in the band, even if it was just their roadie, Tim.

At the night of the Paradise show, I had confused Tim with Jeff because they both had dreads. Although I didn't know it then, Tim and Jeff were actually brothers.

Dogboy was attending Westfield State College in Westfield, Massachusetts, which was ninety-five miles away. He couldn't come back for the show. So I took Dann, who was another friend and also a member of my band, Yellow #1. He was a big KMFDM fan. This show was going to be perfect for him too.

We showed up on Lansdowne Street with plenty of time to spare. It was at least two hours before doors even opened at Avalon.

Lansdowne Street was like another universe. Although it was a short street, about one-fourth of a mile long, only clubs were along it. Each venue touched the next. If you were to look down from the sky, it would look like one long roof. What made the street really unique was the fact that it was tucked underneath the bleachers of Fenway Park. It also made going to a concert on a Red Sox game night almost unbearable at times.

We stood outside the door where the bands loaded and unloaded their gear. We hoped that anyone from God Lives Underwater would pass through. I was nervous and anxious about seeing the guys again. I kept looking up and down the street. I never took my full attention off the closed door.

Tim came through the door first. My heart jumped. I almost felt like Tim was my personal messenger for the band. He must have been sent out to specifically see if I would be out here, to hold me to my word of always being there for David.

I had purposely worn my *Rocky Horror Picture Show* baseball hat again, just in case the band had completely forgot who I was and needed a reference.

"Tim!" I yelled.

He recognized me. I was a welcomed sight! "Are any of the guys inside?" I asked.

"Yeah. I'll tell them you're here," he replied.

I felt like I had won a golden ticket from Willy Wonka. The guys in the band definitely saw me as more than a fan. I was their Boston supporter. More important, I was their friend.

It was October, so there was a brisk chill to the air. It took some time for someone to come out after Tim had disappeared into Avalon. The door opened again, and David was there. He wore sunglasses, even though the sun was setting. He also had a chain wallet attached to his waist. He wore cut-off shorts and long johns.

I was so nervous as he walked down the steps toward me. He was coming to me on his own accord. He actually wanted to talk to me. I realized that wearing my *Rocky Horror Picture Show* baseball hat was just a paranoid overreaction. It was obvious to me then that it wasn't necessary for him to see the cap to remember who I was.

He had a very specific way of greeting me and saying, "*Hey, man.*" It was more like, "Hey, me-han." His accent could change a one-syllable word into two.

"How do you know Rocky?" David asked Dann as I introduced him.

Dann replied that we were in high school together and in Yellow #1.

As we stood on the sidewalk outside the club, several emotions flashed inside me all at the same time. I was with a man who I greatly admired, and I owned both of his albums. I couldn't help but wonder how much more than an acquaintance I really was to him. He seemed genuinely happy to see me; there was no doubt about that.

Of course I had to tell him what I thought of *Empty*. I said that I thought "Weaken" was their strongest song, even though it wasn't my favorite. I told him that my favorite was actually "We Were Wrong."

He looked at me and nodded. I realized that I didn't always need to tell him how I felt about his music. Over time it tended to be the least significant part of our conversations.

"I have a question about the song '23,'" I said. "It's in a

pretty weird time signature, isn't it? It sounds like it's in five-four."

Since I had written songs for Yellow #1 on a drum machine, I felt that I had a pretty good grasp on identifying tempos and time signatures. I also wanted to feel like I could talk about the technical aspects of David's songs with him. The truth was, I was bullshitting my way through a topic I knew very little about.

He looked at me blankly. "No. I don't think so." David hummed the song and clapped his hands.

Somehow my comment had made him doubt himself. If he only knew that I really didn't know what I was talking about. However, it felt good that he entertained the idea that maybe I was right.

"Nope. It's definitely in four-four. The song 'Empty' is in five-four. Maybe that's what you were thinking. Adam has a tough time playing 'Empty' live, because of the odd timing. Sometimes he just plays it in four-four instead, so we have to remove the last guitar lick to compensate in order to stay in time with him!"

"Yeah, maybe that's it." I said.

I was too embarrassed to admit that I wasn't thinking of "Empty." I changed the subject as fast as I could. I asked him if he had eaten. He said the club had provided some food, but he would rather get something real to eat. I asked him if he wanted to go down the street. Maybe for some pizza.

I realized then that what I had just suggested was a very important question. On one hand, David might decline. Maybe he really wasn't that interested in hanging out with me except for in a club setting. Maybe that would confirm how I had been perceiving our friendship. His answer could either cast me back into being just a fan or let me know that I was, in fact, something more.

David not only accepted my invitation to dinner but he genuinely seemed very enthusiastic about it as well. We even left the rest of the band behind. The line of fans was already forming around the club. We were just three people, all equal.

We went inside Boston Beer Works, which was right near Fenway Park. A spot at the bar opened almost immediately. I sat on one side of David, and Dann sat on the other. Dann was quiet. He was probably just adapting to the fact that we were actually sitting at the bar with the singer of God Lives Underwater.

I felt obligated to play some sort of middleman between them, in order to get David and Dann to open up to each other. David didn't have any rapport with Dann yet like he did with Dogboy. I felt that it was my responsibility to create the best atmosphere between them that I could. Little did I know at the time, but Dann and David would actually become closer friends than Dogboy and David ever did.

David ordered a beer. Dann and I ordered nonalcoholic drinks and some appetizers. We discussed everything from the *Empty* album to the most recent Depeche Mode album, *Songs of Faith & Devotion*. It was surreal to think that we were sitting at a public bar with the singer of God Lives Underwater and that he would be playing a show not more than three hundred yards away. No one else even paid him any attention. He was all ours.

Dann finally got more comfortable with the situation and relaxed. We discussed *Empty* even more, and the correlations between it and the *GLU* album. I would like to think that David opened up to Dann because David trusted me. Anyone who I brought into our friendship was automatically deemed okay.

Perhaps I was just being narcissistic, but David had already trusted me in ways that even people I had known for years didn't. I had to ask myself, where did this trust come from? Was it because I wasn't part of his usual drug scene? Did I interject different desires for a friendship that neither of us had experienced yet?

David had also completely opened up about his ex-girlfriend and his substance abuse problems to Dann. David reiterated to Dann what I had been told at the Paradise show about Heather: the addiction, drug use, attempts to get clean, deception, and ultimately feeling that she was just as toxic to his well-being as the drugs were.

That was something David always seemed to carry with him when he talked about Heather and his drug abuse. A sense of betrayal. They had become one and the same. His ex-girlfriend and his addictions had become synonymous and interchangeable to me.

As David went through the story of Heather again for Dann's sake, I made sure that I got all the details. David seemed to focus on what I could see was really the central point of his pain and inspiration for the two albums. I could see how betrayed he felt by the sequence of events that she had dragged him through.

Dann also listened very intently. I'm sure he didn't know what to make of it all. He had probably never expected to have this kind of conversation with someone who he looked up to as well. I was glad that they had opened up to each other.

One of the many endearing qualities about David was his ability to immediately sense who was good for him and who was bad. That didn't necessarily mean that he never associated with the bad; it just meant that he knew. Maybe he had some sort of second sight at that moment, where he could see how he and Dann would become good friends too.

"What do you think of the vocals in 'Fool'?" he asked me.

"What do you mean?"

"Well, I've heard that I sound too much like Scott Weiland from Stone Temple Pilots in that song."

I was afraid to say anything else. Not only had I already recognized the resemblance myself but apparently so did almost everyone else I had spoken to who had heard the album. So I changed the subject.

Eventually, when we walked back to the club, we crossed Lansdowne Street, and David turned to me.

"Seriously, Rock. There are two ways that I could sing 'Fool.' I can't decide how to sing the song live. Tell me what you think."

David sang the first verse of "Fool" just as it appeared on the album.

"Here's the other way I think it could sound."

He went through the first verse again in a completely different vocal style and intonation. What was great about that moment was that his voice actually echoed and bounced off the outside walls of the Green Monster at Fenway Park.

Dann and I listened intently. I thought it was neat to hear the same lyrics, sung by the same singer, in completely different vocal styles.

"David," I said when he was done. "I like that second style a lot! However, everyone who has the album already is used to hearing the vocals the way they are."

I wish he hadn't agreed with me, because it would have

been amazing to hear them play "Fool" live with completely different vocals on a song that their fans were so familiar with.

There was a light bounce in David's step as he walked back to the club with us. He noticed a street vendor who was selling sausages and pizza. David stopped, pulled out his wallet attached to a chain, and bought a slice of pizza. A homeless man who sat against a wall next to the pizza vendor asked us for money. It surprised me when David took his change from the pizza and dropped it into the street guy's white paper cup. The coins made a metallic clinking sound as they collided with the other change the homeless man had already collected.

As the three of us continued toward the club, David ate his pizza.

"Well, I'm going to the van," he said as we got closer to the venue. "You're on the guest list with a plus one."

Dann and I got in line. When we reached the box office, I said that I was on God Lives Underwater's guest list. The woman at the box office asked me for my name. When I told her, it didn't even dawn on me that David still didn't know my full name.

She flipped through the papers and shook her head. "Nope. I don't see a Brian Paone here."

I panicked. How could I get her to understand that I was supposed to be on the guest list? I was friends with the band!

Luckily, Dann saw David walk by the line again.

"Hey, David!" I yelled. "My name isn't on the guest list!"

"It might be under Rocky Horror," he yelled back as he kept walking.

"Try Rocky Horror," I said to the lady.

There was a pause, and she looked at me suspiciously. She looked back at the page in front of her.

By this time, I was really nervous. All of the guys in the band, including Tim, were already inside.

She flipped through her list again and found *Rocky Horror +1* on the guest list. "Do you have any ID that says that's you?" she asked.

At first I thought she was joking. Then I realized that I needed something to prove to her that David's nickname for me was Rocky. Thankfully the ID that I needed was on the top of my head. I pointed to my hat. "That's what the guys in the band call me."

I couldn't tell if she was amused by me or annoyed. Either way she crossed my name off the list and hesitantly let us into the club. I smiled to myself when I realized that I had just used a baseball hat as my ID.

We couldn't help but feel that there was a lot of history in Avalon. An oddly placed disco ball over the wooden floor gave us the immediate impression that a diversity of events happened right here. Railings sat about six inches higher than the floor and separated it from the bar, which was great for vertically challenged people like me to be able to see the bands. The bar area was furnished by a red carpet that had a certain stickiness to it that reminded me of the floors of certain movie theatres. The stage was much higher than the Paradise's.

God Lives Underwater was going to play first. Dann and I pushed through the crowd and found a spot near the front barrier. As I looked at the railing, I thought, *I hope David notices us this close and lets me sing again. Or at least that he knows we're up here.*

We were so close to being in that front row. The worst part about the handful of people who were in front of us was that they were definitely not here for God Lives Underwater.

As the lights dimmed, Dann and I pushed through again and finally made it to the very first row. I placed a hand on the barrier for support. I was determined to let David, Jeff, Drew, and Adam know exactly where we were. I wanted them to know that I didn't let them down. I fought for them.

Their set was only thirty minutes long, and we yelled every single lyric. We jumped up and down. It was more for the crowd around us that didn't know just how amazing God Lives Underwater really was.

There was a moment of silence between two of their songs. As David dialed the next song into his sampler, Drew tuned his guitar. Some punk in front of Drew mockingly yelled, "Nine Inch Nails!" Drew looked up and just stared at him. I could see the discontentment in his face.

Although I love Nine Inch Nails, it must have been so insulting to Drew and the rest of the God Lives Underwater band members to have somebody yell the name of the most commercially successful band in their genre. Especially when God Lives Underwater was trying to solidify their own style!

I looked at Dann, and we both just shook our heads. We knew that if that guy didn't shut up, Drew was going to jump off the stage and crack him in the head. Drew never took his gaze off the heckler.

As I watched Drew perform the next song, I could see so much more aggression in his stage presence. He never broke eye contact. I literally thought that we were about to be in the middle of a God Lives Underwater versus the fans of Life of Agony battle royal. Thankfully, it never happened.

When God Lives Underwater finished their set, Dann and I watched the guys walk off stage to go outside. I really wanted to just forget the next two bands and follow them, but we stayed through KMFDM's set for Dann since he was such a big fan.

I didn't see David, or anyone else from God Lives Underwater, during the remainder of that night. However, that was fine with me. I knew things would never be how I had feared. The Paradise show wasn't a one-time fluke. David and the rest of the band saw us supporting them during their set. David would always come through. I would never have to worry about getting into one of their shows.

David hadn't let me down.

On the afternoon of November 9, 1995, I was driving my very first car, a 1989 blue Ford Tempo. It was a gift from my father when I got my license in 1993. I called it "Midnight Cowboy" after the Faith No More song from the album *Angel Dust*. There was even a plaque glued to my dashboard to let everyone know my car's proper name.

My girlfriend, Christine, with her brother, Scott, and I were driving on Route 95 North in New Hampshire. Christine was in the passenger seat, and Scott was in the back. We were on our way to an all-ages club in Portsmouth called the Elvis Room for a local hardcore show. There was a band playing that Christine wanted to see.

Since my car's stereo console only consisted of a tape player, I had attached a disc player to my stereo via a cassette adapter. Unfortunately the disc player was of such poor quality that it skipped whenever my car went over a bump. This made it practically impossible to listen to music without getting aggravated. Especially if we were singing along.

The radio has always made me mad. Maybe it was because they played the same songs. My musical tastes in bands just never got any airplay. So what was the point of listening to any radio station? Unfortunately there wasn't much of an alternative. My disc player was just giving us more problems than it was worth. I reluctantly turned on the radio.

The only three stations that I listened to in the Boston area were WBCN, WFNX, and WAAF. WBCN was mainstream rock; WFNX was alternative; and WAAF was metal. I tuned the dial to WBCN, the station that had originally sent me to my first God Lives Underwater show back in June.

I was half-paying attention to the radio and half-paying attention to the conversations that were happening around me. Then all of a sudden, WBCN played "All Wrong." My heart quickened its pace.

I immediately told Christine and Scott to be quiet. This was a very personal moment. Neither of them could understand. I didn't want them to understand.

The version of the song played was the edited-for-radio version. When it was over, I heard the deejay say what I had feared the most.

"And that was God Lives Underwater, who is playing tonight at Avalon, opening for Lords of Acid and My Life with the Thrill Kill Kult."

I had become such an elitist in my own head—not only with David but also with the band as a whole—that I thought that I should always have some sort of inside scoop. If information was passed to me about the band that I didn't know, and it had gotten to me in such a way that it wasn't from the band itself, that would somehow discredit our friendship.

Everything stopped.

Christine let a few minutes of silence pass. "Did you just hear that?" she asked.

"Yeah," I said. "I heard that."

I felt every inch of that road passing underneath the car as we were heading north. Boston was south. The road itself closed in on me. I just had to turn the car around. We had to abandon our original plan of going to New Hampshire. I needed to not let David down. There had to be a spot on the guest list for me that read, *Rocky Horror +1*. I needed to be there.

"Go ahead," Christine said. "Let's go. Turn the car around. I really want to meet this guy that you have been talking about so much anyway."

I was so relieved to hear her say that. But I was also concerned. "David usually does just a plus one for my guest list. We have Scott. He's only fourteen. Avalon shows are eighteen-plus."

"Don't worry about me," Scott said from the backseat. "I'll just stay in the car if I can't get in."

"We could always take him home," Christine suggested.

I looked at the digital clock on the Tempo's dashboard and did a quick mathematical equation in my head. "We don't really have time to take him home," I said. "Especially if they're opening."

I had already turned the car around.

"Let's just chance it. If he doesn't get in, then I'll stay outside with him. You can go in and watch their set. Just come out when they're done," Christine suggested.

That sounded reasonable enough.

I accelerated the car to a speed that I felt comfortable

with. We actually made it into Boston well before the doors opened. I parked the car, and we walked toward the Avalon. It felt so odd to me to be here, since I was just on my way to the Elvis Room in New Hampshire for a completely different show.

We stood outside the club. My gaze wandered everywhere. I was looking for anyone in the band, even Tim. Someone came out of the side door that led to the backstage. I asked if anyone from God Lives Underwater was inside. They said yes, and I thanked them.

The cold was getting to us, and were shivering. As much as I felt bad about putting Christine and Scott through the cold for a band they could have cared less about, I was determined not to move until I saw someone I knew.

Once again it was Tim who I saw first. He had recognized me. Since this was such short notice, I wasn't wearing my *Rocky Horror Picture Show* hat. I hoped that this wouldn't cause a problem at the door.

"I have my girlfriend and her brother with me this time, but he's only fourteen. Is that going to be a problem?" I asked him.

It's funny, when someone thinks that they might have some pull, how quickly they start to test the rules.

"Hold on. Let me tell the guys you are here," Tim said.

That was reassuring. At least there was going to be an effort to help get Scott into an eighteen-plus show.

After a few more minutes of jumping up and down to stay warm, Jeff came out next. I left Christine and Scott where they were.

"What's up?" Jeff asked.

"I'm here with my girlfriend and her brother, but he is

only fourteen. We wouldn't have brought him, but we just found out about the show about an hour ago."

"Okay. Stay here. I'll see what I can do."

Jeff disappeared back into the club. There were no signs of David yet.

I turned to Christine and told her that we were just going to have to hold on a few more minutes. They were working on getting Scott into the show. I couldn't believe how much pull I already had with the band!

The backstage door finally opened again, and there he was.

"David!" I yelled as I walked toward him.

"Hey, me-han!" he said with that signature greeting again.

He walked down the steps and joined us in the cold.

"David, this is my girlfriend Christine and her brother Scott."

"So, you're Rocky's girlfriend!" he said as he shook her hand. "I think the best way to do this is for you guys to just follow me."

We enthusiastically followed David to the front entrance of the club. He flashed the bouncer his Band Pass. "They're with me."

The bouncer nodded, and we walked right inside. No ID checks. No age checks. No guest list checks. We were inside the club before the doors even opened.

"Okay, guys. Just find a place and act like you belong here, or they'll throw you out." He looked at me and asked, "You all set?"

"Yeah, man. Thanks!"

"No problem!" David replied.

He left us and went back through the backstage area. We

found a spot and did our best impression of people-who-were-supposed-to-be-here. It wasn't until after the doors finally opened that we felt safe from being thrown out.

The club filled up. I was surprised that the two headlining bands had that much of a draw. Lords of Acid was touring on the *Voodoo-U* album. My Life with the Thrill Kill Kult was touring on the *Hit & Run Holiday* album. A local band, called Women of Sodom opened the show. They seemed to be more of an S&M act than actual music.

I felt uncomfortable that Scott was with us, but it would have to be the price I paid to see God Lives Underwater live so soon after the last show.

After the local act was finished, God Lives Underwater came out. This time we stayed to the side for their set. I still did just as much jumping and singing as I had for the last two shows. David knew I was here somewhere. Jeff knew I was here too. That's all that really mattered.

There was no reason to sit through two more bands. Especially since Christine and Scott were so accommodating about missing the original show that we were headed to see earlier. I made the suggestion that we should just leave when God Lives Underwater's set was finished.

"You can't come back after you leave," the bouncer said to us as we left the club.

I thought that was funny. I almost replied, "The most important band of the night is done playing. Why would I want to go back in?"

Lansdowne Street was cold and quiet. It felt awful to leave the show without at least saying good-bye to David. But he would understand because there was always a next time.

We got into the Midnight Cowboy and headed home. I

still couldn't believe that I had just seen God Lives Underwater for the third time. Although I was feeling guilty about how little time I had spent with David, especially after he had even got Scott into the show. David was always going out of his way for me. I felt like I had to find a way to repay him for all of his accommodations.

Just six weeks later God Lives Underwater returned to Boston. The lines between David and I blurred even more.

Since the next show was highly publicized, I knew about it well in advance. God Lives Underwater was going to open for Deluxx Folk Implosion at T.T. the Bear's Place in Cambridge, Massachusetts on December 19, 1995. The gig was also going to be part of WBCN's Xmas Rave concert series, a very high-profile series of shows that happened over a week in every club around the Boston area. Deluxx Folk Implosion were touring with a huge hit, "Natural One" from the *Kids* soundtrack. They were fronted by Lou Barlow from Dinosaur Jr. and Sebadoh fame. The venue, T.T. the Bear's Place, had a capacity of only three hundred people.

I found out about the concert almost immediately after God Lives Underwater's previous Boston show. I had plenty of time to plan for it. It also happened to be during Christmas break, which meant Dogboy was going to be home from Westfield State. When I told him about the show, he was more than eager to go with me. I could tell that he felt like he had somehow let David down by not going to the last two shows.

I wanted to make sure that we got there before their white tour van even arrived. We drove into Cambridge and arrived at the club by four o'clock.

Since it was December, it was very cold. A typical New England wind ripped through us. However, that didn't deter either of us from standing outside on the corner as we waited patiently for their van to arrive. We anxiously darted our focus every time we heard a vehicle. Even though we were counting every second in our heads, we didn't realize just how cold we were. The excitement of times like these was enough to keep us warm.

The back corner behind T.T. the Bear's Place was where two one-way streets met. Across the street, on the other corner, was the famous goth/industrial club Man Ray. Connected to T.T. the Bear's Place was the Middle East, a club where many local and national bands played if they had a larger draw than T.T. the Bear's Place but not enough to get into the Paradise. Boston clubs are all about the numbers, which usually dictated which club a band might play at when it tour here.

I was afraid, if we left our corner, that would be the moment when God Lives Underwater showed up. We kept our ground.

Since this was a radio show, and it was twenty-one or older, maybe David wouldn't be able to get us in. Or maybe he wouldn't want to risk trying. So far all of David's moments with me had been stress-free and effortless. I was nervous. I knew that this was a real test of the length he would go to as my friend.

As my thoughts were consumed with this dilemma, my toes and fingers had gone beyond numb. Then I finally spotted the dirty white van on Brookline Street. It headed straight for us. I stepped off the curb. I walked toward the middle of the street, so they would see me. I wasn't nervous anymore. I was full of confidence and pride.

I approached the oncoming van as it slowed down. I strained my eyes to see who was inside. The driver's side window rolled down. Jeff was at the wheel.

"What's going on?" Jeff asked. "Do you know where we go?"

"The parking lot is right around that corner." I pointed to the corner where Dogboy was still standing.

David was in the passenger seat wearing big sunglasses. I knew he was looking at me even though I couldn't see his eyes. I realized that we didn't even need to say anything to greet one another. We had already said hello and had bridged the gap since the last show, all in that one moment.

"Alright. Thanks," Jeff said. He rolled up the window and turned the van to the left, toward the small parking lot.

I walked in the middle of the street behind the van. I grabbed Dogboy, and we turned the corner.

Jeff pulled the van in front of the dumpster in the lot and shut off the engine.

Dogboy and I stood outside the van, and the sliding door opened. Tim, Adam, and Drew came out of the backseats. David and Jeff also came out. We all stood in a messy circle.

The guys stretched their arms and legs. Dogboy and I tried to feel as natural as we could. Jeff and Adam recognized Dogboy and shook his hand. David came around to say hi to him too.

Dogboy openly apologized for missing the last two shows. He explained that he was away at college. David and Jeff didn't even flinch. They let Dogboy know that no explanations were ever needed.

"Have you seen anyone from WBCN or any of the other bands yet?" Jeff asked.

"No. We haven't even been inside."

"Alright. Let's go in and see what's going on."

We walked toward the front door. I walked beside David. "How was the rest of the last tour?" I asked him.

"Tiring. We're only able to go home for Christmas, and then we're going right back out again."

"Hey. Before we go in, I just want you to know that this is a twenty-one-and-over show. I'm nervous they aren't going to let us in."

"Don't worry about it. I'll take care of it."

We reached the front door.

"Can I help you?" an employee of the club asked.

"We're the band," David answered.

"Which band is that?"

"God Lives Underwater."

David still hadn't taken off his sunglasses.

"All of you are in the band?"

"Just the four of us," Jeff said. Then he pointed to Tim. "And him."

"Everyone have IDs?"

Everyone pulled out their lanyard with the God Lives Underwater mantis logo on it.

"What about those two?"

"They're with us," David said.

"Can I see their licenses?" the guy asked.

I figured honesty was the best policy. I hoped that having the singer of the band vouch for us would help. I reached into my wallet. "We aren't twenty-one though."

"Can't come in," he retorted.

I paused. Time just stopped. My worst fear had materialized. I was waiting for someone to step up and help me.

"They're with us," David repeated.

"Doesn't matter. Unless they have a lanyard, they have to be twenty-one to get in."

I still didn't feel defeated. I had the entire band backing me. There was no way David was going to let me down. There was no way the genie had fallen asleep inside the bottle. This just couldn't be happening.

"Okay, Rock. Why don't you guys wait outside? We'll try to figure something out."

We were being left outside! Although I wasn't about to give up hope, it sure did make me feel vulnerable. The door closed. David just went through a set of doors that I had been denied access to.

Dogboy and I watched cars go down the street. We did anything we could to keep our bodies warm and to keep our thoughts from panicking. I actually thought, *What if we don't get into this show?*

Enough time had passed that I had gone from being sure that David would come through for us to looking at my watch and thinking that we would probably be home soon. The doors to the club finally opened, and David and Adam came out. I waited eagerly for either of them to say something.

"C'mon. You guys are carrying Adam's drums. Don't look or talk to anyone. Once we get in there, find a corner to hide in."

We walked to the back of the van. David unlocked their trailer. Adam handed both of us two large drum cases, and we quickly headed for the door.

"Hold on a sec. Wait for us," David said.

We stood there and shivered. Were we really that cold or just nervous? This was The Big Plan. If it didn't work out, we would be heading home soon.

David and Adam grabbed some gear. We walked back toward the front of the club. When we got to the doors, there was no one there. We never slowed our pace. We were able to follow them right into the back room.

I couldn't get over how small the club was. The backstage area was really just another room the size of anyone's bedroom.

We put the drums down.

"If you guys want to help set up the equipment once we get it all in here for soundcheck, that would be great," Adam said.

The band made a few trips with Tim to get the rest of the equipment. Since Dogboy and I were actually inside the club, we didn't dare leave for anything.

After all the gear was brought inside, we found out that the soundman wasn't even here yet. We were told to sit tight. We decided to bring the gear onstage and set it up anyway. Dogboy and I helped Adam with all of his drums. Adam stood onstage, and we passed everything to him.

The soundman finally arrived. The club was still empty. Even Deluxx Folk Implosion hadn't arrived yet. The soundman set up the microphones and levels. Dogboy and I sat on the stage, right in the middle of David and Jeff. This was going to be like a private show, just for us. We twisted our bodies, so we could look at the band properly. We also didn't want to look too conspicuous to the guy who had already denied us access to the club.

This was the first God Lives Underwater soundcheck that I had ever been to. This was also the first soundcheck I had ever been to period.

There was no need for the soundman to speak through the monitors, since the club was so small. Instead, he just spoke in a normal volume across the floor. He gave the signal for them to play a song all the way through. The opening synths of "All Wrong" began.

Although I felt like we were at a friend's house, watching their band play in a garage, I still felt entirely too vulnerable. At any moment we felt like we were going to be discovered.

I was hearing something that had become so natural to my ears. The sight of the guys in the band had also become very familiar to me. My view of David as the singer of the band had minimized almost to the point where I couldn't even view him as that anymore. He was slowly becoming just an average person to me.

We bobbed our heads to the beat of the song. We paid more attention to the musicians than the music. When the song was over, we all looked at the soundman for any critique or instruction. It never even crossed my mind to put my hands together to clap. The silence when the song ended just felt so natural.

The soundman was happy with the mix, both in-house and in the monitors onstage. He told the band that they were all set. We stood up. David jumped off the stage.

"How did that sound?"

"Awesome," I told him.

"We're gonna go get something to eat. I don't think it's a good idea if you guys come with us. I don't know if I could get you back in again. The club is offering us pizza, but I think we want to get something different."

"That's totally fine."

I was disappointed but didn't want to risk being rejected at the doors again.

"Just find a corner. Don't move until I come back."

We agreed and walked toward the bar. There was a pool table and a large-screen television nearby. We could see a table in the farthest corner of the club with two seats against the window that faced the street. That way we could see when the guys came back from dinner.

We were so happy to be inside, yet we were constantly watching our backs. I was sure we were going to be discovered. Every moment that David was gone felt like forever. As long as he was here with me, I felt safe. Now I felt like we had been thrown to the wolves.

We sat quietly and watched the line stretch down the street outside for the sold-out show. When the doors finally opened, Dogboy and I could finally breathe easier.

The bar area filled up. The floor in front of the stage was getting crowded with fans. People were sitting down at the tables all around us.

Since we were already on such a personal level with the band, I felt very possessive of the situation. Through the big windows my gaze kept trying to catch sight of any member of the band coming back to the club.

Instead, two girls sat at the table next to us. One of the girls had hair that reached past her waist and snug red velvet pants. She was on the shorter side, maybe an inch taller than me, and very thin.

She started a conversation with us almost immediately upon sitting down. "Who are you guys here to see?"

How should I have answered that? How should I have told her that I was actually here not just to see a band but to spend time with my friends, especially since they weren't even there with us? How should I have said that, without sounding like I was bragging? I was having a hard time trying to conjure up anything that sounded intelligent.

"God Lives Underwater," Dogboy answered for us.

"Really? Me too!" she exclaimed. "But don't tell anyone that I'm only eighteen. I used a fake ID to get in."

Even though I applauded her, I was also resentful. I'm friends with the band, and I was almost sent home because of my honesty. She had walked right in. By lying!

"Have you ever seen them before?" she asked.

"This is my fourth time," I replied.

"Wow. How have you seen them so often?"

It was just too much for me. I had to get an edge on her. I felt threatened. "I'm actually friends with the band. I'm really good friends with David, the singer."

Her eyes lit up. "Really? This is my first time seeing them. I'm just so excited. I want to be right up front."

All of a sudden she wasn't a threat anymore. I felt myself let my guard down. I realized that I had been like a lion protecting its cub from danger. I didn't even notice how deep my caring for David ran until I was faced with a situation that felt threatening. Even if she was just a fan.

"If you want to meet the band, just hang out with us."

That statement probably sounded so shallow and creepy, especially coming from a guy she had just met, but that's not where my intention was rooted. It was the most sincere, yet awful-sounding thing I had ever said to someone I didn't know in regard to the band. She had gone through the trouble and risk of making a fake ID to see God Lives Underwater. It was the least I could do.

The girl and her friend sat with me and Dogboy at our

table. She was definitely attractive, but I didn't want anything I had said to come off as a pick-up line.

After some time of talking and getting comfortable with them, David suddenly appeared behind me.

"Hey, me-han."

I turned around and introduced David to the girls. I wish I could remember their names or at least the name of the girl I was smitten with. I could see that she was starstruck by David's presence. She must have been pretty impressed that I wasn't fabricating my comment about being friends with the band.

"Jeff's going crazy outside right now," David said.

"Why? What happened?" I asked.

"When we got back to the van, there was a fifty-dollar parking ticket on the windshield. He's trying to get it fixed and move the van."

"Oh, man! That sucks!"

"Yeah. The other band isn't even here yet."

"Really?" I couldn't believe it.

"I don't know what that means, if they don't show up. Maybe we'll get more time." He shrugged.

This almost felt like a small local show, not a big national radio concert. The whole time David stood here, no one else even paid any attention to him.

"We're gonna hang out in the back room until we go on. Do you guys want to come along?"

I was already getting up. He didn't need to ask me twice. I looked at the two girls. They were still shocked that the singer of God Lives Underwater was standing with us.

"Is it okay if they come too?" I asked.

"Sure. Doesn't matter to me," David answered.

I turned and looked at them. "Do you want to come hang out backstage?"

Christine and I were taking a break with our relationship. We would continue to be separated until June 1996. I had also heard that she was seeing someone else. I didn't feel guilty becoming infatuated with someone else for a change.

We followed David into the back room. He closed the door. The static noise of the club was instantaneously sealed out. It felt like we had just entered a completely different building. Adam, Drew, Jeff, and Tim sat on a bench that circled the wooden room. We could see graffiti everywhere from bands that had played here before.

One thing that always impressed me about David was that, during his steady climb in popularity, he never seemed to care about girls backstage. In fact he seemed to be more focused on making sure that I got into the show and that we had enough time to hang out. My whole perception of the wild backstage antics of rock bands was skewed because of him.

The girls sat quietly and didn't take for granted that they were here. They understood what an honor it was.

"What happened with the parking ticket?" I asked Jeff.

"I must have parked the van in a no-parking zone. I tried to fight it. Tim had to move it to the other side of the street."

I felt bad. I assumed that they would probably have to pay the fine out of their pockets.

"Hey," I said, turning to David. "I noticed that in the lyric book to *Empty*, there are words for 'Still' that aren't in the song."

"Yeah. Those lyrics were originally in the song before we recorded the album. All of the lyrics were submitted to the label before we finished the recording. They accidentally got printed. The UK version doesn't even have Drew's face in the band photo, but it has the right lyrics to 'Still.' So you either get the right lyrics without Drew's picture, or Drew's picture and the wrong lyrics. They accidentally printed the mantis logo where his face should have been. Either way, we can't win."

The door opened, and the guys from Deluxx Folk Implosion, led by Lou Barlow, filtered in. I felt like they had just barged in on our private conversation. They had arrived late and were dragging their equipment through a packed crowd.

It seemed that more than half of the audience was there to see them. I wondered how many people knew more than just their hit "Natural One."

There was an uncomfortable silence when we all stopped talking. Then the activity from Deluxx Folk Implosion's arrival filled the room with noise. It was one of those moments that had a very us-versus-them feeling to it. It made Dogboy and I feel like we really were part of the band and not just casual observers.

It wasn't even fifteen minutes after Deluxx Folk Implosion's gear was dragged into the room when David got word that the club was almost ready for them to play. David looked at us.

"Since the show is starting so late, there is a very small change-over window for the equipment. Your jobs are to grab Adam's drum kit when we are done and get back here as fast as you possibly can. We're closing with 'Don't Know How to Be.' When that song starts, get with Tim. As soon as it ends, just grab stuff."

It felt amazing to have such an important job that David

was going to trust us with. We had instructions! The last thing I wanted to do was let the band down and look untrustworthy.

After WBCN's deejay made his opening remarks to everyone, I heard him say, "And give it up for God Lives Underwater!"

The crowd cheered.

I couldn't help but feel like I was part of the band at that moment. Dogboy and I walked out of the back room with the band, Tim, and the two girls. The lights dimmed, and it was hard to see the crowd. The band headed for the stage. We cut right in front of the first row of people.

We found a spot right at the stage. We even forced some people to take a step back. Dogboy immediately became protector of the stage. The stage was only a few inches off the floor, and no barriers were installed. He spent the majority of the show with his back to the band, half sitting on the stage, and watched the crowd for any unwanted craziness. That was Dogboy's comfort level. We really felt more important than just the casual fan in the audience. We wanted to make that known during the show too.

During God Lives Underwater's set, the girl with the velvet pants and long hair danced with me. I stood behind her with my hands on her hips. I could feel her hips move under the fabric of her pants. Her hair kept brushing past my face. She was quickly becoming yet another reason why I didn't want the night to end.

The ceiling of T.T. the Bear's Place was very low and consisted of tiled paneling. Many of the tiles were either broken, or missing, from years of damage and wear. During the show, Adam was drumming so hard that a stick slipped out of his hand and went straight into the air. It disappeared into a black hole of the ceiling. I'll always remember that look on his face as he reached for another stick. He must have been wondering where that stick wound up.

"All Wrong" started, and I knew we were coming to the end of their set soon. I anticipated making our way to the side of the stage. Tim also put himself into position. "All Wrong" caused the club to erupt in a sing-a-long.

I noticed, while watching David, that part of his stage presence was to never actually make eye contact with the crowd.

"Don't Know How to Be" had a very distinct opening synth line. As soon as we heard it, Tim, Dogboy, and I jumped onstage next to Drew against the wall. I spent more attention anticipating the ending of the song than I did watching the band play.

When the song ended, it was like a pistol went off. We rushed to Adam's set. We disassembled it in record-breaking time. Tim packed up Jeff's rig like it was on fire. David grabbed the keyboards and helped Drew with his amps. We all jumped offstage with equipment and brought it into the back room, only to turn around, and sprint back onto the stage to grab more. I was determined to show the entire band, not just David, how efficient and reliable I really was.

As quickly as we cluttered the tiny backstage room with the gear, Deluxx Folk Implosion brought its gear out at the same time. The door to the back room was only big enough for one person with one piece of equipment to fit through at a time. We ultimately created roadblocks with our urgent respect for the time restraint.

The Deluxx Folk Implosion band members hadn't even said anything to us all night.

Dogboy jumped back onstage but still had to weave and dodge Deluxx Folk Implosion's equipment. He grabbed Adam's bass drum, practically the last piece of the kit that needed to be taken down. All that was left was his seat, which I took. I signaled to David and Adam that we had everything. There was no reason for them to come back. Dogboy jumped offstage with the bass drum, and I followed him.

At the same time, Lou Barlow came through the door with his amp. Dogboy couldn't see him over the curve of the bass drum. Maybe Lou wasn't able to get out of Dogboy's way in time. Maybe he was just too much of a pompous ass to care. Either way, the bass drum and amp collided in the middle of the doorframe.

"Watch where you're going!" Lou yelled at Dogboy.

Dogboy knew, even though we felt as if we were part of the band, that we still didn't have the right to get in the way. Dogboy did the admirable thing and backed up with the heavy drum in his arms. He moved to the side, so Lou could get by comfortably with an amp that rolled easily on wheels.

"Jesus! What's your fucking hurry?" Dogboy retorted as Lou passed him. "We're just trying to get the shit offstage so you can set up faster."

Lou stopped and glared at him.

My money would have been on Dogboy if that altercation had escalated any higher.

Lou broke the stare and continued to the stage.

"Asshole," Dogboy whispered.

After David was satisfied with the inventory of the equipment in the back room, he announced that we needed to get everything to the van. They didn't want to leave it in that room longer than necessary. However, we quickly realized that we would have to travel the length of the club through the crowd while Deluxx Folk Implosion was playing to transport the equipment. If we started immediately, we just might be able to finish before the next band started their set.

We grabbed as much as we could. We pushed through the crowd. Even when they clearly saw that we were trying to get the band's equipment out, people still didn't want to move.

I loaded up my arms with the smaller drum cases and held onto whatever else I could. Jeff ran outside to swing the van around, so it was closer to the door.

Every time we passed by the girl with the long hair, I looked at her to see if she was watching me. I was also checking to see if she saw what I was doing, how close I was with the band, and to see if she was still interested in me even though the set was over. Almost every time I looked at her, she was looking at me too.

It only took a few trips to get all of the gear outside. Every time I went back in to get more, I made sure I passed directly by her.

When the last of the gear was brought outside, our body temperatures had finally adapted more with the outside cold than the inside heat. We shivered.

"Thanks, me-han," David said to us. "You guys can go inside if you're too cold. We're gonna stay out here and pack up the trailer."

I became terrified that our visiting time would be over. I needed to make sure that, if we went inside, it wouldn't be a replacement for hanging out.

"Are you coming back inside?" I asked him.

"Yeah. We want to check out the next band."

That was enough to give me comfort that they weren't just

going to jump in the tour van and speed away. Plus I was still thinking of the long-haired girl in red velvet pants.

Dogboy and I returned to the club. The door guy didn't even flinch. Deluxx Folk Implosion was already playing. We found the two girls. They hadn't moved from the spot where we had been during God Lives Underwater's set. I immediately felt a sense of apprehension with the long-haired girl. She didn't seem as interested anymore. She was concentrating on the band instead, and all of her body language was different.

David came through the front door and stood next to me. We watched them play. I didn't feel the need to even keep looking at him to check if he was still there or not.

"What do you think of these guys?"

I shrugged.

"Do you know any of their songs, other than 'Natural One'?" he asked.

I shook my head no.

"Me neither," he replied.

After a few songs that we couldn't decipher the difference between, Dogboy made a motion to leave. Since the rest of the guys in the band were still outside, it wasn't going to be that difficult to get David to leave with us.

"We're gonna go after this song," I yelled to David over the music.

He nodded.

I didn't want to leave just yet, without at least asking the girl for her phone number. I also didn't want to do it in front of David, in case I was rejected. I wasn't ready to let my guard down in front of him that much. I actually wanted to impress him more than I wanted to impress her.

The song ended. David headed for the door without even another warning. I finally got the girl's attention.

"Hey. We're gonna be heading out. I want to hang out with the guys a few more minutes outside before they leave. I was just wondering if I could have your phone number?"

Without hesitation she opened up her purse, and looked for a piece of paper and a pen. The band started playing their next song. The noise level grew to the point where, if we wanted to say anything else to each other, we would have to yell.

I had hoped that David would leave the club before I asked for her number in case she had rejected me. But after she was so eager to give it to me, I actually wished he had stayed. It would have been a perfect opportunity to impress him. If I had known it was going to be that easy, I would have done it sooner.

She leaned into my ear. "Where do you live?"

"Lynn," I replied.

"You don't go near Nashua, New Hampshire, do you?"

"Not even close. Why?" I asked.

"We don't have a ride home. Maybe my friend will just call her dad."

For just a split second I thought that maybe it wouldn't be so bad to drive them all the way home to New Hampshire. Sure, it would have put at least ninety minutes both ways on our trip home, but it would have scored major brownie points if I wanted to go out with her after all. In the end, the desire to spend more time with David and get home at a reasonable hour overrode any impulse to drive them home.

"Sorry. I don't know how long I'm gonna be hanging out with the band. That's really out of our way from here," I answered.

She gave me a very big hug, and we said good-bye. I never saw or spoke to her again.

Dogboy and I reached the front door. The cold hit me like a freight train. Adam was closing up the back of the trailer. David stood by the side of the van on the sidewalk.

"What's going on now?" I asked. I was hoping that we could hang out with him even more.

"We gotta hit the road. We have to drive through the night just to get to the next show on time."

Even though I was disappointed, I understood. I couldn't be too greedy. It seemed that we were getting further into the band's inner circle at every show. I didn't want to be an overbearing friend. I had to let them go, even though I had no idea when or where I would see him next.

As I approached David to shake his ring-laden hand, he instead pulled me into a solid bear hug. I wrapped my arms around his skinny frame and hugged him back. We pulled away. I felt somber as I watched him get into the van and close the door.

As I waved good-bye, the van pulled away.

"Do you want to go back in and hang out with those girls some more?" Dogboy asked.

"Nah," I replied. "The night can't go anywhere from here."

At the end of February, 1996, God Lives Underwater was opening for Spacehog. This seemed rather peculiar to me. I didn't think that the two bands were anything alike. I thought that God Lives Underwater's singles "No More Love," "All Wrong," and "Don't Know How to Be," were much more popular than Spacehog's single, "In The Meantime." It should have been God Lives Underwater headlining the tour.

This time the show was going to be at the Paradise again.

Dogboy was in Westfield at college. Christine and I were back and forth with our relationship break. Dann wasn't old enough to get into the show. I was flying solo. Even though I would be technically going to the show by myself, I felt as if I was still going there to meet up with friends.

That morning I had to report for jury duty at the Salem, Massachusetts, courthouse at eight o'clock. I wasn't particularly worried about being selected and having to stay there all day. I figured I would check in, sit in the room, read the book I had brought with me, and then be dismissed.

I sat quietly reading Stephen King's *Rose Madder*. I kept a watchful eye on the clock. After an hour or so, they called out a few numbers. There was a case moving forward. If my number was called, I had to report downstairs and wait to be briefed by the judge.

I was still in denial when I heard the lady call out the number I was holding. I closed my book, stood up, and filed out of the room with the rest of the selected jurors. It was early enough in the morning, so I wasn't that nervous. I still had some time.

We were ushered through a metal detector. After we had all passed through, they let us sit in a large room with long tables. We were handed pamphlets about the responsibilities of serving on a jury as an American citizen. All I really cared about was getting out of here. I didn't want to miss any time with David.

To pass the time, I talked with another guy who was roughly the same age.

I got nervous when the clock read noon. The judge hadn't come into the room to start the hearing yet. We didn't even know what kind of case we were going to be involved with. As the small hand on the clock kept moving forward, I got even more nervous. I actually wondered about what would happen if we didn't get out until it was too late. Then my paranoia set in. I thought about what would happen if we were sequestered on some murder case.

Like a blessing in disguise, the judge walked into the room and asked for our attention. We quickly quieted down and breathed a sigh of relief when he announced that it was a civil case. The lawyers had just settled it! We were no longer needed. Our civic duty had been fulfilled.

I looked at my watch. I left the courthouse so fast!

I made sure I was at the venue in plenty of time before the van pulled up for soundcheck. My back was against the same bricks that I had leaned against just eight months ago on the day that we had met. I looked at the marquee that also doubled as an awning over the front door.

Spacehog was written in huge letters. It took up at least 75 percent of the sign. *God Lives Underwater* was written underneath it, just three words, forced to squeeze into the bottom. It was disheartening.

I didn't expect to see a full-size silver tour bus pull up in front of the club. Tim came out of the bus. They had finally made it to the big leagues. I hoped that they wouldn't get so big too fast and that I would be left behind.

I pushed myself off the brick wall and walked toward the bus. David came out next. It looked so unnatural for him to get off that huge bus. I felt that, at any moment, it was going to devour him.

"Hey, me-han," he said.

"What's up? I see you guys graduated to the big time," I said.

"Yeah. The label can actually spend more money on us now that the records are selling."

I had always looked at the tour van as a vehicle that was fair game for anyone. This bus looked like a home on wheels. I was a little intimidated by it. Maybe because it was the first sign that I might lose the band to popularity. The last thing I wanted was to have to fight for time with David. Maybe I was just intimidated because big things were happening for the band. It reminded me that I didn't always know about these changes until I saw them.

"You want to help us get the gear inside?"

"Sure," I answered.

"Who are you here with?"

"No one this time. Nobody was around."

"That's okay. Right?" he asked in the form of a statement.

"It's fine with me. It just means I get you more to myself," I joked.

The gear was stored underneath the bus in cargo compartments. I helped the band bring the equipment through the front door and down the long dark hallway. There was no one around to bother us or to question who I was.

"C'mon," David said after all the gear was brought inside. "We gotta get you a pass."

I followed him to the box office. He showed them his lanyard and said that I needed a VIP pass so I could come in and out as I pleased. The box office lady asked him who I was.

He said that I was with the band. She filled out a VIP sticker with the date on it. I stuck it to my shirt.

"Are you hungry?" he asked me.

"I could eat."

"Do you want to go grab a bite? There's a McDonald's on the corner. I can't be away too long though. Soundcheck will begin soon."

As he started to take a step toward the door, he looked down and noticed my sneakers. "Hey, Rocky. Are you trying to copy me or something?"

I didn't really know what he was talking about. I looked down too. Sure enough, not only were we wearing the same sneakers, but they were the same color. We both had on the new plastic Chucks in shiny black.

"Hey, we're kinda like brothers," he said. "But next time you gotta call me so we don't start wearing the same clothes!"

We headed toward the door, down the hallway, and then into the sunlight. Even though it was the end of February, David put on his sunglasses. He looked like Layne Staley from Alice In Chains. We walked the short distance to McDonald's.

While standing in line, I looked at him without him knowing it. It felt really good to be able to pick up right where we left off.

He placed his order. Then he looked at me. "Go ahead. It's on me."

I felt really guilty taking David's money. It was one thing to be on the guest list at a show and get free stuff like T-shirts and posters. It was another thing to have his cash pay for me.

He could see how uneasy I looked. "Don't worry about

it. It's not even my money. It's the label's. We get a food allowance."

That made me feel comfortable enough to order a combo meal. I didn't know when I would eat next, so I even supersized it. David ordered a chocolate milkshake to go along with his meal.

We took our trays and found an empty table, almost right in the middle of the restaurant. As we sat down, I noticed he was wearing a new nose ring. It wasn't as large as his last one.

"What happened to your old nose ring?" I asked.

"The double-zero gauge one?" he asked.

"That was a double-zero?!" I retorted.

Since I knew about body piercing, I just couldn't believe that his was that big!

"Yeah. I lost it one night on tour. At the end of a set, I jumped into the crowd. Someone just ripped it out. I looked for it after the club emptied out, but I never found it."

"That sucks."

"But when we were on tour with Filter in the UK last month, I found this one on the floor of a club, so I just threw it in."

The blood drain from my face, as if the earth had tilted and all the status that we had with each other slid in the opposite direction. I felt like a parent who just heard that their toddler had tried to eat gum that they had found on the sidewalk.

I had to pause and replay what he had just said in my head, before I asked him to repeat it. "I'm sorry. You, what?!"

"I missed having a nose ring. I didn't want to buy a new one. I found this one at a club," he said nonchalantly. He took another bite of his food.

"David, that's so gross! You just can't do that!" I scolded him. "Seriously. You have no idea where that's been. Or whose nose that was in before you found it! What would ever possess you to think that was a good idea? I can't believe you would ever do something like that! If you're that hard-up for a new ring, I'll buy you one. Okay?"

He stopped eating and stared at me.

Everything I had felt about being tactful, as well as David's perception of me, went right out the window. My intensity for what he had just told me overrode any boundaries that may have still lingered between us. I was disappointed with him, and I wanted him to take me seriously. "I want you to take that out right now."

He was still completely motionless. He stared at me.

"David, I'm serious. You're acting like a little bitch, keeping that in. I'm horrified at what you did. Take it out."

"Rock. I have put worse things than this in my nose before."

"Yeah? Well, you haven't done any of that in front of me. I can see this thing in front of my face. That's what I am concerned about at this moment. Take it out."

David looked like a hurt child. I didn't want to back down. I felt like I was taking my role of big brother even further, and I wasn't going to let him talk his way out of it. There was only one solution that would satisfy me.

As he sat there, I could see the wheels turn in his head.

"Listen, David. I'll make a deal with you. If I buy you a new ring, will you take that one out and throw it away?"

"You don't have to do that, Rock!"

"No. I do, David. I want to."

"Okay, fine. Just don't get me anything under an eight gauge."

"Agreed. You know what? I still don't know when your birthday is."

"May 5. It's easy to remember. Just think of Cinco de Mayo."

"Alright. Let's call the ring a birthday gift then. If it doesn't look like you guys are gonna be back here before your birthday, I'll just mail it to you."

"Deal."

Even though I was content with our arrangement, I had surprised myself. Sure, I had known that he was a drug user. That didn't bother me as much as the nose ring did. It was seeing it right in front of me that set me off. David must have picked up on that. Because of this, David always tried to keep me safe from that ugly side of him.

We watched people walk past the windows on Commonwealth Avenue. He told me about the small town in Pennsylvania where he had grown up. We spent at least a half hour after we finished our dinner just watching and commenting on whoever walked by.

There were quite a few people who came into McDonald's who were also going to the show. It still baffled me how many fans looked in our direction but didn't even flinch when he was right there.

David hardly drank any of his chocolate shake. As we were talking, he amused himself by placing his finger over the straw and lifting it out of the cup so that the straw filled with liquid. He then proceeded to release his finger so the shake dribbled all over his red tray. It became so repetitive that he didn't even realize how much he had siphoned onto the tray until there was a thin coating creeping toward him.

"I think it's time we start heading back," he said, laughing.

As he stood up, the edge of the tray caught on his chain wallet and lifted. More than half a cup of milkshake was knocked all over the table. As the cup struck the surface, the lid popped off. The chocolate shake came out like a fountain! It literally covered the entire table. I froze.

As I made my way toward the bin of napkins, David suddenly had a mischievous smile on his face. "Let's get out of here, Rock! Quick, before they can catch us!"

David laughed as he sprinted toward the door. He ran like he had just robbed the place. His blond hair flew behind him. Everybody stared at us. I didn't know what else to do, so I just dropped the napkins and ran after him.

I caught up to him outside, and he was in hysterics. Once I realized the absurdity of what had just happened, I laughed uncontrollably with him. He still had chocolate milkshake all over his hands. He wiped them on his pants.

"Oh, me-han," he said. He wiped tears from his eyes. "C'mon! We really gotta get inside for soundcheck."

As I sat through another God Lives Underwater soundcheck, I thought about how quickly the band was getting more popular. Maybe it was because of the surprise of the bus and their ever-growing percentage of fans, but I was terrified that they would slip through my fingers before I knew it had happened.

I thought about how difficult it would be to get on their guest list and find any time to hang out with David. Things wouldn't be at our personal and intimate level that we currently shared. Maybe the band would even be protected by security.

As much as I wanted God Lives Underwater to be the biggest band in the world, I also wanted their shows to stay personal. I didn't want to be left behind as they grew in popularity. I had seen just how fast a band like Korn could rise to the top. Maybe God Lives Underwater would too. However, I didn't want them to have any more friends in Boston other than me.

The club was packed even before they hit the stage for their opening slot. David and Jeff's signature dual keyboards faced in opposite directions and already adorned the stage. They were becoming tighter as a band with every show. Even though their set didn't change that much, I could still see that they were perfecting their live songs with each gig.

Lights flashed. Their music was thick and textured. Every note of the songs, either on their albums or live, was so familiar to me that I didn't even need to really pay attention to know what was happening.

I looked at the crowd, and I could see everyone's intensity and how many people were really God Lives Underwater fans. David's lyrics were just as important to all of these people as they were to me. More than half the club sang along to every word with such conviction.

I was so proud of every fan who knew every song, not just the three radio hits. There were so many times when the majority of the audience, especially for an opening band, only knew the songs on the radio. It seemed like people were actually buying the albums and had really listened to each song they had!

After the set was over, I made my way toward the backstage door of the Paradise. David popped his head out and said he would meet me by the bus. Spacehog was giving them some problems, and he didn't want to hang out backstage. It seemed like more than half of the crowd filed outside as well. I realized that there were more people at the show to see God Lives Underwater than there were for the headlining band!

When David met me by the bus, he told me that they had to pack up and get going. They only had four days off before the next show in Virginia. They had a rare chance to stop by home for a few days. He invited me into the bus, but I could only stay for a few minutes.

When I had seen Maids of Gravity again at T.T. the Bear's Place on December 3, 1995, I had the opportunity to hang out and shoot pool with their singer, Ed Ruscha. I had told him that I had become friends with the guys in God Lives Underwater. Ed had expressed to me how much he would love to tour with God Lives Underwater again.

On the bus, I told David this. I thought he would be flattered. Instead, he seemed sarcastically amused.

"Did you guys hear that? Rocky says that Maids of Gravity wants to tour with us again!"

There were some snickers from the guys, and David chuckled. I had no idea what that was all about. I decided to drop the subject and not bring up Maids of Gravity again. I never did find out, but it was time to go. I could tell that David and his band members were tired and antsy to get home.

I gave him a hug good-bye and told them to drive safe.

David told me sometime later, when Spacehog was brought up in a conversation, that God Lives Underwater was kicked off that tour right after a Florida show, four shows after the Boston one. At every show, the clubs would empty out after God Lives Underwater's set, and Spacehog was upset. By the time Spacehog hit the stage each night, they would have to play to almost nonexistent crowds at every gig.

The solution wasn't to flip the order of the bands and go on first, which would have given them a solid audience every night. They chose to throw God Lives Underwater off the tour instead.

Around the same time, I had met a girl online named Annie, who lived in the northwest part of the country. It was a platonic friendship. We shared the same music tastes and movie preferences. Her parents were going through a divorce. We had a lot of fun talking in private chat rooms, America Online's biggest attraction for teenagers just like us.

Annie consistently mentioned how much she wanted to visit the Boston area. She was also a huge God Lives Underwater fan. We discussed making plans for her to come for a weekend based around the next show. After a few months went by, God Lives Underwater announced their first headlining tour.

Sure, I had seen them headline once before, but that wasn't even really a tour. It was a radio show with win-only tickets. This was different because it was backed by their label. They finally had a big enough draw to headline a tour across the country, while only being on their second album.

This was definitely exciting! They would get to play longer than thirty minutes. A longer set meant hearing some of the songs that hadn't been played live before. There would also be less aggravation getting on their guest list.

The tour dates were announced. They were coming to Boston to play Axis on May 8, 1996, just three days after David's twenty-fifth birthday. The band Far, from California, was going to be their opening band. The club booked Kilgore Smudge, from Rhode Island, as the local band.

Annie and I both thought it would be the perfect chance for her to visit. I discussed it with my mother and stepfather, and they ultimately agreed to let Annie stay at our house. Annie bought her plane ticket. She would land the morning of the show and then fly home just two days later.

I picked her up at Boston Logan International Airport, and we went to Claire's Boutique at the Liberty Tree Mall in Danvers. We searched through a bunch of body jewelry. I picked out a nose ring that wasn't too big, but it was still one that I thought David would really like. I paid for it, and we left for the show.

We arrived at Lansdowne Street in plenty of time. The sun hadn't even set yet. We found a great parking spot right outside Axis. As usual I looked around for anyone in the band. The big silver tour bus was already parked on the street. I felt like we were late. Maybe I was just used to getting there before they arrived.

Just like so many times before, it was Tim who I spotted first. "Hey, Tim! What's going on? Where is everybody?"

"Adam and Drew are eating somewhere. David and Jeff are at the WBCN studio. At five o'clock, they're going live on the air for an interview and some acoustic songs."

"Really? Shit! I wish I had known that so I could've taped it."

It was almost five o'clock. I wondered who I could call to record the broadcast for me. I called Matt, and he said he could do it.

We walked back to my car and turned on the radio. If I couldn't be in the studio to witness it, I certainly wasn't going to miss the broadcast. We didn't have to wait long before we heard the last song the station played—"Tahitian Moon," by Porno for Pyros—before the interview started.

"Ladies and Gentlemen, God Lives Underwater," the deejay said.

The opening riff of "Stripped" came through the speakers. David's voice sounded so raw and frail over the acoustic strumming of the guitars. When the song was finished, the few people inside the studio clapped.

A loud squeal of feedback pierced through the speakers.

"We have feedback! Make it go away!" the deejay yelled.

"That was the first time we played that," David apologized. "So it was a little bit choppy."

"Thank you very much for doing this," the deejay said. "This is an extreme departure for you. You made a great exception in doing this. Not only that, you just got off a bus from Portland and the gig. How was the gig?"

"It was… fun," Jeff answered hesitantly.

"Is Portland a place you've been before? You've been to a lot of places like Portland."

"Yep. We've been to a lot of places like Portland—" David began, but the deejay interrupted him.

"You're very small-town people like myself. I think we have that in common."

"We're from a real small town," David added.

"Exactly how small?" the deejay pried.

"Like, four hundred people," David answered.

"How small is that? Is there a store?"

"There's one store," David said. "There's a gas station, post office—"

"And that's it," Jeff added.

"Everyone in the town knows everyone," David finished.

"There is a post office?" the deejay asked.

"Yeah."

"Alright. So your town is so small, if one person left, it wouldn't be a town anymore."

"More or less," Jeff said.

"My town was so small, and maybe yours was the same, that all eight grades of school were in one room. This is true. This is not a lie. There was one teacher," the deejay said. "The eighth grade person was like sitting beside the first grade person. So beat that!"

"Well, all eight grades were in the same"—David took a long pause as a woman cackled in the background—"couple buildings for me."

"Well, we had to get bused like twenty miles to get to our school," Jeff said. "Because all the little towns made up one school. They had to cover an area, like, as big as Texas. So top that!"

"You're near Three Mile Island?" the deejay asked.

"Yeah. We could see it from my house," David laughed.

"You could, really? Because I think everyone has forgotten how intense that was," the deejay continued. "Do you remember it at all?"

"Yeah. But we're not really anywhere near Three Mile Island," David replied.

"Alright," the deejay said. It sounded like David had just confused him.

"I lived near Limerick Power Plant," David clarified. "Sort of the same thing, but never melted down."

I laughed. I knew exactly how David's morbid and dry humor worked. It was especially effective because his delivery was always monotone. I wondered if the deejay knew he was being mocked.

The deejay changed the subject.

"How much of a project is it to take—" He paused to reword his question. "Your songs are extremely electric, and probably written electrically..."

"They're written all different," Jeff answered. "Some of them are written like this. But actually, since that was a cover song of another electronic song that we decided to try and do acoustically—"

"Although I heard that Martin from Depeche Mode writes all his songs on acoustic guitar," David interjected. "So, go figure. He probably heard it like this before."

"Is this your first time on the road at any great length?" the deejay asked. He sounded bored.

"No. We've pretty much been on the road since last February," Jeff answered. "With not more than a month break in between."

"When you first went on the road, what were the surprises? The things you did not expect? The lurching in your lifestyle?"

Jeff chuckled.

"You know what? I never expected to see kids singing the words to all the songs on the album," David said. "Most places, people only know one song. Two songs. That was kind of a surprise."

"That's good."

"That's the good surprise. Bad surprise? How bad the bus could smell!" David said. He laughed again.

"I have tickets to the gig tonight at Axis. I don't usually do this, but what would be a good question for someone to answer to win the tickets? Something not too insanely difficult, but something that would ensure that it was a real fan who won the tickets." There was a moment of silence. "You can take your time. I have coffee over here."

I heard that woman laugh again through the speakers. It was so forced and fake! Who was this woman with them? Why was she even there? I should have been in there with them! What gave her the right?

"They can tell us which record the next song we're gonna play is on," Jeff suggested.

"Excellent!" the deejay proclaimed in his best *Wayne's World* voice. "Very, very good. We'll do it right now. Okay?"

"Might be too tough," Jeff added.

"Oh? That's alright."

"Are we ready to go?" David asked.

"Let's do it!" Jeff answered.

"Alright. One, two three, four."

The fast strumming of the song "Weight" began. David sang, *"Some say it's nothing to all / Some say it's nothing to take the fall."*

I felt heaviness in the air. His voice was so alive with levels of raw emotional walls. What a paradox! Shaky vocals. Textured lyrics. Vulnerability. So many emotions! Even when his voice cracked, it didn't make him sound like a bad singer. It just made him sound human.

"God Lives Underwater. Tonight at Axis with Far and Kilgore Smudge," the deejay advertised before moving onto the next question of the interview. "You guys grow up together?"

"Yeah."

"Like way, way back?"

"Pretty far back," Jeff agreed.

"This is what you do. I'm assuming—and correct me if I'm wrong—this is what you do all the time. So motivation must be easier. People breathing down your neck, 'Write the next hit!' But in those early days, when it was just sort of an impossible dream, what was the motivation? How did you find the thing necessary to put it all together?"

"We just wanted music to listen to that was cool, pretty much," David answered with reserve. "We lived out in the middle of nowhere, and there was no scene. We had a little computer knowledge and some limited equipment. So we just wanted to make good-sounding music that we could listen to."

"And anything you did that day, that was enough. 'Hey, that's cool. Look at that!' And then you'd go on with the rest of the day. So, it wasn't like, 'We're gonna be rock stars, dammit.'"

I could hear David and Jeff agree.

"We really didn't think anyone would ever dig our stuff because a lot of people were like, 'You guys would be really cool if you didn't have those stupid keyboards.' And then other kids were like, 'The songs would be really cool if you didn't have those rock-star guitars.' And then 'You guys would be really cool if your singer could sing or you guys were good-looking'."

This led to laughter from the deejay and woman in the background again. No one else laughed, not even in my car. I could hear David's insecurity through the speakers. He must have been so uncomfortable. I didn't find anything funny at all. I really just wanted that stupid lady to stop laughing!

"So you guys go from the day-to-day thing of, 'That's cool,' and 'That was enough,' to somebody discovering it and decided, 'Well, we can make a lot of money off this stuff. Let's give these guys a break.' What were the chain of events that led to that?"

"One of those songs leaked out through a little network of people to labels. And then like five labels called us. We didn't have a band name then. We thought maybe we should pursue it a little bit more. So, we did," Jeff answered.

"So, if you have a good song these days, you can get out there?"

"Believe it or not, you don't have to have a fancy cover or fancy gimmick or anything," Jeff answered.

"No. You just need to be good at making tunes," David added.

"It used to be that everybody had to go into terrible hock to get studio time. But in these days of the digital audiotape and things, it's really decentralized, and everybody has a better chance," the deejay said.

"Well, if you're kinda smart," David answered, "or not even that smart, and you have a little knowledge of recording gear and stuff, you can make a record at home for nothing. That's why our record label likes us so much."

"We haven't been into a studio yet," Jeff added.

There was a moment of silence. "Wow!" the deejay exclaimed.

"Nope. Everything in the bedroom. Very efficient."

"You put your guitar down. Does that mean we don't have any more songs today? That can be okay if you don't want to. But if you could, I'd love it!"

"We could do one more song," David said.

"I'd love it! Yeah, yeah!" the deejay said. "Please do one more, and then we'll let you go get some lunch."

There was that damn woman laughing again. What was so funny?

"Sounds good to me," David said.

"Lonely Again" started. It sounded really full the way they put one guitar in one speaker and another guitar in the other. David's voice was still cracking, but he sounded like he had more self-confidence.

When the song ended, the deejay said, "Yeah! Thank you! It's so excellent now—you know—I have a picture of you guys in my head when I hear the song. I will have an entirely different feeling when I hear the song, and I hope that's the same for everybody out there who heard you guys."

"On the record," David interrupted, "I play all the right notes on the guitar."

"Still, that sounded pretty cool."

"I couldn't really see what I was doing because of this weird mic situation thing."

"Because you're left-handed!" the deejay said.

"Because I'm weird, you know."

"You've got a couple mics, and you're left-handed, and that really does muck up the normal situation."

"I gotta play upside down, play the guitar the wrong way. I gotta be looking at it the whole time I'm singing. If I want to sing good, I can't look down. It's kinda a toss-up with what you get. Good guitar or good voice."

"As I watch you guys, I realize once again, simple is best. You don't need to be any freaking guitar freak. You just have to have, sort of, a thing in your head. Work it out on the cuff or guitar. Very simple."

"Yeah. We're really not guitar freaks at all," David said.

"In fact we're not very good at playing any instruments. We actually learned how to play a few chords and then started songwriting. That was like the most important thing to us."

"Which something that anyone, who really wants to do it, can do, and that's what's cool. Thank you very much for coming by. Tonight, God Lives Underwater in an entirely different situation. Plugged in, megajuice. Very, very electric. I'll see ya there tonight. I hope I see all you 'BCN people there tonight as well at Axis. Thanks guys!"

The last thing I heard was David's voice.

"Thanks for having us."

As Annie and I sat in my car once the broadcast was over. I almost didn't know what to do with myself. I knew there would be a bit more time before the guys returned to the venue from the station. David didn't even know I was here yet. I looked at Annie. I suggested that we should just continue to wait for the guys to come back. She agreed. She was just excited that she had the chance to meet the band.

Time felt like it dragged on forever. David and the rest of the band finally arrived at Axis. Annie and I got out of my car and greeted them in the street as they came out. David told me that they were going to go inside to eat the pizza that the club had supplied.

"You guys are more than welcome to come in and eat," David said.

We walked with him toward the back door of the club. David's chain wallet swung down by his side. His blond hair and lanky frame were exactly how I remembered. He showed the bouncer his pass and told him that we were with the band.

"We're gonna try to do 'Stripped' for the first time tonight. The problem is that Adam doesn't really know the song, so we're going to use soundcheck to teach him," David said as we walked inside.

Axis was on the smaller side for a venue. There was a bar to the right and a separate lounge area with televisions on the left.

A woman stood at the back of the room. Although she was trying to look inconspicuous, she radiated a level of command presence about her. She had short, spiky red hair and carried a thin folder with her. She probably looked more important than she actually was. I immediately didn't like her, but I also couldn't put my finger on why yet.

We stood in front of the bar as the bartender set up the stock of booze for the night. I hoped that David didn't think I was taking advantage of his hospitality, by always showing up with a new person at their shows and by expecting him to get us in each time.

We kept our distance from the spiky red-haired lady who made me feel uncomfortable. God Lives Underwater took to the stage for soundcheck.

"Whenever you guys are ready," the soundman said.

David stepped up to the microphone. The room was quiet and empty. I thought it was strange how I could see him in his proper environment, and yet I noticed how awkward and out of place that environment really was.

"If you don't mind, we're going to work on a new song," David said.

"Doesn't matter to me what you do, as long as you guys are playing. I just need to get my levels."

The spiky red-haired lady laughed. It was more like a cackle—that same skin-grating cackle that I had heard during the radio interview. At least I could put a face to the voice that

I had despised so much during their radio broadcast! I shook my head and directed my attention back to the band onstage.

David and Jeff knew the song like the back of their hands already. I could see how much it meant to David to be able to play it live. David took complete control of the moment. It very rare when I could witness him taking charge like that. Both David and Jeff stopped the song when Adam didn't get a part perfect, so they could explain and go over the part again.

Annie and I heard God Lives Underwater practice the first minute of "Stripped" at least ten times.

"If y'all don't think you can pull it together before the show, I don't think you should play it tonight," the spiky red-haired lady said with a very commanding tone.

I looked at David to see how he would handle the situation. I had never seen David, or anyone else, have to make such an internal decision with the band in front of me. He just stood there. He wanted, so badly, to make it work. I could see how much he didn't want to argue either. David just wanted it to work itself out.

"Give us a few more minutes," David said.

"Alright," she whined. She threw up her hands in defeat.

"If we don't think we can get through it tonight, we can always pass and work on it later."

The room suddenly felt a lot emptier than it did just moments ago. The space between the band and the lady grew even wider. David and Jeff turned their backs to the soundman and faced Adam behind the drums. I watched God Lives Underwater play "Stripped" all the way through, for the very first time. When someone had challenged their territory of creativity, David and the rest of the band just pushed twice as hard and made it happen.

"You guys want to play one more song all the way through?" the soundman asked.

"Sure," David replied.

They played "All Wrong" and finished the soundcheck. David jumped off the stage. His feet creating a loud *thump* that echoed through the empty club. He went to the bar where Annie and I stood.

"What did you think?" he asked me.

"I think 'Stripped' is going to sound awesome," I replied.

"Yeah. I'm just afraid of playing it live, you know? What you guys just saw was the only experience Adam and Drew have with the song."

"I think it's going to be fine," I said optimistically. "I have something for you, since it was your birthday last week."

"Oh, Rock, you didn't have to do anything."

"I know. But the whole nose-ring thing really pissed me off. So, here," I said. I dug into my pocket, felt for the small plastic envelope that his new nose ring was in, and pulled it out. "Please put that in and don't ever put anything in your nose that you didn't know where it came from. Okay? Even if you lose this one, let me know. I'll replace it. I'd rather keep buying them for you, and know that you aren't being an asshole and picking shit up off the ground."

"Thanks, me-han!"

David looked very touched that I had actually bought him a new nose ring and that I cared so much about what he had done with the dirty one. At the same time, he looked embarrassed.

"You even got the right size!" he said.

"Of course," I answered. "Happy birthday."

"What size is it?" Annie asked.

"It's a zero gauge. The only size that feels okay in my nose. All the cartilage has started to rot away from the cocaine," he said as he lifted his head and pushed up the tip of his nose, so she could see. "That's probably what gives me my singing voice. Watch this."

He unclipped a padlock from his chain wallet and opened it.

"David, you're not…" I knew exactly what he was going to show her. He slipped the padlock right through his nose and locked it. He put his hands down by his side. I lowered my head in disgust.

I was ashamed that I had just bought him a new nose ring, so he wouldn't put anything in his nose that wasn't sanitary. Did he really have to wear a padlock from his nose to show Annie how large the hole had become? It was insulting actually. Somehow I had an easier time accepting that drugs caused the hole than I did watching a padlock swing from his nose. I was mortified. "Okay, David. Please take it out," I said. I just couldn't take looking at it anymore.

He removed the padlock, clipped it back on his belt, and wore the new ring I bought him instead. I actually felt like I was babysitting.

"Did you guys hear about the radio station contest where we were just interviewed?" David asked me.

"WBCN? No, what? All I heard was the trivia question to get tickets for the show."

"No. Not that," David chuckled. "They had a win-dinner-with-God-Lives-Underwater contest this week. Some lucky contestant and a friend could win dinner with us at a restaurant."

We walked out of the rear door of the club and back outside onto Lansdowne Street.

"Wait, what?" I asked in disbelief. "I don't listen to the radio that much so I must have missed that."

"Yeah. How crazy is this? Some girl won. I have to be there in fifteen minutes. It's right around the corner. She's there now with her friend and representatives from the radio station."

"Do I get to have dinner with God Lives Underwater?" I asked, laughing.

"That's not funny. This is one of the most ridiculous things I've ever been a part of. It wasn't even us who did this. The radio station that's promoting the show tonight set it up themselves. What are we going to do? The most I'm going to say to her is something like, 'Please pass the salt.'"

"Oh, man! Can we come to at least keep you sane?"

"Rocky, believe me, if I could, I would ditch this, and we would go grab a pizza and a beer somewhere."

We walked up Lansdowne Street, and I shook my head. I thought about how introverted and shy he was around people who he didn't know. Maybe I was actually glad that I wasn't invited.

"Why don't you guys just hang out here? I promise I'll make this as fast as possible. We should still have time to hang out before doors open."

"Alright, man. Good luck," I said to him. I really meant it. I knew David's personality and how he got intimidated around people he didn't already know.

"Thanks, me-han. This is so ridiculous."

Annie and I watched David walk up the street by himself toward a dinner that he really didn't want to be a part of. It was actually a pretty good idea for a contest. Who wouldn't want to win a dinner with their favorite band? It was just a bad idea for David.

I felt so helpless as we watched him. I knew how much he wanted the dinner to be over already. Of course he wanted to meet fans and make their night special. He was just forced into a situation he didn't feel comfortable in. I sympathized with him. He was only comfortable in situations he created when it came to people he didn't already know. Especially with fans of the band who treated him like a hero.

Annie and I waited around the club for at least an hour and a half. We became friends with the bouncers. To kill time, we talked with some of the band members of Kilgore Smudge and Far.

The entire time David was gone, I was distracted by thoughts of him being at dinner. I knew David's personality very well. David didn't have a very convincing poker face. His demeanor toward the fans during the dinner could very well reflect how much he dreaded being there. Surprisingly, I felt worse for him having to muddle through it than I did for the fans who might be disappointed with David's sour attitude.

Eventually, at some point before the two-hour mark, we saw David walking toward us.

"Do you guys mind coming back to the hotel room we rented so I can take a shower? I really need one before we play tonight."

"Where's the hotel?" I asked.

"Around the corner on Boylston Street, I think. If we take your car, I can show you."

"Okay. My car is across the street."

We walked back to my Ford Tempo, the Midnight

Cowboy. David got into the backseat, and Annie sat up front. He insisted that she rode shotgun. He gave me directions to the hotel. I immediately shut off the radio when I started the car's engine. A God Lives Underwater album was in my player, and I thought that might be just be a little too creepy for him.

After a few moments we pulled into the parking lot of the hotel and got out of the car. We walked past the front desk and got into the elevator.

"Our manager rented this room so we could all take turns to shower. We aren't going to sleep here, but it's nice to have a place where we can clean up."

We followed him to the room and went inside after he swiped the key card. The bathroom was immediately to the left when we walked in. The small hallway gave way to a typical hotel room with a queen-size bed.

Annie sat on the bed. David undressed to his boxer shorts. After he had taken off most of his clothes, while talking to us about random stuff as if this was the most natural situation in the world, he walked into the bathroom and turned the shower on.

I stood in front of the open bathroom door as he was talking to us. I stepped backward so that I was out of his view. I heard the shower curtain pull closed, and he was still talking.

He felt Stabbing Westward had ripped him off with their song, "What Do I Have to Do?"

I decided that it was easier to just go into the bathroom while he showered to have the conversation, so we wouldn't have to yell over the water. I sat on the toilet while he showered. If David was comfortable with it, so was I.

"Listen to our song, 'Weaken,' and then listen to their song. It's the same note progression into the chorus."

The bathroom was getting foggy from the steam. I thought of Annie on the bed in the other room. Just then David turned off the water.

"Hey, Rock. Can you grab me a towel?"

I grabbed one of the generic hotel towels and handed it to him through a small crack he had made in the shower curtain. He dried himself off and stepped out with the towel wrapped around his waist. I excused myself from the bathroom so he could put on clothes.

I sat with Annie on the bed. After a few minutes, David came out with his hair all wet, tucked behind his ear, and dressed in new clothes.

"Well, that's it. Are you guys ready?"

We took the elevator to the lobby and walked out of the hotel. David sat in the passenger seat this time, and Annie took the backseat. We drove back to Lansdowne Street with a clean and fresh-smelling David Reilly.

All of a sudden, David chuckled as we drove.

"What?" I asked.

"I haven't told you yet why we can never, ever play the song 'Tortoise' live ever again."

"No, you haven't. Why not?" I was really curious to why that would be. If David was serious, that meant that we had just lost a song forever.

"Well, all the synthesizer lines on that song came from a keyboard that we built ourselves. It's one of a kind. We can't buy another one, or even fix it, if it ever got broken."

"I didn't know that," I replied.

"Yeah. After a show just recently, we were loading the equipment, and the keyboard was accidentally dropped. It shattered into a million pieces."

"Are you serious?"

"Yeah. Unless we play that song acoustically, which I don't think will ever happen, it'll be put to rest forever. I can never rebuild that keyboard."

I let out an "Oh, man," as I realized what he had just said, even though "Tortoise" was my least favorite song on *Empty*. As much as it was awful that the song was sent to the God Lives Underwater graveyard prematurely, it was easier to take, all the same.

We arrived back at Axis. David said that we should go inside for the show. He wanted to get some rest on the bus before they had to go on. The first band was already playing. Annie and I went inside, and saw the last half of Kilgore Smudge's set and all of Far's set.

God Lives Underwater came out with no frills, no stage gimmicks, and the band members even wore the same clothes they wore during soundcheck. There wasn't even a funky backdrop or an over-the-top light show. It was just the band rocking out as hard as they could.

They played for over an hour and covered almost every song from both albums. The only songs from their catalogue that they did not play were "Drag Me Down," "We Were Wrong," "Tortoise," "Scared," and "Weight."

The band returned to the stage for a final encore. David's new nose ring still hung over his top lip. I just knew that they were going to play "Stripped." This was do-or-die time. This would be much different than during soundcheck in an empty club. This was The Show. I knew how David felt about The Show.

We almost didn't recognize the song until David's voice came through the speakers. The crowd cheered loudly as

David sang the first line of the lyrics. No one in that audience could ever know that they were witnessing the very first live performance of a song that everybody knew so well. Furthermore, no one in that audience could ever know how close the band had come to not play that song live at all.

I couldn't help but smile. Annie and I knew. I had been a personal witness to their struggle. They pulled it off perfectly!

After "Stripped," they closed the show with "Weaken" as the big finale. Adam and Drew walked offstage, and left Jeff and David with just their keyboards. They always had this battling keyboard thing going on. It eventually had so many overdubs and loops that it just became noise with the strobe lights flashing overhead. They walked offstage and left the synthesizers to loop indefinitely with what they had just played.

I could see the confused soundman. He was probably wondering whether or not the show was actually over, just like everyone else was thinking too. He appeared reluctant to turn down the volume of the keyboards in the house speakers.

The entire band was probably already in the bus. The stage was empty. The lights were still flashing. The club was filled with static and noise, backed with a looping beat. Still, no one knew if it was really over. Eventually the house lights came up. The soundman still didn't know if he should kill the sound. Some people filed out of the club. Others stayed, expecting the band to come back out. I found this situation extremely amusing.

The soundman took a gamble and killed the noise. Annie and I headed for the door with the rest of the crowd.

On the way out I grabbed a poster for *Empty* from the wall. I remembered that Drew was the only one left who hadn't signed anything. I was determined to have all four members' signatures on something at least.

We got outside and went straight to the bus. I knocked on the door. Fans hoping to catch a glimpse of the band, or even just to have a few words with any of them, already surrounded the vehicle. The door opened, and Annie and I walked inside, just like that.

David was sitting on a bench opposite the dining table. I sat down next to him. I told him how confused everyone was with the ending of the show. He laughed. He told me that was the point.

Then I asked Drew to sign the poster for *Empty*.

"Brian, we're friends. That's kind of weird, signing something for you."

I asked him to just do it anyway. He took a pen and completely defaced the poster with his name. He wrote DREW in huge letters and made all these lines underneath to destroy the artwork on the poster. I actually thought it was pretty funny.

"You know when you have spent too much time with your own songs when you can mimic the opening synth line with just your voice," David said.

"Okay. Go ahead," I challenged him.

He chose "Don't Know How to Be." I couldn't believe what was coming out of his mouth! It sounded exactly like what was on the album!

He smiled.

It was like some sort of beatbox. I was completely dumbfounded.

We spent some more time on the bus just eating pizza and drinking soda. I didn't know where they had to go next on the tour, but after a while, their bus driver made a very loud and obnoxious announcement that they were leaving. Anyone not in the band had to exit the bus.

He basically just meant me and Annie. No one else had come onto the bus but us.

David stood up and gave me a hug, shook Annie's hand, and told her that it was nice to meet her too. She thanked him for everything. David walked us off the bus.

"Hey, Rocky. I'll see you soon, okay? Thanks for the nose ring!"

"Of course. Just don't piss me off again!"

David laughed. Annie and I walked away. The door closed. Yet another God Lives Underwater night had come to an end.

A lot happened to me between their last show and the next time that I saw David and the rest of the band again. Christine and I had actually gotten back together in June. She signed up for City Year in Columbus, Ohio, and would be leaving in August for eight months. My band, Yellow #1, was in the studio finishing up our debut album, *Bottle of Rain*.

Every year the Boston radio station WAAF had an outside festival called Locobazooka with three different stages made up of bands from all over New England. They also booked a national band to headline, which helped with the ticket sales.

The gates would open at nine o'clock in the morning. The first band would be on around 9:15. The headlining band would go on around five o'clock, so they could be off by the six o'clock noise ordinance curfew.

God Lives Underwater was booked to be the headlining band that year. The radio station promoted the headlining band the most, to get more of a draw. For weeks before the show, at nearly every commercial break in WAAF's programming, there was an advertisement for Locobazooka. A clip from a God Lives Underwater song was featured in almost every ad. WAAF also played "No More Love," "All Wrong," and "Don't Know How to Be" in almost sickening rotation. There were full-page advertisements of the show taken out in local music magazines. It was almost a bombardment of God Lives Underwater music. In addition the radio station, along with Strawberries Music, was going to set up a meet-and-greet signing session with the band.

I was again without someone to accompany me. Christine had already gone in Ohio. Both Dogboy and Dann were also away at college. My stepsister Lauren was only thirteen years old. She had really gotten into the band by hearing them constantly from being around me. She really wanted to go and see them live. As it was an outside all-day, all-ages festival, Lauren's mother told her that she would be allowed to go with me, if I could promise that she would be home before eight o'clock. There was just no way that I could promise something like that. Plans with David were always so unpredictable after shows. Lauren would just have to wait for a different show. I was flying solo for this one as well.

I woke up around seven o'clock on the morning of September 22, 1996. I was soon out the door and on my way to Worcester, Massachusetts, which was about sixty miles from where I lived in Lynn at the time.

When I arrived at Green Hill Park, the large field that WAAF had rented out for the day, there were already security guards directing people where to park. I hoped that I had made it here before the band did. It would be much easier for me to wait for them than to have to convince one of the security guards that I really did know the band. At a show this big, that would be nearly impossible.

The parking area for the show was in a dirt lot. There was a long paved road to the front gates of the field. No vehicles were allowed on the road except for the bands' and any emergency apparatuses. The road was about three-fourths of a mile long. It's canopy was a ceiling of overhanging tree branches and leaves which made for a shady walk. There were two security guards positioned at the entrance of the road from the parking lot to make sure no unauthorized vehicles tried to get in. Neither a ticket nor a pass was needed to travel this road. Only at the gate to the field itself when a ticket was necessary to enter.

I headed toward the gate with everyone else. I saw Metalheads, Skinheads, Burnouts, slutty girls, Jocks, families with children, Rivetheads, and Punks. Pretty much anyone and anything was here.

I reached the front gate and found someone who looked somewhat official. I needed a foolproof angle. "Excuse me," I asked her. "I'm with God Lives Underwater. We came together in two vehicles, and I think I may have beaten the rest of them here. Do you know if the van with the gear has arrived yet?"

"Let me check. Hold on a moment."

She grabbed her walkie-talkie and asked someone if God Lives Underwater had checked in yet. The person on the other end, who was obviously inside the field, confirmed that the band had definitely not shown up yet.

I thanked her and walked back down the road. I felt a bit like a salmon swimming against the current. I could already feel the warmth of the sun on my arms and legs.

I decided to leave for a visit to a convenient store to buy some soda to tide me over. I used the payphone there to call Christine. I wanted to tell her that the band Tree, who was Christine's favorite local band, was also playing the show on the main stage.

After buying my soda and talking to Christine, I walked back toward the parking lot, which was rapidly filling up with fans. I made my way toward the gate that led to the road.

I sat down on the curb and talked to another security guard. I told him how I had beat the rest of the band here and that they had the van. I was just going to hang out until they showed up. He seemed very sympathetic and accommodating. He told me to let him know if I needed anything.

I watched the crowd for about an hour and decided to take a walk down the road to the main gate again, just to kill time. My watch went from ten o'clock, to eleven o'clock, to noon, very slowly. I was thinking that maybe they weren't coming. Maybe they canceled. I would never know.

My soda was almost gone. The sun was getting much hotter, even under the protective covering of the trees. There was an almost constant low-end *thump* from the bass of whatever band was on the stage.

The worst part was that I didn't know how much longer I would be waiting. David and I had never discussed what time they were planning on arriving.

Just shy of one o'clock, I had been here for almost five hours when I finally saw an all-too-familiar van finally pull around the corner into the parking lot. The driver's side window rolled down.

A security guard pointed to the access road. "Is this them?"

"I believe so," I replied.

The van made its way toward me, and I stood up. The security guard that I had been talking to all morning greeted the driver. I still couldn't make out who was driving or how many people were inside.

The driver and the security guard exchanged a few words. He leaned his body away, pointed toward me, and then continued talking. The security guard waved me over, and I ran to the driver's side. Jeff was driving.

"Get in," he said to me.

I heard the sliding door of the van open on the other side. I ran around the front and stepped inside. Adam, his girlfriend, and Drew were in the back row. David was sitting by himself. Tim was riding shotgun up front with Jeff. David was wearing his sunglasses. I took the empty seat next to him.

He nodded lethargically at me.

"What's up?" I asked rhetorically. I was just so excited not to be sitting on that curb anymore. I didn't even know what else to say.

"Hey, me-han," David replied.

"I didn't know what time you guys were going to be here. I got here before ten this morning."

"We had a show last night in New York City," David said. "We got lost on the way here this morning."

Something didn't seem right with him. I couldn't put my finger on it. David seemed almost like he was trying to hide something. I realized that this was the earliest that I had ever been with David during the day. He seemed to be more like a mannequin.

We slowly drove up the road toward the front gate. We had to inch our way forward so we didn't hit any of the pedestrians. The windows to the van were tinted. As people stepped aside for us, almost every one of them glanced in to see if they could make out who was inside. The air-conditioning was on. It was very quiet.

Adam introduced me to his girlfriend, Melissa, who had come with them from Philadelphia to New York, and then this show for the weekend. After the introduction, I looked at David.

"Hey, are you okay?" I asked him.

"Yeah, me-han. I'm just really tired. I didn't get much sleep from the show last night. I'm exhausted."

I studied his face as he looked away and out the window next to him. My realization of the truth came down like a ton a bricks. There was a line that could be crossed between us—for example, when I got mad about the dirty nose ring. In addition there was also a line that David didn't want to cross with me either. That line was disappointment.

I could see that David was tired. But I had also seen David tired almost every time that we had hung out. This time, however, David was high. I knew what he did and what he used, but, up until this moment, it had always existed in dialogue format only. Everyone in the van knew that he was high. For whatever reason, he used tired as an excuse. Not only was I disappointed in him, I was also ashamed.

We sat in silence as the van pulled toward the front gate. Jeff rolled down the window to speak.

"We're God Lives Underwater. Do you know where we go or where we get passes?"

She looked at her clipboard. "Okay. You guys are down for six passes. Is everyone here with you?"

David leaned forward over Jeff's shoulder. "There are actually seven of us."

"Your management only forwarded us six names. That's all we have passes for," she said to David.

"There are seven of us now. Please get us another pass. Thanks," David said and sat back in the seat.

The original quantity didn't include me. My heart was racing. I didn't know if this was actually going to happen or not. I had never seen David that definitive with anyone before. "Thanks, man," I whispered.

The van idled in its spot while the lady left. She came back with a handful of bright-yellow laminates with a robot on it attached to a green lanyard.

"These are band passes," she said. "They get you full access anywhere on the field and access to all the food in the tents. Please keep these visible around your necks at all times while walking around."

She stepped aside. The gate lifted for us to drive through. Jeff handed the passes to everyone. We drove onto the grass and followed a dirt path behind the stage where all the bands' vehicles were.

After we found a spot to park the van, Jeff shut off the engine. We all got out. David tied his pass to the belt loop of his shorts. It hung down to his knees. I always thought his style was unique for that time period, especially the way he wore long johns under his shorts instead of pants.

Behind the stage, there were other bands everywhere. They practiced on drum kits and ate food. Two long tables were under a tent filled with food and drinks, basically buffet style.

"Anyone hungry?" Jeff asked as he headed toward the food.

David and I walked to the tables, got in line, and piled food on our plates too. There were tables set up all over the backstage area. We found a table and sat down.

"How's your band going?" David asked me.

"Good. We're in the studio about twice a week or so, laying down tracks for the album."

"I'm trying to put out a Depeche Mode tribute album," David said, in-between mouthfuls of food. "I have a few bands interested in submitting tracks for it. I'm focusing on that right now since the touring for *Empty* is finally coming to an end."

"Really? That's awesome. Depeche Mode is one of my favorite bands."

"No one has done a good tribute album yet," he said. "If I can get a label to back it, I'd like to release it sometime around the next God Lives Underwater album. I need to get a good batch of songs. I already have The Smashing Pumpkins, The Cure, Deftones, and Rammstein all signed on. I'm going to call it *For the Masses*."

"I would love to do something like that," I said as I stuffed some more potato salad into my mouth.

"What song would you do, if you could?"

"Probably 'Waiting for the Night.' That's a song I think Yellow #1 could pull off the best, in our style."

"Well, I can't make any promises, but if you can get me an unmastered copy of the song, I'll see if there would be room for it."

"Wow! That would be amazing! Thanks! Are you going to use 'Stripped' as the God Lives Underwater song?"

"Nope. We've already solidified 'Fly on the Windscreen' instead. Oh," he said. He paused to swallow the food that was in his mouth. "Did you hear the rumor about me dying?"

"I actually did hear something about it. I just didn't pay

any attention to it, since I had gotten an email from you after the supposed-death. I forgot to ask you about it."

The rumor that David from God Lives Underwater had died was spread within the same two weeks that Mike Patton from Faith No More and Trent Reznor from Nine Inch Nails had also died. The rumors weren't exactly believable.

"Yeah. Some asshole soundman in Rhode Island started the rumor online. I guess we pissed him off when we played there, so he got back at me by posting that I had overdosed and died."

"Can you do anything about it?"

"I'm sure gonna try the next time we play Providence," he said, chuckling evilly. "I don't know what that guy's deal is with us."

"That's still pretty shitty though, saying that."

"Eh. Fuck 'em. Right, Rocky?"

"Exactly."

We finished our lunch, stood up, and walked over to where the rest of the guys stood near the other vans. Adam leaned over and whispered something to David. I had to squint my eyes from the sunlight. I tried not to make it look so obvious that I was trying to hear what they were saying.

"We're gonna run an errand," David suddenly said to me. "You can either stay here or come with us."

"I'm gonna walk around and check out some of the other bands, if you wanna stay with me," Jeff suggested.

"Yeah, okay. I'll stay with Jeff," I said. I had a feeling that might be a better idea.

"Okay. We'll see you when we get back."

David, Adam, and Adam's girlfriend, Melissa, got into

the van and headed toward the access road. None of their equipment was in it anymore. It had all been unloaded and left at the bottom of the backstage ramp. Tim and Drew watched over it.

Jeff and I ventured into the crowd together and walked along the semicircle perimeter of the audience. Food and drink stands were every few yards. The ground was littered with people either sitting or lying on blankets as they watched the bands. There were circles of Hacky Sack games, guys with their shirts off, girls in bikini tops, long lines at the Porta Potties. It definitely was a typical outside festival.

As I walked around with Jeff, I had to admit that I too had a cocky bounce in my step. People looked at our band passes around our necks as we passed by them.

We stood and watched a random band play for a few minutes.

"Have you ever heard of this band Tree that's playing today?" Jeff asked me.

"Yeah. They're probably the biggest local band. They've played Warped Tour and Lollapalooza. They're part of the hardcore scene. They just released their third album, *Downsizing the American Dream.*"

"I knew I heard something about them before! I was surprised when I saw their name on the bill. I didn't know they were from Boston."

We walked toward the entrance to the backstage area again. I hung out with Tim and Drew for a bit. We waited for David and Adam to come back. When the van returned, I made my way to them. Adam and his girlfriend immediately walked toward the crowd area.

"Did you check anything out?" David asked.

"Yeah. Jeff and I went out for a bit and watched one of the bands. There's a pretty big crowd out there."

"That's good. Hopefully they're all God Lives Underwater fans. Or if they aren't yet, they'll buy our albums after the show."

"Yeah. What's up with that booth setup, by the way?"

"I don't know. It looks like we just have to sit there and sign some albums at a table that Strawberries Music is setting up for us."

"What should I do while you guys are doing that? Are you gonna be able to hang out afterward?"

"I really don't know what's going on after the show. We don't leave until tomorrow morning though."

They were here for the whole night! I was really thankful that I didn't bring Lauren with me after all.

"I'm sure you could just hang out behind the table while we're doing the signing," David said.

We stopped talking and listened to the thump of the bass from whatever band was playing.

"David?"

"Yeah, Rock?"

"I know that it was just a rumor, but I just want you to know that one of my biggest fears is waking up one day and finding out that you died of an overdose. Although I can't tell you what to do, and I would never think less of you for using, I just want you to know that I have that fear. I believe that you and I have become close friends. Even if the only time we spend together is surrounded by a show. If that's all we can get, then I'll take it. I just worry about you. Probably a lot more than you know."

David's face showed complete shock that I brought up drugs so bluntly. "Okay. Let me explain something to you," he began. "The reason why junkies overdose is because they don't know how much their body can take. Or if they get clean for a while and go back to using, they think they can use the same amount they were using right before they got clean. The reason why you never have to worry about me overdosing is because I know exactly how much my body can take. Continuing to take the amount that I use at this point is actually preventing me from overdosing or getting sick."

I listened to everything he said like it was gospel. This was such a foreign conversation for me that I didn't have any rebuttal. I had to accept it and just blindly trust him. "Okay, David. Like I said, I'll never look down on you because of anything you do. I just want you to know my concerns. I have always admired you, but I also feel that the lines between fan and band were blurred right from the beginning. I feel like I have the right to voice my concerns."

"And I thank you for that. You're right. You can tell me anything."

"I just worry about you, that's all."

"Listen, Rocky, I promise you this much. If I'm going to die before old age or before my time, it will be because of something else. It will not be because of an overdose or drugs. That's not my style. You know that."

"I know," I said. I felt embarrassed.

"Plus I'd rather go out in a much more glamorous way. Like dropping dead while playing Wembley Stadium or something." He laughed.

That didn't really give me any more comfort than before.

"Alright, man. I trust you. I just want you to know how pissed off I would be if I find out you just lied to me about this," I said with a smirk.

"I'm not going anywhere any time soon." He put his arm around my shoulder. "I'm always in complete control of my body. I know exactly when too much is too much, or too little is too little," he finished with conviction.

I had never heard David so sure of his own words before.

"Do you want to take another walk around so I can see what's going on out there?" he asked.

"Absolutely."

We exited the backstage area and walked through the crowd. People actually recognized him. They whispered and pointed at us. We never slowed our pace. David seemed oblivious to the other people noticing him.

At one point a group of teenage girls debated whether or not to talk to him. When one of them got enough courage, the other two followed.

"Excuse me," the girl said shyly. "Are you David from God Lives Underwater?"

"I am."

"We're your biggest fans! We just saw you guys at Pearl Street in Northampton. You rocked!" The girls giggled embarrassingly.

How could God Lives Underwater have played a show in Northampton, Massachusetts, that I didn't even know had happened?

David morphed into his meek and shy demeanor, an automatic reflex that he recoiled into when someone he didn't know approached him with such overbearing admiration.

"Thanks, guys," he answered.

That was his way of trying to paint himself out of a social situation that he no longer wanted to be in. At the same time, though, he felt obligated to be respectful enough to stay here.

I stood with a smile on my face and my band pass across my chest. David's laminate flipped around at his knees. Deep down I silently cursed these girls for attending a God Lives Underwater show in Massachusetts that I hadn't known about.

"We won't bother you anymore. We just wanted to come over, say hi, and tell you how much we can't wait for the show."

The girls finally excused themselves, and we continued to walk around the outskirts of the crowd.

"David!"

We both looked up as a female with dyed-red hair in her mid-twenties came trotting in our direction.

"Hey!" David replied.

I followed him until we were all standing together.

He gave her a hug. "Kerrie, this is my friend Rocky. Rocky, this is Kerrie."

We said hello and shook each other's hands. I could tell, with the first handshake, that we were already jockeying for a position. Neither of us really knew who the other one was.

"Do you know anybody playing today?" David asked her.

"Not really." She pulled out the festival's program, handed to her at the gate, complete with the current lineup.

"Is that the bill?" David asked.

"Yeah," she said and handed it to him.

David opened it up, and I looked over his shoulder. A short bio was provided for each band. At the end of the pamphlet, a full-page bio of God Lives Underwater had been printed along with a picture of the band.

"Nice sneakers," Kerrie said to David.

"Yeah, you wanna see something cool? Show her, Rocky."

I held up my right foot in the air and showed her that we had the same sneakers.

"Aw, isn't that cute!" Kerrie said mockingly.

I hoped that she didn't think I was some sort of obsessed fan-boy that followed the band around, harassed the singer, and dressed the same way.

I didn't know if she felt like she needed to one-up me, but, out of nowhere, she babbled something along the lines of, "When I was on the road with Cracker and also The Cranberries…"

David then suggested that we should be getting back to the gear and the rest of the guys.

"Is there room for me to come too?" Kerrie asked.

Oh, God. Please, no! I thought.

"Sorry. We had just enough passes for the band, Melissa, Tim, and Rocky."

"I'm here by myself though. You can't just sneak me through the gate?"

"Nah. I don't think so."

"Alright. Try to find me after the show," she said.

That was exactly what I didn't want. As we walked toward the stage, I asked David about her.

"That's just Kerrie from Rhode Island. She comes to the Rhode Island shows. She's one of those types of people who just wants to hang out and be close to whatever band is the flavor of the month. Did you notice how she made sure she worked in the fact that she knew Cracker and The Cranberries into the conversation?"

"Yeah," I said. I was satisfied that David knew who was sincere or not.

"She's harmless and a little annoying, but she's cool. I'm sure she'll move on when the next big thing happens."

We made our way behind the stage just as the sun was starting to go down. There was a slight chill in the September New England air, especially when it blew across the field. I followed David to where all their equipment was laid out, so he could take inventory. They were scheduled to go on in less than an hour.

"Where should I be when you guys are playing?" I asked him.

"I don't know. I guess you can just come up with us and hang out on the stage, if you want. I don't think anyone would say anything about that."

"Really?!"

This wasn't some small venue show. I was expecting him to tell me that I should go into the crowd so there wouldn't be any problems with security. I thought about being on the stage with God Lives Underwater and looking out over ten thousand people, all pressed against the barrier below.

"Hey, Jeff!" David yelled. "Rocky's gonna be on the stage with us while we play. Is that cool?"

"Yeah. If you want to, you can just hang out by my guitar cabs."

"Sounds like a plan," I said. I tried so hard not to act too giddy.

"Hey, have you seen *Toy Story*?" David asked me.

"Of course! It was so funny. I saw it in the theatre."

"Do you know who my favorite character was in that? The

aliens with the claw."

"Those guys were great!"

"Hey, Jeff!" David yelled. "Remember the aliens in *Toy Story*?"

"*The claw!*" Jeff yelled back, mimicking the aliens' voices perfectly.

"Me-han, that part killed me," he said.

It was finally time to get the equipment onstage. I stepped aside to let Tim and the guys grab their gear.

"Are you just going to stand there or are you going to grab something?"

I didn't realize that I was just watching them move stuff. I grabbed anything I could, and helped them move the amps and drums up the ramp to the stage. Once we were done, Jeff told me to stand at the side, near his amps, while they got their levels right.

It was so exhilarating to look over a crowd of at least ten thousand fans, all of them pushing toward the barrier below; to be able to stand where I was and watch the line check. All of the waiting that I did earlier in the day was worth it.

I also hoped that, wherever Kerrie was, she could see that I was up here with them, not her. I didn't know where this animosity or jealousy came from, but I felt threatened somehow.

"Go ahead and just sit on it," Jeff said, motioning to his guitar amp.

"Are you serious?"

"Yeah. You won't hurt it."

I pulled myself up and sat right on top of Jeff's amp. My feet dangled in front of his speaker, directly next to his foot pedals.

I watched their entire set from the top of Jeff's amp. The crowd went crazy. There were so many crowd surfers. Almost everyone in the first ten rows sang every single word. Mosh pits started everywhere in the crowd and sent dust rising into the air.

Their sound was awful onstage. Even though I was hearing the songs only through Jeff's monitor, I could barely hear David sing. Jeff was too loud. All I really got out of that set was the guitar riffs for every song, and the low end of the drums and keyboards. If I didn't know their lyrics as well as I did, I wouldn't even have known what David was singing. Even still, I wouldn't have traded that moment for anything.

I didn't sing along to any of their songs, and I didn't clap when the songs were over either. I was way beyond partaking in normal audience responses.

They played their usual set for the *Empty* tour, so I already knew what song they were going to close with. When they were finished, I followed them down the ramp.

David was complaining how outside festival shows never sounded good and that he couldn't even hear himself in his monitors. I didn't have any comforting words for him since I didn't really hear anything myself, except for the guitar riffs.

The equipment was allowed to stay on the stage since they were the headlining band. They headed over to a long table on the other side of the field that was set up for the band to sign copies of their albums.

"Are you coming?" David asked me.

"I guess so."

A rep from Strawberries Music, who was sponsoring the signing, met us halfway there. She ushered us hastily to our designated spot. Already a substantial line of fans was at the table. Four seats were set up with a stack of God Lives Underwater posters next to piles of both of their albums.

"Only people who buy one of your albums at the table can get it signed. Then everyone can get a free poster at the end of the table," the representative explained. "If they brought an album from home, they can't get it signed, but they can go through the line, meet you guys, and still get a poster."

"So, what you're saying is that, if one of our fans comes with a copy of our album that they have already bought, we aren't allowed to sign it?" David asked suspiciously.

"That's how we have it set up," she answered.

"Well, that seems really fucked up to the fans who already have the album and came to meet us!" David retorted.

I was expecting a full blow-out at any moment. I could see David's point of view. I knew how he felt about their existing fans.

"Think of it as an incentive for them to buy a copy of your albums for a friend or family member," the representative said. She was obviously trying to justify the point that David had just made to her.

"I'll tell you right now. I don't like the way this is set up. We were unaware of these rules," he said.

I was thinking that he was about to cancel the meet-and-greet altogether. Maybe the only thing that drove David to continue it all was the line of fans that got longer by the second.

The band took their seats behind the table. Tim, Melissa, and I stood behind them. That's when I finally saw Kerrie. She looked like she was just waiting for this part of the day to be over.

I overheard someone making fun of Melissa for never

having fried dough before. I didn't realize that it was a New England–only thing. As she was from Philadelphia, she had never heard of it. This was a big deal to me too. So much of my childhood centered around a piece of fried dough at a fair or carnival.

"You've seriously never had fried dough?" I asked her in disbelief.

"No," she said with a chuckle. "Why is this such a big deal?"

"Because they're just so good!" Adam answered. "You can put powdered sugar or cinnamon on them."

Coincidentally there was a fried dough stand at the show. The guy at the booth was still selling some to the crowd.

"Come on. I'll buy some fried dough for us," I said.

I walked with Melissa to the fried dough stand and bought two pieces. We walked back to the table where the guys were signing. The line was actually getting even longer. We ate our fried dough, and she loved it!

I could see how many people were actually buying copies of God Lives Underwater's two albums to get signed. Most of the fans were really excited to meet them. I heard quite a bunch of people thank David for his lyrics. They tried to convey to him just what his words meant to their own lives. David kept smiling. However, I could see how uncomfortable he was with that kind of praise.

At one point I goofed around with Jeff. I stood behind him as he was signing stuff. I took two of his long black dreads, held them in the air, and flopped them back and forth so they looked like two antennae. He swatted me away and gave me a dirty look. I couldn't help but laugh.

We continued to watch them sign their albums, shake

hands, and receive compliments. The end of the line filtered through, and the event was finally finished.

Kerrie made her way to the table. David gave her a hug. She paid him a compliment about their show, and David rebutted with something negative about it. David had a hard time taking a compliment and just leaving it alone.

"So, what's the deal now? Do you have any more time to hang out?" I asked.

"Actually, Rock, I think I'm gonna go back to Kerrie's."

"Oh, okay. That's cool. I have a long drive home anyway." I tried to hide the disappointment in my face.

"That's fine, right?" he asked. He must have realized that I had other plans in mind for us.

"Of course, man. I'll see you soon. I'll shoot you an email later this week."

The tour manager joined David and Kerrie.

"You need to sign this release form. It basically states that you'll have David back at the bus safely no later than ten o'clock tomorrow morning. You take full responsibility for his safety and punctuality."

I turned and walked away. Kerrie took the clipboard from the manager to sign the release form so David could stay the night.

By that time I had made my way to my car in the parking lot. As I pulled onto the road, the last thing I saw was David as he got into Kerrie's car that had been parked not too far away. I honked my horn and waved. David turned, waved, and yelled something to me.

Kerrie didn't see or hear anything as she disappeared into the driver's seat.

A year had passed since God Lives Underwater had played the WBCN Xmas Rave at T.T. the Bear's Place with Deluxx Folk Implosion. Their popularity had exploded so much that, with this Xmas Rave, they were booked to open for Social Distortion at the Paradise in Boston.

It was December 3, 1996, and Dogboy was home for Christmas break. Since he had gone with me to the last Xmas Rave, he promised me that he would not miss this show.

Although the band wasn't on tour at the time, they made the trip from Philadelphia specifically to play this show. What was also different about this show, other than it not being part of a tour again, was that they came with two surprise guests.

Dogboy and I arrived later than the band. The tour van was already parked out front. I asked the door guy if he could grab anyone from God Lives Underwater. Surprisingly, he obliged and went inside.

A few minutes later, Jeff greeted us. Because they were the opening band, they were already setting up their equipment. I noticed that the stage was more cluttered than usual.

David jumped down from the stage when he saw us. "Hey, me-han!"

"What's that?" I asked, pointing at the extra set of amps.

"We thought that our live sound was too thin, compared to the albums, so we brought our friend, Dave Alverado, from Philly, with us to try adding extra live bass to our show. We've been working with him since we got back from the last tour." David yelled to the new guy, "Hey, Dave! Come here for a sec! This is Rocky. He's our bestest friend in Boston!"

"Nice to meet you!"

We shook hands. It was weird to meet a new fifth member of the band after knowing the rest of the guys so well. Dave went back to setting up his gear.

"How does it sound with him?" I asked David.

"Very full. I don't know if it's going to work out full-time yet, but we're going to try it tonight and see what happens. We've played a few shows with him back home. This will be the real test."

David walked with me toward the right side of the stage. We stopped in front of a booth that had a guy and girl in it. My second surprise of the night came here.

"Rocky, I want you to meet someone else. This is Heather. Heather, this is Rocky."

I stood face-to-face with David's his ex-girlfriend Heather, the person who so many specific lyrics were written about. I wondered if she knew that David had told me all about them.

"Hello," she said and shook my hand. "David told me about you. He said I would be meeting you tonight."

She was sweet and small. Even at my five-foot-four height, I still felt tall next to her.

"Yeah. David has told me a lot about you too," I said. Then there was a moment of awkward silence. "All good by the way."

"Yeah, I'm sure," she said sarcastically.

"I gotta go finish with our soundcheck," David said.

Dogboy and I were left with Heather and the other guy in the booth.

"You came with them for the show?" I reiterated.

"Yeah. We left Philly this morning just to play Boston,

and we go back tonight. I figured it was the perfect show to come to, since it's not really part of a tour or anything."

I noticed that Kerrie hadn't shown up yet. I was hoping that it was just going to be us for the night.

I felt immediately comfortable with Heather. There was no jealousy or hostility. She was easy to get along with and talk to. I felt like we were already friends.

"I'm gonna go outside. Do you guys want to come and get some air?" David asked.

Heather, Dogboy, and I got up and walked down the long hallway of the Paradise with David.

"Did you hear about the video game that Jeff and I are composing the sound track for?"

"No."

"It's called *Slamscape*. We wrote all the music for the game, and they put some of our videos on it too."

"That's really cool."

"Not really. The game is absolutely terrible."

I laughed. "Really?"

"Yeah. We just didn't know that much about the game when they asked us. It's completely unplayable. It's that bad."

"That sucks."

"Oh, Rocky! Look at this new ring I got!" he said. He held out his hand to show me a large spiked ring on his middle finger. "It's a motorcycle gear that I found. It fits perfectly."

I had to admit, it did look really cool. It really matched his personality and style.

"I have something for you too," I said. I reached into my pocket and pulled out a keychain of the aliens from *Toy Story*. "Merry Christmas, man."

"Oh, Rocky. You didn't have to get me anything!"

David took the keychain and clipped it to the belt loop of his pants.

"It lights up too," I said.

David squeezed the alien's torso, and the whole face lit up, yellow and green.

"Oh, me-han. That's great! Thanks, bro!" he said. He giggled and gave me a hug. He turned to Heather and said, "Rocky and I were talking about *Toy Story* last time we played in Boston. We had talked about how the aliens were my favorite part of the movie."

"Aw. That's really sweet."

David gave the alien toy a pinch again to watch it light up. "Hey, you work at a video store, right?" he asked me.

"Yep. Suncoast."

"Do you think you could get me *Billy Madison* and *Happy Gilmore*?"

"Sure! Absolutely."

"Okay, cool. I'll get you some money. If you could just ship them to my sister's apartment in Ambler, that's where I'm staying."

"Nah. Don't worry about the money. I get an employee discount anyway. Consider it another part of your Christmas gift."

"Thanks, me-han!"

Jeff came out of the club, and David stopped him.

"Hey! Look what Rocky gave me for Christmas."

When he showed Jeff the keychain, he squeezed the alien's body.

"No way! That's hysterical!" Jeff said.

"Yeah. He's gonna send us a copy of *Billy Madison* and *Happy Gilmore* too, so we can have them for the bus."

"Right on," Jeff said. He excused himself and left us in front of the club.

Doors opened, and it was a sold-out show. Dogboy and I went to the balcony with Heather. We positioned ourselves to the right of the soundboard on the balcony, so that we had a clear view of the stage.

Something was wrong with the sound. David was getting frustrated with the monitors, even though it sounded amazing through the house speakers. The extra bass filled in some of the gaps, but I wasn't completely sold yet. Some of their charm was the spaciousness of their sound.

I could tell just how upset David was getting as they went through each song. They only had half the amount of time they were used to. Halfway through the set, I noticed David was completely pissed off. Whatever was wrong was either not being fixed or getting worse. To distract himself from the problem, he spent the rest of the set with his mouth to the microphone singing, not moving, and just squeezing the *Toy Story* alien over and over again.

Despite his apparent hostility, it was comical to see a dark stage with the aliens from *Toy Story* flashing to the beat of each song up against the singer's leg. Flash-flash. Flash-flash.

Heather and I looked at each other.

"He's really pissed off right now."

"Yes, he is," she agreed.

They closed the set with "Weaken." When the song reached the end, everyone left the stage except for Jeff and David, who stayed there with their keyboards while they looped and layered sounds and beats until it all just became undecipherable noise. David finally punched the top of his keyboard, knocked it over, and stormed off.

This could either have gone over really well with the fans or made them think that he was being a jerk, throwing a temper tantrum. I never really found out how people felt about how David just gave up, halfway through their set.

That was the last show of the *Empty* era.

I accompanied Heather and Dogboy outside to the van, and David met us on the street. He apologized for what happened. He said that he couldn't hear anything at all in his monitors, and it got worse as the set went on.

Because Social Distortion hadn't played yet, no one was exiting the club. We had the opportunity to talk outside without being bombarded by fans.

I could see how mad he was. Heather suggested that we all get something to eat. I felt that it wasn't my place to tag along or invite myself. I was just happy that Kerrie never showed up. I also felt that David needed to go vent and be alone with Heather.

When she asked if we wanted to come along, I took it upon myself to decline for both of us. I did promise David again that I would send him those two movies before the month was out though.

He gave me a hug and apologized again for the show. I told him that he didn't need to apologize. I would talk to him soon.

Little did I know it then, but another fourteen months would pass before I saw him again—not until their third album's tour in 1998 for *Life in the So-Called Space Age*.

We waved good-bye to Tim as he came out of the club for a smoke. That was the last time I would ever see Jeff's little brother. He passed away in August 2006.

She has a name, and I hate her for it.
She has a name, and I regret he learned it well.
Goddamn you, Heroin, for taking one of my best friends away.

MANTIS THREE

*"A shot in the arm / Or a shot in the head. /
It's killing me / Or all my friends."*
God Lives Underwater: "The Rush Is Loud" - Life
in the So-Called Space Age

A lot can happen in fourteen months.

David and I kept communicating through emails and phone calls. Most conversations were surface chitchat about the recording of the new album with some semipersonal stuff tossed in. Our best quality time was always when we were able to meet in person. Phone calls and emails were reserved more for staying in touch and updates than anything else.

Christine and I did not survive her term at City Year in Ohio, and we broke up in April 1997. That same month, I moved out of my mother's house in Lynn and moved in with my father in Peabody. I met my new girlfriend, Sue, a few months later.

My band, Yellow #1, had released our album, *Bottle of Rain*. We played a respectable amount of shows for being a regional band, including even opening up for Godsmack in Salem, Massachusetts, on their debut album tour. Yellow

#1 eventually broke up before we could write a second album.

I joined an industrial hardcore band called Drop Kick Jesus in July 1997. We immediately wrote and sculpted the songs for our debut album. We also played some shows to promote our music.

Drop Kick Jesus's first show ever was as at an after-party for WAAF's Locobazooka festival, which had featured Faith No More and Limp Bizkit. That same festival God Lives Underwater had headlined the previous year. Faith No More was touring on the *Album of the Year* album. Limp Bizkit was touring on the *Three Dollar Bill, Y'all* album.

God Lives Underwater got to go home for the first time since March 1995, so they could write and record their third album. American Records, which had released both *GLU* and *Empty*, had dropped just about every band on their roster, except for Slayer and System of a Down.

Instead of God Lives Underwater finding a new label, God Lives Underwater's manager, Gary Richards, started 1500 Records and signed God Lives Underwater. The band went to Hollywood to write and record the songs that would eventually make up the album, *Life in the So-Called Space Age*. The band began their touring schedule for the album in February 1998, even though it didn't actually come out until March.

I drove to the Boston show on February 21, 1998, with nervous anticipation. Mostly because it had been the longest length of time that I had gone without seeing David. The band would also be playing new material that I hadn't even heard yet. It was going to be very weird to be at a God Lives

Underwater show and not know their songs. Even before *Empty* came out, I had received that promo tape in advance.

I took Sue with me to the show. She was really excited about finally getting to meet them. We arrived at the Middle East Restaurant & Nightclub in Cambridge later than I would have liked. This was the first and only time that God Lives Underwater had ever played there.

After we parked in the garage around the corner and made our way to the side of the club, I could see that we were much later than I had originally thought. The tour bus was already parked out front. I really didn't want to be forced to search for David, especially since it had been fourteen months since I'd seen him. I really had wanted to be here when they arrived.

The Middle East was right next to T.T. the Bear's Place. As smaller bands played T.T. the Bear's Place, larger bands with more draw would play the Middle East. The club even offered an inside restaurant, separate from the show area. In order to get to the club, we'd have to walk through the restaurant and down a set of stairs once inside. The building had almost a speakeasy feel to it. The club itself was adorned with a deep stage, and the crowd area was almost a perfect rectangle, from the front to the back.

I led Sue into the front restaurant part of the club. The anticipation of seeing the guys again was killing me. We walked by a few occupied tables and continued on toward the doors at the top of the stairs.

We were greeted by an employee of the Middle East who was probably going to be the one collecting tickets when the doors opened.

"Do you know where the guys from God Lives Underwater are?" I asked.

"I believe that some of them are eating in the restaurant."

I thanked him and turned around to look behind us at the almost-full restaurant. We walked back toward the tables, and I immediately spotted Jeff seated with a group of people. We made our way to their booth at the farthest table in the back, right in front of the doors to the club itself. My heart beat just a little bit faster. I didn't see David yet. Just seeing Jeff made all the familiarity come back in a rush.

I also noticed Drew sitting at the table with Jeff, alongside a new guy with red hair that I had never seen before, and then someone else who I glanced at quickly.

"Hey, Jeff," I said nervously.

"What's up, man?"

No one at the table made an overly enthusiastic greeting. If I didn't know better, I would have thought that I had just walked into a serious band discussion, or a band fight of some sort, and was interrupting more than I was welcomed.

"Do you happen to know where David is?"

The guy sitting in the outside chair at the table to my left leaned back. "I'm right here."

I turned my head and looked at him. I was so embarrassed that I didn't even recognize him because of the way he looked. He had cut off all his dreads; his hair was shorter; his face was sunken in, and he was so skinny that his clothes hung off him. An invisible cloud of melancholy seemed to surround him. He looked like he had aged fourteen years instead of just fourteen months.

I tried to disguise my embarrassment of not recognizing

him and forced a haphazard smile. "Oh, man! I didn't even see you! What's going on?"

"Nothing much. Just back on the road again for the new album."

I didn't even get his trademarked, "*Hey, me-han.*" I felt like I was much more eager to see him again than he was to see me. Something was different.

Jeff slid over so I could have a seat. I introduced Sue to everyone. I didn't know the new guy with the red hair yet. I also wondered where Adam was.

David was definitely in a weird mood. He said hello to Sue but didn't even try to engage in any conversations with her. He didn't make any of his usual sly, sarcastic remarks.

I sat next to Jeff, and Sue grabbed an extra chair to sit at the head of the table. There was a peculiar thickness in the air.

"Want to see what I got in Hollywood during the recording?"

"Okay," I replied. I was uneasy with how blunt David was acting.

He pulled up the sleeve of his shirt and held out his right wrist. I looked at it for a moment. I must have had a confused expression on my face.

"It's my new tattoo!"

A solid black line wrapped around his wrist. It looked like he had put a hair-tie around it.

"It's my favorite," he added.

"David. It's… a… line…" I said. I paused slightly between each word to make sure I wasn't missing some hidden joke.

"I know! Isn't it great? I also got this."

He pulled up his sleeve even higher. A black circle on his

bicep looked like someone had taken a black Sharpie to draw a perfect circle.

"A circle and a line," I said.

"Yep. I got them from a guy who was doing tattoos on a boardwalk."

I was feeling so uncomfortable at that table. I wanted more than anything to just get up, walk away, go outside, come back in, and start this whole experience over from the beginning. I just wanted David to act like his old self. The way the night had begun was so unsettling.

"You should get a line around your wrist too. All the cool kids are doing it."

"Nah. I think I'm all set. I'll leave the line tattoo to you," I said cynically.

"Oh, that's right. You're the piercing guy."

Was there a hidden attack in that statement? I couldn't tell if he was mocking me. I did sense that he was in a bad mood, and I felt that he was taking it out on me. All I wanted to do was just hang out again. I looked at Sue. I could tell that he wasn't making a good first impression on her at all.

"Did you hear about what happened to Adam?" he asked me.

"No. What happened with Adam?"

"Not to go into a long story or anything, but we all decided that it would be better if he didn't continue with the band after we got home from the *Empty* tour. We did some searching, and we found Scott Garrett. He used to be the drummer for The Cult."

I looked at the new guy with the red hair.

"Scott, this is Rocky."

I was surprised that David had never told me about Adam leaving, or the band hiring a new drummer, during any of our communications over the last fourteen months.

"He really does change the sound of the band," David explained. His mood seemed to be getting better. "Even the new album has a different feel than the first two albums. When we play live, the new sound makes everything much tighter."

"Well, that's good," I said. "I can't wait for the new album to come out. I really wish this show was next month, so the album would be out and everyone would know the new songs."

"Yeah, but we thought it was important to tour earlier to promote the new album and test out some new songs before people knew how they were supposed to sound. The stuff on the new album is a lot harder to play than any of the songs on the first two albums."

"Did you remember to put my name in the thank-you section in the album insert?" I joked.

"Actually the new album doesn't even have anything except for artwork. The inside is a continuation of the front cover, so you can only see the whole picture when you open the insert. It's just one big piece of art. We really wanted to just skip all the lyrics and thanks."

I was more disappointed than I thought I would be. "Are you happy with the new album, compared to the first two?"

David and Jeff both agreed. They felt this album was what they had been trying to achieve since the band had formed.

We were in the middle of discussing the specific tones and atmospheric mood of the new album when Kerrie walked through the front doors of the Middle East. I had completely forgotten about her. Since she wasn't at the last show in Boston when I had met Heather, and David hadn't mentioned her in any email or phone call in the past fourteen months, I had actually purged her out of my mind. I didn't think I would ever see her again. Especially since David said she was a band jumper and it had been over a year since God Lives Underwater actively toured, I figured she had just moved onto someone else. But nope. There she was.

David pushed his chair over slightly, so that she could stand next to him. There wasn't enough room for her to pull up a seat. Sue took up that space. Kerrie leaned on David instead and said hello to everyone.

"This is Rocky's new girlfriend…" David said. He tried to introduce Sue, but I could see that he had forgotten her name already.

"I'm Sue," she said awkwardly. She extended her hand.

"Did you show them your new tattoos?" Kerrie asked him.

"The line?" I asked. "Yeah, he showed me."

"Well, look at this," Kerrie said.

She held out her arm. She showed me the same exact line tattoo on her wrist. Was I living in the *Twilight Zone* right now? Was there some sort of secret gang that I didn't know about? She also showed me her mantis tattoo as well.

The praying mantis was not only God Lives Underwater's official logo but it was a way for fans to show their loyalty to the band.

"I got mine after I flew to Hollywood and stayed with David while they were recording the new album," she bragged.

I didn't want to know any more. It seemed that she couldn't wait to find a way to taunt me with the time that she had spent with David or that she had been present while the band recorded the new album. Moreover, she was the one who rolled her eyes at me when all I did was accidentally wear the same sneakers as David one day! However, getting the same exact tattoo as him is okay. Sheesh!

"Does anyone have any change? I need to use the payphone to make a call," Kerrie asked.

We all dug into our pockets and produced enough money for her to make a call home.

"She's gotta call home and check on her kid. Something about the kid's father this weekend and court. She's really worried," David whispered to me.

"I didn't know that you still talk to her," I said.

"Yeah, sometimes. You don't like her too much, do you?"

"Not really. She makes me feel like everything is a contest."

"Don't pay that any attention."

"Would it be okay if I took pictures of the set tonight for you guys?" I asked. I wanted to get my request in before Kerrie came back. "I brought my camera. It's a sold-out show, and I'd rather not be crushed at the barrier."

"Sure. I'll talk to security and see if we can get you on the stage again. I might have to get you a press pass, but I don't think it would be a problem."

"That would be awesome. I don't know if I told you or not but my band, Yellow #1, released our debut album since the last time I saw you. I have a copy in my car for you. I'll give it to you after the show."

"Thanks, Rock! We've been watching *Billy Madison* and *Happy Gilmore* almost every day on the bus."

"Have you seen that new show, *South Park*?" I asked him.

"I caught a few episodes, but I don't have much time to

watch a show like that regularly. What I've seen though is hysterical."

"I've been taping them every week. I have every episode so far. I can make you a copy and mail you the VHS tapes."

"I won't get them until we get off the road for this album sometime in the summer."

"That's cool. Every time I fill another tape, I'll just send it off to you. It'll give you something to watch on your downtime when you get home."

"Thanks, me-han! Just send it to my sister, Gretchen's, house. She'll make sure I get it. I'll give you the address tonight."

"Okay, great."

Kerrie joined us at the table again, and the rest of the conversation was actually quite enjoyable with her. She dropped whatever bad vibes she had around me, and we talked about other stuff instead of just David and the band.

Then all of a sudden, she really shocked me.

"I'm gonna give you my home phone number."

"Okaaaay..." I said suspiciously.

"You talk to David more than I do. It would be good for you to have it in case of an emergency, if something happens and you need to get in touch with me."

I took the small piece of paper with her phone number on it and realized that maybe this wasn't a power struggle after all, but just my own jealousy. I programmed her number into my phone, then hit Save.

"Drew's parents are coming to the show tonight," David said.

"Really?" I said and looked at Drew inquisitively.

"Yeah. They're in town, so they're coming. When I see you after the show, I'll introduce you."

Finally time came for the doors to open. The band had a meeting with their manager, Gary Richards, who had flown in from Los Angeles that afternoon.

Sue and I went downstairs into the club and found a spot on the left side. We stayed there through the opening band, Seaweed, until it was time for God Lives Underwater. The club was jam-packed, and the audience was pressed like sardines firmly against the barrier in front of the stage.

We pushed our way up to the bar area, which was at least three steps higher than the club floor. I leaned over the barrier and yelled to Jeff at the side of the stage. He came over. I asked him about the press pass and if we could watch the show on the stage instead.

"I'll be right back," he said and left to find a security guard. When he came back, he said, "Okay. Here's the deal. You don't need a pass, but they are being really strict due to the show being sold out. They said you have to sit on a chair off the stage to the side, and it can only be you. Your girlfriend has to stay in the crowd. You can't get off the chair at all during the show. If you do, you'll have to go back into the crowd."

"Okay, I guess that's fair enough."

I made sure Sue was okay with this arrangement. She knew how important it was to me. Luckily she was able to find a good spot along the railing of the bar area where she wouldn't be pushed around but would still be able to see.

Jeff escorted me onto the stage, and a security guard placed a generic steel chair off to the side of the stage. I was perfectly lined up with Scott's drum set. This meant that I would be looking at David and Jeff's backs and probably wouldn't even see Drew throughout their set, but I would get a perfect view of Scott's profile. What kind of pictures was I going to get with this crappy angle?

When the band came out, the crowd went crazy. Just as I had suspected, I could only see the back right side of David and Jeff's heads. The only time I saw Drew was when he stepped back from his pedal board. He wore a Spider-Man mask during the entire set. All I could decipher were the drums and whatever little bit of music that came out of Scott's monitor.

This was the first time I was able to hear any of the *Life in the So-Called Space Age* songs. From what I could tell, David was right. They definitely were a lot different than the first two albums. In addition to the new songs, they played only about half of the usual songs from *Empty* and *GLU*. I noticed at least seven older songs were dropped to make room for the new ones. This made me sad and nostalgic. I realized I might never hear those songs live again.

David played a tambourine through a lot of the songs and rarely played the keyboard, which was so odd for me to see. He also seemed very unenthused and lethargic during the performance. I was so used to the head-shaking, energetic David. The crowd didn't seem to mind though. Maybe they just didn't care, because they were going crazy either way. I did manage to take a roll of photos of the shots that I could get.

When the band finished the encore, they left the stage. The moment they were done and the house lights came up, security ushered me straight back into the crowd. They were acting as if I was just some lunatic fan who had jumped on the stage.

When I found Sue, I suggested that we should just stay in the club until it emptied. One of the things that I had never liked about the Middle East was that, with a sold-out show, I felt we had to be herded up the stairs like cattle. When it thinned out a bit, I spotted Drew by the merchandise table with his parents.

Once we made our way to him, he actually introduced us to his parents as some of David's friends from Boston. We shook their hands and told him that we would see him outside.

There was a group of people already crowding around the doors to the bus. I went back to my car and grabbed a copy of the Yellow #1 album, *Bottle of Rain*. We pushed through the gathering and knocked on the bus doors. They opened. Sue and I were brought in, and the doors closed quickly behind us. Kerrie was already inside.

There were some snacks and bottles of soda in the bus. We sat down and spent the next hour or so just hanging out. Kerrie really grew on me, which was good.

I gave David the Yellow #1 album, and, after a good amount of time of visiting, we said our good-byes. David gave me a hug. He said that the band would be doing some radio festivals before they would head out on their own headlining tour. He didn't have a festival date booked yet for the Boston area, so we didn't know when we would see each other next.

As we exited the bus and made our way back to my car, I promised to send him those *South Park* episodes again.

I sent David the *South Park* episodes as I had promised before the next time I saw him, which was on May 31, 1998.

The same radio station that had sponsored the Xmas Rave, WBCN, also put together a yearly festival show called the River Rave. Since God Lives Underwater had played two WBCN Xmas Raves already, they were booked to play the River Rave as well.

WBCN's River Rave was a direct competition to WAAF's Locobazooka that God Lives Underwater had headlined in 1996. The River Rave was held at Great Woods in Mansfield, Massachusetts. Great Woods was an outside amphitheater complete with a roof over the seats, but no walls. The seating capacity for the main stage of Great Woods was about twenty thousand.

The River Rave was set up so that the major acts would play the main stage and that the smaller bands would play the second stage. God Lives Underwater was asked to headline the second stage. They would be playing in front of about two thousand people.

Everyone was really pushing *Life in the So-Called Space Age*. Radio stations all over the country were playing different tracks. MTV was running the video for "From Your Mouth" in heavy rotation. Posters were plastered in the national-chain music stores. Articles were being written in major music magazines. It seemed that this could be the album that got God Lives Underwater out of the clubs and into the arenas.

Being asked to headline the second stage at the River Rave was something to be very proud and excited about.

My stepsister, Lauren's, mother was going to allow her to go to this show since she hadn't been allowed to go to the WAAF show in 1996. I decided that it just wasn't my place to ask David if he could get me three guest list spots for a show this big. Sue, Lauren, and I bought our own tickets to the show. This was the first and only time that I had actually paid to see a God Lives Underwater show.

We set off for Mansfield early that morning. I knew that the amount of quality time between David and I was going to be very limited, but I wanted to get there early just in case we would have time to hang out. Great Woods security wasn't like at a club. They didn't care if we knew the band. They also didn't care who we were, and they generally didn't even like to chat with people. At this show I was either going to be as generic as any other fan or have only a small amount of time with David, if he even came looking for me.

I had missed David's birthday by twenty-five days. For his birthday I had bought him the entire *South Park* shot glass set. Each *South Park* character was decorated on a glass in a nice case. I really hoped that I would have an opportunity to give it to him.

I couldn't wait to hear the new songs live again, now that I actually knew them. I wasn't sure how long they were going to get to play. It was tough for me to guess, since this was a festival show and they were on the second stage. I assumed it would probably be under an hour.

Sue, Lauren, and I pulled into the Great Woods parking lot, staffed with employees in orange vests. We followed the flow of cars to a newly started row. I decided to leave the shot glasses in the car in case they wouldn't let me through the front gates with them or in case they broke during the day.

I could see rows and rows of tour buses in the distance secured behind a roped-off area. This made it nearly impossible to know which bus was for which band. I realized that our best option for getting David's attention would be from inside of the venue.

We went through the ticket gate. As soon as we got inside, I wanted to see where our seats were for the main stage. Once we found our seats, I suggested that we head to the spot where the bands at the second stage were allowed to come and go into the venue. I was hoping to catch any members of the band, even Scott. As we made our way there, the venue filled up by the minute.

We stood at a barrier heavily guarded by security. We saw band members, roadies, and managers of a bunch of bands that I didn't even recognize. Once we had been waiting for almost two hours, even after the first band had started playing the main stage, someone from God Lives Underwater came through.

"Jeff!" I yelled.

He waved back. I introduced him to my stepsister. He told me that they had just woken up. David was still waking up too but was going to be coming out soon to get something to eat. Jeff was starving. He told us to wait here and went to search out food.

After another half an hour or so, David finally appeared. Thankfully he was in a chipper mood.

"Hey, me-han! Jeff said you guys were out here."

I introduced him to Lauren. I could tell that she was starstruck in front of him.

"You guys hungry? Do you want to get something to eat?"

"Sure," I replied.

We walked toward the stairs that separated the second stage from the rest of the venue. It was a perfect day outside. The chill was gone from the air, but it wasn't too hot.

"We bought tickets to this show when they announced it because I didn't want to risk not being able to get on a guest list."

"Yeah. We didn't even get a guest list for this show. The label reserved our guest list for press people and label reps only. I probably could have gotten you in on a band pass though, if you had found me outside."

"There was no way I was going to chance that in a place this massive."

"Probably safer this way anyway," he agreed.

We walked down the path inside Great Woods that had food vendors throughout the area, along with bathrooms, novelty stands, and band merchandise.

"What do you think of the new album?" David asked as he stopped to check out a menu at a food kiosk.

"I think it's amazing. I'll be honest. It took me a little longer to latch onto than it did with the first two. You're right though. It does have a different atmosphere than the other two, but I think it's the album that you guys have always been wanting to make."

"Thanks, Rock!"

"My favorite song is 'Vapors.'"

"That's my least favorite song on the album!" He laughed. "Too bad we'll never play it live. We just don't have the means to pull it off. I also don't remember recording too much of it. I was high the whole time."

What a great way to taint my view of my favorite song on the album!

Oddly enough Lauren ran into a few friends who she went to school with. They flagged her down, and I suggested that we meet back up by the second stage in an hour.

It only took a few moments for David to be swarmed by a larger number of fans than I had ever experienced. The crowd gathering around him grew so big that Sue and I got nudged out of the circle, even though we had been standing right next to him. We just had to take a step back and let his fans have their moment to meet him.

Some people pushed their ticket in his face for him to sign. One fan showed David his mantis tattoo on his leg. Another fan told David how many times he'd seen God Lives Underwater live. At one point somebody thought Sue and I were waiting to talk to David also. The fan told us that we could go ahead in front of him. I chuckled a little bit, told him we were all set, and watched.

I could see that David was being humble with the fans, but, at the same time, he was tired, hungry, and just wanted to get some food. He wasn't rude. He just seemed bored. Finally he managed to get the crowd to disperse.

Even after that moment he was recognized along our entire walk around the venue. Occasionally he was asked to sign an autograph or two. Eventually we reached a burrito booth and ordered Mexican wraps.

We walked while we ate our burritos. We talked about the *South Park* episodes I had sent him, and I told him about the birthday gift I had for him in my car. We headed to the second stage to watch some of the bands that were playing and to meet up with Lauren again.

We ran into Jimi Davies, the singer for the band Jimmie's Chicken Shack, who was also playing the second stage. God Lives Underwater had toured with Jimmie's Chicken Shack before, so David and Jimi had become friends. Jimi stopped long enough to chat. I was a big Jimmie's Chicken Shack fan, and this was going to be my first time seeing them live.

Speaking out of turn, I told Jimi how excited I was that they were playing and how much I loved their new album, *Pushing the Salmonella Envelope*. I told him that my favorite song on the album was "Milk." David then formally introduced us and looked embarrassed. Jimi thanked me for the kind words about his band and went on his way.

"Why do you always feel the need to do that?" David asked.

"Do what?" I asked.

"Tell someone what your favorite song is when you meet them? I still remember the night that we met. You told me that 'Nothing' was your favorite song. And then today, one of the first things you said to me was that 'Vapors' was your favorite song on the new album. I even remember you telling me what your favorite song on *Empty* was, at some point."

"I didn't realize that I do that."

"Personally I don't really care. But to someone who doesn't know you, they could take it as you not liking the other songs on the album as much."

I was stunned. Did David just reprimand me? I was speechless. Of course I had never meant anything negative. It was just my way of making conversation.

We arrived at the second stage. David leaned against a plywood wall of the sound booth. Sue and I stood next to him, and we watched the band Cornershop play.

I was still getting over the feeling that David had just brought to light something about me that annoyed him. As I stood watching the band, I glanced occasionally at him.

After a few songs, he took a step toward me and leaned into my ear so I could hear him. "I'm going to the bus. I might be back if you stay in this area. If not, then I'll see you after the show."

I watched him walk toward the buses and disappear.

I finally gave up hope that he was returning after a few hours. We went to the main stage to watch Green Day and Soul Asylum. Green Day was touring on the *Nimrod* album. Soul Asylum was touring on the *Candy from a Stranger* album. Then we made our way back to the second stage, for Jimmie's Chicken Shack.

After a few more hours passed, it was time for the headliners to play. Scott Weiland, the Stone Temple Pilots lead singer, was headlining the main stage. He was touring on his solo album, *12 Bar Blues*. We had been hoping that God Lives Underwater wasn't going to play at the same time. Unfortunately they were.

In order to get a better view of the second stage, we found a picnic table and stood on top. I was in no mood to fight to the front of the stage, and ward off mosh pits and crowd surfers during their set.

The second stage area was packed. God Lives Underwater played mostly songs from *Life in the So-Called Space Age* to promote the new album. They only played the singles from *Empty* and *GLU*.

Even though the band played with high energy, the sound was awful. A constant wind made it appear like their music went with it. It was like listening to a show at different volume levels. I could tell there was a major problem with the monitors onstage as well. Either they weren't mixed to where the band wanted them or they weren't working at all.

The aloofness that David had during the Middle East show was gone. However, it was slowly being replaced by anger as their set progressed. I saw that look in his face as he played. He tried not to let the technical difficulties onstage overpower his ability to keep his energy, but that time his frustration won out.

I knew exactly what David was feeling when they closed with "Weaken." At the end of the song, they traditionally let the two sequencers loop organized noise. Once again the soundman didn't know when to shut it off until he finally realized that the band wasn't coming back.

We headed for the venue exit. If we had any chance of seeing David again, we would have to leave then. Most of the crowd was heading toward the main stage to catch the last few songs of Scott Weiland's set. Only a small percentage of fans like us were actually leaving the venue.

Once we exited the gates, we jogged to the steel barriers that separated the buses from the rest of the parking lot. Luckily I spotted David outside their bus. We yelled and waved our arms. He saw us and let us sneak into the tour bus parking lot.

He asked Sue and Lauren if either of them smoked.

"I do!" Lauren piped up enthusiastically.

"Can I bum one off you?" David asked.

Lauren had a deer-caught-in-the-headlights look on her face as she dug around her purse for her pack. She handed David the cigarette along with her lighter. He lit up, thanked her, and handed the lighter back. Still, to this day, she brags that the singer of God Lives Underwater smoked one of her cigarettes.

"What happened up there?" I asked him.

"Rock, you know me all too well. The monitors didn't have any of the keys coming through them. All we had was guitar. It was so hard for me to know where we were in the song. It was awful."

"Yeah. I could tell by the 'Weaken' ending. And by your face, right from the beginning."

"It was just terrible all around. I'm almost embarrassed."

"I may have something that will cheer you up. Your birthday present is in my car."

"Aw, Rocky! You know you didn't have to."

"Of course I didn't have to! I wanted to. Can you walk with us to my car?"

"Sure. But then we should get going."

"That's fine. We should leave then anyway."

We walked to the Midnight Cowboy, and David stood by the front of my car as I leaned in and grabbed his gift.

"I didn't wrap it. Close your eyes," I said.

"Okay." He laughed and held out his hands.

I gave him the *South Park* shot glasses.

When he opened his eyes, a huge smile came across his face. "Oh, me-han! These are awesome! Thanks, Rocky!"

"No problemo! Something for the road I guess," I said.

"I'm sure Jeff and I will get some use out of these."

David stretched out his arms, gave me a hug, and thanked me again. He said good-bye to Sue and thanked Lauren for the smoke.

David walked away with his birthday present in hand.

It was a weekday night, and Sue was at my house. She was in the bathroom while I flipped through the cable channels for something to watch. It was too late to start a movie but too early to go to bed—one of those kind of nights where I was just hoping to find something interesting to watch.

As I impatiently channel-surfed, two familiar faces flashed across the screen but were immediately gone as I turned to the next channel. I stopped and channeled backward. There they were. David and Jeff both raced down a digital mountain in a virtual skiing arcade game as a veejay from Much Music stuck a microphone in David's face.

I yelled to Sue that David and Jeff were on TV. It never occurred to me to pop in a blank tape to record it.

David gave very short answers. He was obviously more interested in the simulated skiing video game. Jeff was more candid and lively. His replies were a little more detailed. But he too never took his eyes off the screen to face the interviewer.

They were asked questions about the tour, the new album, and their fan-base. No questions were asked that I hadn't already heard the answers to before. The charm of this particular moment was watching them focus on the video game so intently and never looking at the interviewer.

They were in Montreal playing with Econoline Crush, who, at the time was one of Canada's biggest native industrial rock bands. David had mentioned to me that when the Canadian tour was finished, they were going to do a major American tour with Econoline Crush, and Stabbing Westward would headline.

Stabbing Westward was touring on the *Darkest Days* album. Econoline Crush was touring on the *Devil You Know* album. God Lives Underwater was still churning away with *Life in the So-Called Space Age*. Unbeknownst to all three bands, they toured together on the biggest selling albums of their careers. This tour was almost too unbelievable to be real.

The tour was announced, and dates and places were confirmed. When tickets went on sale, venues sold out. God Lives Underwater would be playing their next Boston gig at Avalon on Lansdowne Street on July 21, 1998. It was the best bill of the year by far.

One of my best friends, Sean, who was actually the best man at my wedding, had a ticket to the show. He was a fan of all three bands. I suggested for him to find me before the show and that I would introduce him to David and the guys in God Lives Underwater.

I had also found out that the drummer from the band The The was playing drums for Stabbing Westward. Just the thought of possibly having even the slightest chance of meeting him gave me butterflies. The The had been one of my favorite bands and a major influence on my life since I saw them open for Depeche Mode in 1993. The The had been touring on the *Dusk* album. Depeche Mode had been touring on the *Songs of Faith & Devotion* album.

When Sue and I arrived at the club, there were three large tour buses already parked alongside the club. I knew that we were later than I would have liked. I didn't know which band was getting a soundcheck, but I didn't really care either. My main objective was to just find David. If we were lucky, maybe we would run into some of the other bands' members too.

We did our normal wait-outside-for-someone tactics, and David spotted me first for a change. He just randomly poked me in the back. When I turned around, he had a big mischievous smile on his face and gave me a hug. He cordially said hello to Sue and invited us inside with him.

No one else even noticed us. No security guards or bouncers questioned him or asked who we were, once we were inside the very familiar club with its dark lights, smooshed carpet, and musty smell.

"Do you want to go get something to eat?" David asked.

"Sure! Do you have time?" I asked him.

"Yeah. I'm just waiting for Kerrie. She's supposed to meet me here, and then we can all go for a walk."

For the first time the mention of her name didn't make me shudder.

It was a beautiful summer day. The idea of us walking around Boston sounded very appetizing. We talked about the Much Music interview and how the tour was going. David looked good, besides the normal wear-and-tear from being on the road, of course. He didn't look sick.

As we killed time waiting for Kerrie to show up, Andy Kubiszewski, the drummer for Stabbing Westward and The The, walked by. He stopped to talk with David. I just stood there. I stared at him, in his black T-shirt and cowboy hat, in complete awe. David introduced me to him. Before I could even tell him what my favorite The The song on every album was, he was gone.

Kerrie eventually showed up, and there was still plenty of time for us to head into Boston. She greeted me respectfully, but without an overabundance of enthusiasm. We were still getting used to each other.

She suggested that we walk toward Newbury Street and get something to eat at a café. Maybe go into some of the stores that were known for their chic merchandise: Allston Beat, Newbury Comics, and, oh yes, Condom World.

We set off on foot. David's band laminate swung by his

knees with every step. He had the lanyard attached to the belt loop of his pants.

I got the feeling through casual conversation that Kerrie thought of Sue and me more like little cousins than friends of David. It felt like she was dealing with us because she had to. I tried to compensate and diminish this feeling by forcing myself into every conversation. I desperately tried to prevent her from getting the upper hand.

I didn't realize I was being overbearing until David looked at me and said, "Rocky, do you know who you remind me of? On *Looney Tunes*, there was a small Chihuahua dog that would always run next to the big bulldog named Spike and say, 'What are we doing tonight, Spike? Where we going? Huh? Huh? Huh?' Me-han, that is so you!"

Although I realized he was right, I wanted Kerrie to know that it took more than that to embarrass me. So I laughed. I did my best to act as if I enjoyed David's playful teasing.

And then it happened. It started somewhere around our arrival to Newbury Street. We were browsing different café menus and the wait-time to be seated was far beyond what we could afford to waste. David very quickly became difficult.

Kerrie was trying to suggest every place that we walked by, but each one had something about it that David just didn't want to be a part of. Sue and I walked behind them. We weren't uncomfortable because David was being difficult. We were uncomfortable because Kerrie was still treating us like she was our babysitter, and she was taking the brunt of his attitude.

"Why can't we just find a place where we can sit down, and have a cup of coffee and a snack? Why does every place have an hour wait? Why does every menu have to be far too complicated?" he whined.

Kerrie patted his shoulder and humored him by hoping that the next café would somehow magically be different.

David suddenly started venting, very specifically, about the difference in sales between God Lives Underwater and Stabbing Westward albums, and how frustrating it was for him. Especially when he really believed that his band's songs were of a higher quality than Stabbing Westward's. Once David started his rant, the floodgates opened. There was just no stopping him, as if he had kept all these thoughts and feelings inside, and they were finally coming out. David went from venting about tour support and album sales to his suicide fantasy during a show.

"Do you know how I want to die?" he asked as we turned a corner back onto Newbury Street from one of the side streets.

"Oh, stop it!" Kerrie retorted.

Sue and I just kept walking silently behind them.

"I want to play a really big show, maybe in London. I'll have a rope tied around my neck during the end of the last song. I'll jump from the rafters. The force will be so strong that it will rip my spine right out of my back. Just my head and spinal cord will be swinging on the rope."

"Would you just fucking stop it!" Kerrie wailed.

I walked behind them on autopilot. I couldn't believe what I had just heard. I knew it wasn't David's morbid sense of humor this time either. I really believed that wherever he was inside his head, he was being serious. I felt my heart go numb from shock.

"I'm serious. Then maybe the world would notice. What

the fuck is it all for if no one knows who you are? That would be the best way to go out."

I honestly didn't want to eat anything, even if we did eventually find a place that David agreed to. Kerrie had the exact opposite reaction. She wanted to get David to sit down, eat, and have a good time, to hopefully ease him out of his mood.

The very next place we passed, she made sure we went inside.

It was a mini café and coffeehouse that sold wraps, sandwiches, and high-profile coffee. I really didn't feel like eating. I didn't want to be obligated to say why. I didn't want to revisit that conversation or the image of David's spine coming out of his body. So I flat-out lied and told Kerrie that I didn't bring my wallet and that I did not have any money to eat. My plan backfired way more than if I had just ordered something and didn't eat it.

"What do you want? I got it this time. My treat," she offered.

"No, that's okay, really. You don't have to do that," I said to her. My wallet was actually snug in my back pocket.

It was our turn to order, and she became very assertive. "Look. I'm not fucking playing games. Just order whatever you want, and I got it."

She actually scared me into ordering a sandwich. We got our food and sat at a table. Sue and I split the sandwich Kerrie bought us. How could I tell her that my wallet was really in my back pocket? I felt even worse eating the food.

David didn't get any better. He must have known he was getting a rise out of Kerrie. Within minutes David finally reached his emotional breaking point. He just stood up and walked out of the café.

"C'mon. Let's go," Kerrie said.

She grabbed the food that she had bought for us, threw it away, and followed David back onto Newbury Street.

I was dumbfounded. I couldn't believe what was happening. I was actually afraid that David would do something to hurt himself. I had never seen him take it that far. Kerrie was acting like a mother whose child was testing every fiber of her patience.

We walked back to the club in silence. David's self-loathing continued. I wondered how different it would have been if Kerrie had never shown up. I also wondered what David's real intentions were. I never doubted his frustrations with the comparison of God Lives Underwater and Stabbing Westward, but the suicide act was something new and entirely too melodramatic, even for David.

When we got back to the Avalon, David disappeared to prepare for their set. Kerrie found her own spot to watch the show.

The show was amazing. All three bands played at the top of their game. I wished that my head wasn't filled with the images that David had painted for us.

David never, ever spoke like that around me again. That was the first and only time I had ever heard him sound sincere about suicide.

That was the last time that I ever saw Kerrie. Sure, I spoke with her after that night on the phone when she called me to ask if I knew where David was a few months later. She probably just decided that she didn't want his drama.

Maybe David just became old news, and she moved onto the next big thing.

Autumn had bestowed itself on New England as October 1998 rolled in. God Lives Underwater had finally announced their own headlining tour to support *Life in the So-Called Space Age*. It wasn't going to be like their last headlining tour before the album came out. They would get at least eighty minutes of set time. People actually knew the songs now too. This was finally a real headlining tour for the new album. The Boston date was October 1, and the club was Axis on Lansdowne Street.

I spoke to David via email, and we made plans to get something to eat before the show. Sue and I arrived after the tour buses had pulled in. We had to work and couldn't leave any earlier to get to the show. At this point, finding the band had become such an old habit that I thought nothing of walking to the backstage door and banging on it.

I asked the bouncer if David from God Lives Underwater was there. Before he answered, I could hear "From Your Mouth" playing as part of the band's soundcheck. David's voice floated over the synthesizer lines of the song. I had answered my own question. We stepped back from the door and waited until the rumble coming through the walls was over. We knew that they would be coming out of the club soon.

When David finally appeared, he looked thin and frail. His face was sunken in, and his eyes looked frustrated and tired. He gave us a half-assed "Hey, me-han."

"Do you want to grab a bite to eat at Boston Beer Works?" I asked.

Even though it had only been three years since we had eaten there with Dann, it still seemed like an eternity.

"I was actually thinking of that bar on the corner. I saw it when we came in, and I realized I hadn't been there yet."

"The Casken Flagen?" I asked.

"Yeah. That one."

We walked toward the pub on Lansdowne Street. Once we got there, the bouncer at the pub door asked for all our IDs. Sue only had a Massachusetts ID card due to the fact that she was epileptic and not able to obtain a driver's license until she was seizure-free. I also got worried because Sue was only twenty.

The bouncer looked at David's ID, gave it back; looked at mine, gave it back; and then looked at Sue's. As soon as he took her ID card in his hands, I started explaining.

"She's only twenty, but we aren't going to be drinking anything. We're just here for lunch."

"Sorry. I can't let her in," he said.

"Can't you just stamp her hand or something, so they know she can't drink?"

"Sorry. Those are the rules." He handed Sue's ID back to her.

"It's okay," she said. "You guys go and have your lunch together. It's been a while since you got to hang out alone."

"Hey, me-han. I'm in the band that's playing at Axis tonight. These are my friends that I never see. Can you just sit us at a table in the corner, and we won't cause any problems? You won't even know she's here," David said.

"I wish I could help, but it's my job on the line if something happens."

David nodded and walked into the pub. Sue said she would just meet me back at Axis when the doors opened. I thanked her for understanding.

David and I got a booth on the right side of the pub. He ordered vodka and orange juice, and I ordered a Shirley Temple. After we ordered an appetizer, he told me about his outstanding arrest warrant in Providence, Rhode Island.

"There's actually a warrant out for me. The charge is enticing a riot."

"Are you kidding? What happened?" I asked.

"During one of our shows there, I said that the security guards weren't doing their job, so if people wanted to rush the stage, they could. It got really ugly. We took off. Our manager told me that they had taken out a warrant on me for trying to start a riot."

"That's crazy."

"Yeah. We can't play Rhode Island until I get that cleared up."

"So, first the news comes from Rhode Island that you died, and now there's a warrant out for your arrest. All this coming from the smallest state in the country!" I joked.

"Something's telling me to never go back there again."

Even when David was joking with me, he still seemed downtrodden.

We finished our lunch at the Casken Flagen and made our way toward the club. Sue was waiting for us outside. I was thankful that it wasn't too cold.

We went into the club when doors opened, and it was almost empty.

"This isn't a good sign," I said to Sue.

I couldn't understand it. The radio stations were still playing the singles from the album. "From Your Mouth" and "Rearrange" were in steady rotation. They were getting play on MTV with the video for "From Your Mouth." They were still being promoted in music magazines. Also the band had just sold out at the Middle East Restaurant & Nightclub eight months earlier before the album came out. This was their best-selling album so far and yet the worst attendance I had ever seen.

"Hopefully it'll fill up as it gets closer to showtime," Sue said.

When the opening band finished, we were in the space of time between their performance and God Lives Underwater's. The club was still only about half full. This was very disheartening. Perhaps it was the sudden explosion of heavier bands like Korn, Deftones, and Slipknot that made people move on. Maybe people were just tired of the industrial rock genre.

David and his band took the stage and played their hearts out. The few people who were there got one of the most sonically emotional God Lives Underwater shows I had ever seen, as well as a brilliant mix of all three albums. The songs from *Life in the So-Called Space Age* were played with such ferocity that it was hard to believe they were the same songs from the album. The *Empty* and *GLU* songs were played with a brand new vigor and energy. They were so powerful that, when people left the club, they could just tell that something special had happened during the show.

We caught David outside, and he said he needed to go for a walk, but that we were welcome to come. I could tell that he was feeling worse than he was before the show. Since Kerrie wasn't here, it would be our turn to listen and not just humor him like she did.

Most of the people who were at the show were still milling around, so it wasn't exactly a good time for a walk if David didn't want to be noticed. As we were walking away, a fan came running over. He was wearing a backwards baseball hat, baggy jeans, and some expensive-looking running shoes. He just fit the description of someone who happened to ride whatever bandwagon was passing through at that moment.

"Hey!" the kid yelled to get us to turn around. "I just wanted to let you know that, if it wasn't for your songs and your lyrics, I wouldn't have gotten through so much shit in my life. It was your music and your messages and knowing you were going through it too that kept me going every morning. I just wanted to say *thank you*. Thanks for writing such honest lyrics and thanks for saving me every day. I don't mean to bother you, but I never thought I would actually have the opportunity to meet you in person. When I saw you, I knew I had to say something. Thank you for giving me hope."

David's face looked like it sunk in even further. It would have been amazing if there had been some sort of a magical moment, but there just wasn't. David was emotionally exhausted. The last thing he was looking for was empathy and praise from someone he didn't know.

"I didn't save you. I can't even save myself!" David replied.

The kid just froze and stared at him.

David realized what he had just said. "I'm sorry, me-han. I just had a bad night. Thank you. What you said does mean a lot to me."

The kid turned away like a deer caught in headlights and left us alone.

"I spend all this time writing these songs that contain every honest part of who I am, and it doesn't make me any better. I just keep writing, and I don't feel like they're doing me any good. How can I feel like I'm helping someone else, who I don't even know, when I'm the one writing these songs about my feelings, and I feel like I keep falling down the same hill over and over?" David said. He talked like he needed to justify to me, or to himself, what he had just said to a fan.

I really didn't have an answer for him. It was a rhetorical question anyway. It was better to listen and silently nod than it was to offer some advice that wouldn't do him any good.

David wanted to crash on the bus and just get the night over with. The tour, the album sales, and his own view of himself all weighed down on him.

That night was the last time I saw any member of the band, except for David, ever again. That night was the last time I ever got to see God Lives Underwater play live. This, of course, wasn't known to any of us, especially not the band. It wasn't surprising to me that, when they finally recorded the next God Lives Underwater album, it was the most emotionally charged and honest album of their career.

A lot changed from that night in 1998 to the next time I would see David again in 2001. I had acquired a copy of the fourth and final God Lives Underwater album before it was released. Sue and I broke up in 2000. After that, I dated someone named Jenny.

God Lives Underwater didn't tour for the new album but played only one show to promote it. It was their final show ever as a band on July 13, 2000, at The Roxy Theatre in Hollywood, California.

Their encore album was their greatest achievement as a group of musicians, but yet it didn't get any radio airplay at all. It was released on such an independent label that only die-hard God Lives Underwater fans even knew it existed. The trials and tribulations of an unnoticed, yet brilliant, fourth album would soon come to fruition.

It was called *Up Off The Floor*.

MANTIS FOUR

"I've got some time / But I've got my life to go. /
I wish the best for us all / But I don't know."
God Lives Underwater: "Slip to Fall" - Up off the Floor

David didn't always make the best first impression.

I was working at Suncoast Motion Picture Company one day in 1999 when a customer came into the store. Because of the band T-shirt he wore, eventually God Lives Underwater, and industrial music in general, came up in conversation. We discussed their tour with KMFDM and Life of Agony back in 1995. He mentioned how big of a fan he became after that show. I was glad that I didn't advertise my friendship with David to him. He told me that he had gone to see God Lives Underwater at Axis and had approached David outside the club. "What an asshole," he said.

I just looked at him with my best poker face. I swallowed hard. "Why do you say that?"

"I tried to talk to him. He just acted like he couldn't have given a shit about his fans."

It wasn't my place to constantly defend David's moods. Although I didn't tell this guy that I knew David personally, I did bring up a scenario of people in general having bad days, even celebrities.

Somehow that conversation stayed with me for a long time. Oddly enough I ran into this customer again at a concert in Salem in 2006. There was a local female-fronted goth metal band, Coven of 13, playing that night. They were promoting their album, *Death's Middle Finger*. He looked the same as he had when I had first met him.

I asked if he was a God Lives Underwater fan. He was dumbfounded that someone had even mentioned them. I then asked him if he had heard that David had passed away. He hadn't. He reacted to the news as though his best friend had just died. He actually had to sit down, and he almost cried.

Seven years earlier, he was bad-mouthing David, about what an asshole he was. I didn't remind him of our conversation. I just let him grieve in the moment.

Sometimes the general public feels like they own whoever they support. Sometimes, when the ship goes down, those same people jump off the boat as fast as they can so they don't go down with it.

David disappeared for a while between 1998 and 2000. Other than an occasional email or instant message, we lived our own lives and kept in touch on a minimal scale. I did hear that those two years for David were spent in and out of rehab with a lot of effort and energy expended trying to get *Up off the Floor* written, recorded, and released.

I had my own band that was doing well in my area. Drop Kick Jesus had released our first album, *Splatterguts,* and we played all over Massachusetts, New York, New Hampshire, Maine, Pennsylvania, Rhode Island, and Vermont.

I was about to resign at Suncoast. I had been there six years, and I was even promoted to store manager. I just wanted to go back to college to finish my degree in Criminal Justice.

With no God Lives Underwater Boston shows in the foreseeable future, and with my own band being so busy, David and I were just too focused on other things during those two years to make staying in touch a priority.

Even so, we did have some conversations online about his health. There was never any mention of Kerrie. He told me about the singer of a Canadian band that he was head over heels for, but it was more of crush than anything else. He also talked quite a bit about a girl named Monica who he had met and who he seemed to be madly in love with.

Everyone knew Monica by the name of Seven, a nickname she was given as a child by her family. It had practically replaced her real name for anyone who knew her.

Seven was everything David needed. She was grounded, not a junkie, a girl-next-door type who cared about him deeply, and it had nothing to do with his band. David was so excited the night that he emailed me to tell me that he and Seven had gotten engaged.

One night in March 2000, I was at my computer, and David logged into Instant Messenger. We chatted. I told him about how my band was working on our second album, *Depress the Heart,* and that we had just played a sold-out show at CBGB's in New York City, opening for the band Crisis.

"Drop Kick Jesus has been playing every other weekend in a different state."

"That's great, Rocky," he answered.

"We are really pulling some serious draw into the shows. I think we are really starting to make it."

"What do you mean by 'make it'?"

"I dunno. I just mean that we are playing some pretty good shows at some decent venues. *Splatterguts* is selling really well, and *Depress the Heart* is projected to be even better."

"That's not making it. You have no idea what it means to make it! If I have no idea what it means, than you don't either! Stop thinking that you ever have made it," David retorted cynically.

I felt belittled. I was completely frozen at my computer. It was so hard to talk to him over the Internet because I couldn't hear the fluctuations in his voice or see his body language. I couldn't tell if he was mad at me, sarcastic, or just in one of his moods.

I stopped replying, but I left the chat window open. David also stopped talking. There was a bit of silence while I surfed through different websites online instead.

I had completely forgotten that the chat window was still open behind my browsers when I heard the *bling* sound of receiving a message. When I clicked on the program, I could see that David had invited me into a private chat room that he had created for some fans that were also online. I accepted his invitation.

I mostly just observed the other fans talk to him about God Lives Underwater's upcoming album. I was shocked to find out new things about David that I should have learned on my own. David was clean and had spent a lot of time in rehab over the last year. He was home in Ambler with his sister, Gretchen. He was just trying to stay clean, and get his life and career back on track.

I realized that I could have been a better friend. This was information that I should have found out with a friendly phone call. Instead, I sat and read the words of strangers filling my computer screen. Some random fans in a chat room shouldn't be my update on how he was really doing. It made me feel guilty.

Somehow the conversation turned goofy, and someone asked what David was doing.

"Eating some Fruit Loops," he answered.

Everyone started talking about breakfast cereals. What cereals did David like? Which ones didn't he like? Which ones did he eat while he was high? Which ones made him feel better as he sobered up? This lightened up the conversation, and I felt comfortable finally jumping in. I hadn't said anything yet.

"Hey, everyone! It's my good buddy, Rocky, finally joining the conversation!" David suddenly typed.

I laughed. David sounded like he was in great spirits, clean, and sober.

On July 13, 2000, the very last God Lives Underwater show took place at The Roxy in Hollywood, California. Although I wasn't in attendance, I did manage to obtain an audio recording of it.

There was a brief silence during the crowd's applause as the band took the stage. Neither the crowd nor David and his band members had any idea that this was going to be the final show of the band's career.

God Lives Underwater had hired bass player Kevin Agunas just to play this show with them.

"We already broke something, right? Fuck, yeah!" David said into the microphone. Obviously, something wasn't working properly. "We're God Lives Underwater, and we're gonna play songs from our new album, and then we're gonna play some old ones, and then we're gonna play some new ones. We're on 1500 Records, and those people are here."

Kevin fingered some notes on his bass. Then Scott kicked his bass drum a handful of times.

"Alright! I think we're back in effect," David said.

In the background I could hear the band discuss a broken piece of gear.

"It's brand new," Scott said.

There was another lengthy silence, and then a hum and some feedback.

"What broke?" Drew asked.

"Kick pedal," Scott answered.

"You just broke a brand-new kick pedal?" Drew exclaimed.

"Alright!" David said sarcastically.

Then the signature God Lives Underwater synthesizer line came pouring out of the speakers, and the band opened their very last show with "72 Hour Hold" from *Up off the Floor*.

Then after David thanked the crowd, they immediately went into "No More Love" from *GLU*.

"Thanks. I could use a drink of water if someone's got one," David said when "No More Love" ended.

Without any more banter, the band played "Rearrange" from *Life in the So-Called Space Age*.

When "Rearrange" ended, David did nothing more than announce the next song, "No Way (You Must Understand)" from *Up off the Floor*.

"Hey, thanks!" David said when the song finished. "Is it okay if we play a slow one? Because that's what's next on the list. This is called 'Whatever You've Got.'"

When "Whatever You've Got" finished, David said, "Thanks. We're gonna play another one from the new record."

They played "Tricked" ferociously. It was the only single from *Up off the Floor*.

"Alright, this is called 'Nothing.' This is from our first record," David announced.

Scott clicked his drumsticks together. One, two, three, four. The band blasted into the fan-favorite "Nothing" from *GLU*.

God Lives Underwater took only a few seconds before the guitar riff for "History" from *Up off the Floor* began.

There was very little time between the ending of "History" and the intro to "Alone Again" from *Life in the So-Called Space Age* began.

A female screamed when "Alone Again" finished.

"Who's yelling that?" David asked.

The girl continued to shout randomly.

"I'm twenty-nine now," he replied.

Immediately they kicked into "All Wrong" from *Empty*, in complete unison. When "All Wrong" was finished, David thanked the crowd twice and announced that they had one more song left.

God Lives Underwater had reached their last song, on their final show, ever. This would be the last four minutes that the band would ever play onstage together.

"That's Drew, that's Kevin, that's Scott, and that's Jeff, and I'm David," he introduced.

David had the uncanny talent of being able to perform "Don't Know How to Be" from *Empty* with just his mouth, as he had proved to me on their tour bus so many years earlier. God Lives Underwater retired their show when David announced to the crowd the name of that song.

How many shows on their tours had ended with "Don't Know How to Be"? How many times did I know that was going to be the last song of the night, so I could be ready to rip the drum set down? They ended their final gig with the song that they used to close their sets with from five years earlier.

It couldn't have been a better way to go out.

It was December 1, 2000, my twenty-fourth birthday.

My band, Drop Kick Jesus, had just released our second album, *Depress the Heart*. It was recorded with Grammy-Award-winning producer Neil Kernon in Massachusetts and mixed in Texas.

I had met a girl named Jenny while backstage at a Pitchshifter and Static-X concert in Providence, Rhode Island. Pitchshifter was touring on the *www.com* album. Static-X was touring on the *Wisconsin Death Trip* album. Sue and I had broken up after months of complacency with the relationship.

I had quit Suncoast, gone back to school to finish my degree in Criminal Justice, and got a new day job as a senior sales manager for Eastern Bank.

I logged online the morning of my birthday to check my email, and I noticed that David was also online. I didn't say anything to him as I checked my email. I secretly wanted to see if he had remembered my birthday.

Sometimes David would leave himself logged on for days and not actually be at the computer. Maybe this was one of those times. I decided that, if he didn't message me before I logged off, I would say something after all.

In the middle of reading a birthday email from one of my aunts, the *bling* of the messenger alerted me and there was a message from David. He had remembered!

"Hey, Rocky."

"Hey, David! Do you know what today is?"

There was just silence. And then even more silence. I actually thought that maybe he wasn't there anymore. Then it came, very bluntly, and the exact opposite of a birthday wish.

"Seven died."

Two words on a computer screen that shattered the silence. My hands shook.

"What?!"

"Seven died last week. She was killed."

"What happened?"

"She was hit by a train. She died instantly. They said it happened so fast she didn't even know that it hit her."

"Oh, my God, David. Are you going to be okay?"

"I don't know, Rock. I'm surrounded by friends and family. Gretchen drove me to the hospital to identify the body. We've been home ever since. I just need to be around people who actually care about me."

My brain was already in overdrive, and I thought that I could take a few days off work to make the six-hour trip to Pennsylvania to see him.

"Do you want me to come and stay with you for a few days?"

"That's not really necessary, Rocky. I'm just gonna stay here. I don't feel like talking about it anymore." He suddenly logged offline.

I still entertained the idea of just jumping in my car and driving to his apartment, but my senses got the best of me. Unexpected company was probably the last thing he wanted, and he knew how to get in touch with me if he needed to talk.

It would be six years before I would hear the complete story of her death. Unfortunately it would also be after David's own death that I would be told all of the details and how it really affected him.

Everything fell apart around the beginning of 2001.

The record label for God Lives Underwater went bankrupt, although they had paid for the recording of *Up off the Floor* and had already distributed a cash advance to the band members. This basically meant that the album, which was finished and recorded, would be shelved indefinitely unless another label bought the album from them. God Lives Underwater fans knew that the new album was finished, but then we found out that the album had almost no chance of ever seeing the light of day. David did some shopping on his own to some smaller labels, but the price for the album was too high for smaller labels to be bothered with.

On top of the band's turmoil of being in debt, losing Seven, and having no label, David was ready to just give up God Lives Underwater and move on. He had made the decision to make copies of the last album for any of his family and friends who cared enough to hear it.

In the meantime he worked on a solo project that was purely instrumental and electronic, as well as an ode to Seven. He used only the computer program Orion. The idea of Robot Teen America, as he explained it to me, would be simple.

"I'll only make seventy-seven copies of the album, all burned by me, and each one will be numbered and signed. The first seventy God Lives Underwater fans who contact me for a copy of the album will get one. I'll charge ten dollars per album to help with the duplication and shipping, and so I can have a few extra bucks in my pocket this month. The leftover seven copies will be for friends and family. This whole thing is a tribute to Seven, so most of what I do will revolve around that number."

The album was only four tracks long, had no vocals, and didn't even include any song titles. The album itself was titled *Living in Syn*. The front cover was just a scanned picture of David.

On the official God Lives Underwater website, he announced that he was releasing the Robot Teen America album on a first-come, first-serve basis to the first seventy people who sent him ten dollars. He even used his real address in Ambler, Pennsylvania, as the address where fans could send the money. I told him that I thought this wasn't wise. Any God Lives Underwater stalker would now know where he lived.

About two weeks later I received a package in the mail that had David's handwriting on the outside. I opened it and inside was a copy of *Living in Syn* without any other correspondence. My copy was number *76*.

I called him as soon as I opened up the envelope.

"I just got the package. I can't wait to listen to the album!"

"I'm glad it got there okay. I was nervous that I had an old address for you or something."

"Nope. It got here fine. But I do have one question," I said. "You said there are only seventy-seven copies of the album in existence. You sent me number seventy-six. Who has number seventy-seven?"

"I do. That's the one I'm keeping for myself. I was debating whether to keep number seven or number seventy-seven. I decided to keep seventy-seven because it's double the sevens. In fact you even have the actual master. All of the other copies were made from the disc that I sent you. So you have to keep it safe for me."

"I'll make a copy for myself to listen to and will put this real one away so it never gets destroyed."

"Okay. But make sure you never make a copy for anyone else. That will ruin the seventy-seven theme of the album."

"I promise. You can trust me."

"I know, Rock. That's why I sent you the master copy."

"I can't wait to listen to it. I'll talk to you later and tell you what I think."

We hung up. I put the album in my stereo and my headphones on. The album registered at only eighteen minutes for the four untitled tracks.

I pressed Play.

"The first batch of Robot Teen America discs went out today," David said to me a few days later.

That didn't surprise me. There were countless God Lives

Underwater fans in the world, and this album only had a public run of seventy copies.

"I wouldn't expect there to be any left by the end of the week," I said.

"You think I should do more? I mean, maybe I could do 777, to make some extra cash."

"That's up to you. But the whole reason you made this album was in memory of Monica. You decided on seventy-seven right at the beginning."

"Yeah, I guess you're right."

About a month passed and David sent me an email.

> *I don't know what's going on. I haven't received any more orders for Robot Teen America, and I have been getting really fucked-up emails from people. I want you to read some of things fans have sent me.*

I scrolled down the email to where David had pasted a string of emails from belligerent fans.

- *David, I knew you were always a fucking junkie, but I never thought you would ever do this to your fans!*
- *Hey, man. Fuck you! Stick another needle in your arm and give me my money back!*
- *David, we all believed that you were getting better. I have always supported you, but stealing from your fans is even a little too low for me. Good-bye, from a longtime fan.*

— Asshole. If you needed money to get high so bad, just rob a bank for the cash. Don't rip off your fans!

There were approximately twenty more hate emails that he forwarded to me. Most had foul language, and almost all of them took a direct shot at his drug use. I felt my anger rising. I was just as confused as he was. I could only imagine how David must have felt getting these in his in-box everyday.

I picked up the phone and decided to call him.

"Hey, me-han! Did you get my email?"

"Yeah. What the fuck is that all about?"

"I did some detective work. I replied to all of the emails and asked what they meant. It seems that people mailed me money for the album, their checks were cashed a month ago, and they still hadn't received the discs. When I looked through my old emails, I could see that I had received emails from almost all these people asking if their disc had been mailed out. My reply to all of them was that I hadn't received their money yet. They had all checked their accounts, and the checks had been cashed!"

"What the hell is going on?" I repeated. "How many checks were cashed?"

"Basically all of them. All seventy discs were paid for by the fans, and I didn't even know it. Of course, as a junkie, I didn't have too much credibility to begin with. I don't really blame them for the emails. I probably would have said the same thing."

"Do you know what happened to those checks?" I asked.

"Yeah. My sister's ex-husband, who lives across the street from us, has been stealing my mail knowing that there were checks or money in those envelopes."

"You're kidding me!" I said in disbelief.

"Nope. I don't know how much of my mail he has been stealing or for how long. If it wasn't for this, I would never have known it was even happening. He was depositing the money into his account and forging my signature. All of these people have been sending me their hard-earned cash for my music, and this fucking asshole brother-in-law has been stealing my money. I don't have any money to begin with. Now, I have a whole group of fans pissed off at me."

"Is there anything I can do?"

"Actually there is," David said. "I don't feel safe having anything mailed here anymore."

"Understandable."

"What I want you to do is write up a really nice reply that I can send to everyone who has sent me one of those hate letters. I have saved every single one, and I want to respond to all of them. You're much better at putting cohesive thoughts together than I am. Write up something nice. Explain the situation without giving away too many specifics. I'll send you a list of every email address that sent me a hate letter. You can even say that you're my manager, if anyone asks why the response is coming from you."

"I can do that," I said. I was so proud that David let me pretend to be his manager. "Is there anything else?"

"There is, but I'll completely understand if you don't want to."

"Whatever you need, David. That's what I'm here for."

"I don't trust money coming here, and I don't trust the discs going out of here either. If I send you a list of all the people who have paid for the album, can you make copies from your master and mail them out? I'll send you a stack of the front cover, signed and numbered, and you can package them up and mail them from your house."

"Sure! I can do that," I answered. I couldn't believe that he was trusting me as the duplication center for the Robot Teen America project.

"Also I'm going to change the mailing address for any leftover orders to your house. People can mail the money to you. You can make the disc and mail it out for me. Is that okay with you?"

"That's fine."

"You're probably one of the only people I can trust with my money, Rocky. You do know that, don't you?"

"I do now," I said. "I'll open a new savings account for any money that comes my way for a disc. When all the discs are gone, I'll close out the account and wire you the money. Email me the list of people that claim they paid you, and I'll start burning the discs tomorrow. What are you going to do about the stolen money?"

"It's not their fault that all of their money was stolen. They deserve the album. It's just me that's out all this money. I want, so badly, to go over there and break his neck. Gretchen told me to just call the cops and deal with it legally. So that's what we're doing."

"I think that's a better idea. I still can't believe that he has been doing that to you and caused so many of your fans to be pissed off."

"After this disaster I'm gonna give up music altogether and go work in construction."

"Are you serious?"

"I don't know. Some days it sounds good to just have a

normal job. I think I would be good at construction."

Whether or not he was serious, I still couldn't picture David Reilly, of God Lives Underwater, wearing a yellow hard hat and an orange vest at a construction site.

I did what he asked. The majority of people that were sent a copy of the Robot Teen America *Living in Syn* album, numbered and signed, came from my bedroom and my disc burner.

As the months trudged by into July 2001, David was getting more and more discouraged that *Up off the Floor* was never going to be released. God Lives Underwater was becoming less and less of a band. David was just trying to get the latest music in the right people's hands.

During a phone call one day, David asked me if I would like a copy of the new album. Not only was I flattered but I also didn't know what to say.

"Just remember that it's not mastered yet. The tracks are at slightly different volume levels, but they are equalized pretty well. I don't know what the order of the songs will be when it comes out. The disc I'm giving you will just be in random order. Don't get too excited, Rock. It's just gonna be a burned copy from my laptop of the twelve songs."

"I don't care if they're the demos. I can't believe I'm gonna finally be able to hear the album!"

"They aren't demos. They're the finished and mixed versions. Just do me a favor. You can make a copy for Jenny, but please don't make any other copies. I don't want the songs getting out until they can be officially released."

I had spoken to David about Jenny so much during that

year. He probably knew more about her than he ever knew Christine or Sue, and he hadn't even met her yet!

"You didn't even need to say that."

"I know. I just feel better saying it out loud."

I told Jenny later that night that David was going to send me the album. We had been together a full year at this point, and she was also a really big God Lives Underwater fan. This was just as exciting for her as it was for me.

"You're going to make me a copy! Right?" she stated.

"Of course! David said you were the only one who could have one."

I didn't know how fast the disc would come. It could have taken six months, or it could have taken two weeks. It wasn't my place to hound him for it either. He trusted me with an album of new material, and I wasn't in the position to whine about not getting it quicker.

David really surprised me. About ten days later, there was a small brown envelope in my mailbox addressed to Rocky Horror Paone. Inside was a disc with no markings on it, in a clear slim-line case, and with no track listing. There wasn't even a note or a letter of any kind.

I didn't need any of that. I knew exactly what it was.

My heart beat faster and I got light-headed as I ran up the stairs to my bedroom. I shut off my cell phone, grabbed my headphones, and plugged them into the stereo. I sat on my bed and closed the disc tray door. The screen registered twelve tracks. This truly was *Up off the Floor*!

I pressed Play. I had no idea what it was going to sound like, the quality of the recording, or if the disc was even scratched.

The first song was "Choir Boy." I was disappointed in the

volume. David did warn me that the album wasn't mastered yet. I just felt like the song was playing in another room. I could tell where all the punches of the song could have been but weren't executed right because of the low volume.

The second track on the disc began. "Fame" was so much louder and fuller in sound compared to "Choir Boy." I jumped and almost threw off my headphones.

Thankfully "Choir Boy" was the only song that had any volume problems. Of course I had no idea the song was called "Choir Boy" at the time. In fact, until I had a conversation about it with David, I thought that it was called "Quiet Boy." I thought that was what he was singing in the chorus.

I listened to all twelve tracks with my undivided attention focused on every note and word. I immediately called Jenny when the last song, "Tricked," was over.

"Do you want to know how the new God Lives Underwater album sounds?"

"You got it?" she squealed. I could almost hear her jump up and down.

"Yep! I just finished listening to it."

"How is it?"

"After only one listen, I can honestly say, this may be the best God Lives Underwater album of them all. It's so emotionally driven. The music is exactly what they had been working toward. This may be their masterpiece. David's lyrics are just so honest."

"You better be burning me a copy of it, right now!"

"I will tonight. Just keep in mind that he was right about the volume. Almost every track is a slightly different volume level than the one before it."

"I don't care. I just want a copy of it!"

I listened to the album again as it was burning for Jenny. I fell in love with it twice as much the second time around.

When I went to bed that night, I looked forward to waking up the next morning just so I could listen to it again as I got ready. Jenny and I had plans to drive into Boston for the day. I knew that we wouldn't listen to anything else on the way.

The next day Jenny drove to my house that I shared with the guitarist of my band Drop Kick Jesus, K.J., and another close friend, Mike. Jenny and I took her car into Boston. The moment I got into the passenger seat, she held her hand out for the disc. I gave her the copy I made for her. She ejected Finger Eleven's *The Greyest of Blue Skies* album and put in *Up off the Floor*.

"I can't make you a track listing because David sent it without any song titles."

"That's okay. You know I memorize track numbers and not song names."

I tried to say something else, and she shushed me. We didn't speak until all twelve songs had played through her speakers and the album repeated back to track one again. By this time we were on one of the ramps from Route 93 to one of the tunnels in Boston that would bring us into the North End.

"What do you think?" I asked.

"It's amazing."

"I told you."

"We should call David."

At this point Boston traffic was backed up, and we were at a standstill on the highway. I took out my cell phone and called his number.

"Hey, David. I got the disc yesterday. Jenny and I are in her car listening to it again."

"I'm glad it got to you in one piece. What do you think?"

"Seriously I think it's the best thing you've ever written."

"Tell him how much I love it too!" Jenny said.

"Jenny says that she loves it too. We both think it's amazing. When this album gets released, if you could get the song about the train on the radio, it could be a huge hit for the band. This album has the potential to commercially be your biggest album yet. Every song on it could be a hit."

"Thanks, me-han! The song about the train is called 'Whatever You've Got.' We already decided that the first single is going to be 'Tricked' when the album comes out. What did you think of our cover of 'Fame'?"

"It was fantastic!"

"I'm glad you think so too. 'Fame' is going to be in the movie *15 Minutes* with Robert DeNiro that's coming out this year. We're shooting a video for it too. The director is going to splice scenes from the movie with a fake house party where God Lives Underwater plays the song live. They mentioned putting the video as part of the bonus material on the DVD when it comes out."

"Wow! Sounds like the wheels are moving for the band again! Could you tell me the names of all the songs?"

"I have them saved on my laptop. I'll email them to you tonight."

"Yeah, that works. You know me and my OCD with song titles."

David laughed. "Here's something you don't know. The album was originally going to be called *The Mantis Returns* while we were writing it."

"Why did you change it?"

"I wanted something that reflected the meaning of the lyrics on the album more."

"That makes sense," I said.

"And then it was called *Drowning in Air*, the entire time we were recording it."

"I actually like that title better. It really goes along with the name of the band!"

"Yeah. That's the reason why we didn't go with it. It sounded like we were trying too hard to match an album title with the band name. It sounded too cheesy."

"I can see that. What else are you up to?" I asked.

"Not much. I just sit around most of the day on my computer. I really need to get out of here."

There was a moment of silence.

"Do you want to come hang out and stay with me for a weekend?" I finally asked.

There was an awkward pause.

"I would love to but I don't have a car. I don't even have my license anymore. They suspended it. I don't know how I'd get there."

"What about the train? Amtrak dumps right into South Station in Boston. Is there a train station near you?"

"Yeah. It leaves from Philadelphia. I don't have any money right now to spend on a ticket."

"How much could it be?" I asked.

"I don't know. It could be just as much as a plane ticket."

"Really? Yikes! Okay, we'll talk about it later. We're heading into a tunnel, and I'm going to lose service soon. We'll talk in a few days."

"Alright, Rock. I'll email you the track listing for the disc tonight."

We said good-bye, and I realized that I had talked to David for almost as long as the length of the disc. It was getting ready to start over again. Jenny and I let it repeat for the third time.

That night I checked my email, and, sure enough, David had sent me the track listing. I copied the names of the songs into a program that prints out CD inserts, so I could have a homemade back cover of the album with song titles.

The titles and order of the songs, according to David's email, were as follows:

1. Choir Boy / 2. Fame / 3. White Noise / 4. Step Off / 5. Take Whatever You Got / 6. You Must Understand / 7. 72 Hour Hold / 8. 1% / 9. Slip To Fall / 10. Miss You More Than Anything / 11. Positivity / 12. Tricked

Some of the song titles eventually changed from David's email to what they were actually called when *Up off the Floor* was officially released in 2004.

- "1%" was lengthened to "1% (The Long Way Down)."
- "You Must Understand" was lengthened to "No Way (You Must Understand)."
- "Take Whatever You Got" was shortened to "Whatever You've Got."
- "Step Off" was completely renamed "History."

The next day at work, I had some downtime so I went on Amtrak's webpage. I researched times and prices for a train from Philadelphia to Boston. I planned to have David arrive on a Friday afternoon and leave on Monday. With that plan, we could have three full days together. All I had to do was find a Monday that landed on a holiday so that I could have a long weekend off from work.

I looked at the upcoming schedule. The next long weekend was for Labor Day on September 3, 2001. I checked the prices of a round-trip train ticket from 08/31/01 to 09/03/01. It would cost $180 total. After I thought about it some more, I decided that I could afford to spend that much money.

I didn't really know what we would do yet, but since it was Labor Day weekend, anything was possible. There would definitely be enough barbecues to go to. Plus I could show him the North Shore of Massachusetts.

I called David on my lunch break in the parking lot of the bank where I now worked. It was a beautiful July afternoon, and I didn't feel like talking inside the bank offices. He answered the phone, and I gave him my proposal. "Would you come for a long weekend if you didn't have to worry about how to get here or spend any money?"

"Of course I would."

"I just checked the schedule. How would you feel about spending Labor Day weekend here? Don't worry about the ticket. I'll buy it for you. While you're here, you won't need money for food or anything. It'll basically be a free vacation."

"Are you sure you want to do this, Rocky?"

"Yeah! I really think it would be fun. You can kick back, get your mind off things. No pressure."

"Okay. If you want to spend the money, I would love to come."

"I'll go back to my desk, look up specific times, and get in touch with you tonight."

"Sounds good. The only thing is, you'll have to send the money via Western Union to me. I have to buy the tickets myself. You can't buy them for me. You can't send me a check or money order either, because I don't have an account to cash it. I have to use Western Union for all my transactions."

"Okay. So I'll just wire you the total amount of the ticket, and you'll go buy it?"

"Yeah. I'll buy the ticket on the day of the trip for both ways."

"That sounds doable. I just have no idea where there is even a Western Union near me."

"You can look up their locations online. Send it to my name using Rocky Horror as a password."

"Why am I not surprised?" I laughed. "Okay, man. I'll talk to you tonight. I really should get back to work."

After we hung up, I questioned how much faith I actually had in David's ability to follow through. I didn't doubt that he wanted to come visit. I just didn't know if, when the time came, there would be some kind of excuse why he couldn't get on the train. I tried not to get too excited that he was going to come and visit. I still had a nagging feeling in the back of my head that, when the weekend actually came, David just would not show up for some reason or another.

I pushed aside any negative thoughts and moved forward with the plans as if I knew that David was definitely coming. I looked up the train schedule again and wrote down the best times. Then I looked up Western Union locations.

There was actually one inside a Lynn's supermarket right down the street from where my office was. All I needed to do was talk with David about the schedule options. We needed to confirm the trip before I went ahead and sent him the money.

Although I didn't expect to hear from David until later that night, it seemed that he had been thinking of the trip as well. He was getting even more excited about coming to visit. A few hours later my cell phone rang at my desk. I was on the phone with a customer, so I had to let my voice mail pick up.

When I saw that it was David, and he had left a message—which he never, ever did—I immediately put my work phone on hold so I couldn't get any more calls.

I listened intently to the message. He sounded different. He sounded both ecstatic and bored at the same time.

I got up and asked my supervisor if I could take five minutes to make a phone call. I told her that it was an emergency. Someone had left a message on my phone, and I needed to find out what was going on. It was a slow day anyway. My boss didn't mind letting me off the phones.

I walked into one of the empty cubicles to have some privacy. I called David from the phone on the desk. My cell phone didn't get the best reception inside the office, and I didn't want to chance losing a signal.

David answered after a handful of rings. He sounded terrible. He didn't even sound like the same person I had been talking to earlier.

"David! Are you okay?" I asked. Something just didn't sit right.

"Yeah. I'm just a little sleepy. I came up with an awesome idea!"

"Okay," I said suspiciously. I was nervous that David might be canceling his trip.

"If I'm going to be there anyway, why don't we try to set up a solo acoustic show somewhere in Boston?"

"Like a God Lives Underwater acoustic show?"

"Sort of. More like a David Reilly solo show featuring songs of God Lives Underwater. Or something like that."

"That would be amazing!" I replied.

Then there was silence.

I was dragged into the hole with him. This definitive conversation with David after six years of friendship, turned the tables and I became more of a brother to him than anything else.

The silence was curious and confusing. I could hear David breathing heavily. So heavy, in fact, that I could actually hear the air being pulled from the space around him and into his lungs. The silence was deafening to me.

I didn't know what was happening, but it terrified me.

"David?"

Nothing.

His breathing didn't even feel natural. I felt helpless. I had no idea what was going on. I didn't know if I should say his name again or how loudly I should say it. I felt like I was intruding on something disgraceful every time I said his name.

"David?" I stopped and listened. His breathing was deep, but regular. I heard his lips smack, and he came back to me.

"Rocky?" he croaked. His voice was raspy. It sounded like he had been sleeping for a while.

"I'm here."

"Sorry about that, me-han."

"That's alright. What happened?"

"I'm so tired. I just fell asleep. My brain keeps shutting off."

"We were talking about a solo show in Boston."

"Yeah, yeah. What do you think?"

"I think it's a great idea! I have a lot of connections at the clubs. I think Bill's Bar on Lansdowne Street would be the best place. The capacity is somewhere around two hundred people. I'm friends with the booking agent there."

"We played there before, right?"

"Sort of. You guys played on Lansdowne at Avalon and Axis."

"That's right. That's a great street for clubs…"

I waited for him to finish some sort of thought, but all I could hear through the phone was that heavy breathing again. The second time around was much creepier. It just feel so unnatural.

I decided not to say his name again. Instead, I waited for him to wake himself up. There was something about saying his name into that heavy breathing that felt dirty to me.

I heard the phone slide away. That must have been enough to startle him back to consciousness. I heard him put the phone back to his ear.

"Sorry, me-han."

"That's okay. Is there something else going on?"

"Yeah. I've been clean for fifteen days. This is the hardest time of the detox for me. My brain goes through withdrawal and shuts me down every few minutes. I doze off and then I startle myself awake."

"No shit. I'm happy that you're clean, but that must suck."

"This will only last a few days. Once I'm over this last part of being dope-sick, I'm a new person." "So, if Bill's Bar won't do it or doesn't have that weekend open, I can always go to T.T. the Bear's Place, the Paradise, or the Middle East."

"Yeah, me-han. I'm down for anywhere."

"Once a club is booked, Jenny and I will make a flyer on her computer. She's really good at Photoshop. We'll plaster flyers all over Boston and in all the music stores."

"What am I gonna do about equipment?"

"What would you need? I can just rent it from Daddy's Junky Music."

"Probably just two acoustic guitars."

"We can get those the day of the show. I'll also try to get an interview or some radio spots on WFNX. Their office is in Lynn."

"Rocky, if you really think you can pull this off, it would be a great show for me. Maybe I'll play some of the songs off the new album too."

I couldn't believe what had just happened. I was actually in a discussion about booking the first David Reilly solo show! He was putting every aspect of this show on my shoulders.

I didn't even notice that David had drifted off to sleep again. I listened to his deep exhales, and I took advantage of the pause in the conversation to make a mental list of things I needed to get working on. David woke himself up and apologized again.

I told him that it was okay, but the truth was that it really wasn't. It made me uncomfortable. It reminded me that David was sick because he was an addict. I hated every labored breath, down to my core.

"I'm going to go to Western Union right from work. I'll wire you the money for the train ticket. If, for some reason,

I can't find a club to host the show, would you still want to come and visit?" I asked cautiously.

I just wanted to confirm that the possibility of a show wasn't the only reason he wanted a trip to Boston.

"Of course, me-han! I'm really looking forward to a vacation. You're like my safe place. You know that, right? When I'm around you and your friends, I never feel pressured into anything. That means a lot. This will be good for me."

"That means more to me than you could ever know, David."

"Hey, you know what I just thought of? I'm gonna have to go through all my songs and see which ones I can actually translate acoustically and practice them. I plan on staying clean this time. When that weekend rolls around, I want to be on top of my game."

"I'm really excited," I said.

"Me too. You do you realize that you just gave me something to wake up for again, right? Putting this show together will give me something to work toward. Thank you."

"David, you never have to thank me. Just get your ass here safely."

"Yeah, me-han. I promise. You'll send the money to me tonight?"

"Right from work."

"Okay. I'm gonna have to ask my sister to drive me to get it tomorrow or something. I should let you go. I know you're at work."

"I'll give you a call as soon as I find a club that'll book the show."

"Okay, me-han. Peace."

I put the phone back on its cradle.

Every time I thought about those weird silences, my skin crawled. I prayed this was the beginning of a better and healthier chapter in David's life. A chapter that would start with a long weekend getaway at my place and his first solo show.

When I left work that night, I drove straight to the Western Union office in downtown Lynn. I handed over the cash and filled out the form with all of the pertinent information using the password Rocky Horror.

I was eager to get home and send an email to Shred, the booking agent at Bill's Bar. I was almost positive that he would book the solo show in his club. I figured that we could advertise the show almost as an unplugged God Lives Underwater show, even though it would only be David Reilly performing.

I talked to Jenny about everything. She was just as zealous to design a flyer as I was to confirm the show. She agreed that Bill's Bar was the best club for it.

I fired up my computer the moment I got home and wrote one of the most important emails I had ever sent.

Shred,

This is Brian from Drop Kick Jesus. I have both a huge favor and a proposition for you. I'm very good friends with the lead singer of the band God Lives Underwater. I'm actually helping him set up a solo unplugged show in Boston on Labor Day weekend. I'm writing to you first about booking him at Bill's Bar because of how great you've been to Drop Kick Jesus. It has to be either Friday or Saturday of Labor Day weekend. We'll be doing our own advertising for the show to make sure we get the word out to every God Lives Underwater fan in the area. Please get back to me soon. Is this something you would be interested in? I hope that we can work something out.

I sent the email.

My band had a pretty solid working relationship with Shred from our previous shows already, so I was confident that he would jump at the chance to book a show like this. If he didn't bite, then I was planning on contacting the Paradise, T.T. the Bear's Place, and Middle East next.

A few days went by.

David's visit, along with organizing his solo show, consumed my every waking thought. I had butterflies every time I checked my email. I was hoping for the best, but I prepared for the worst. Finally I got a reply. Shred was no longer booking shows at Bill's Bar. He suggested that I contact T.T. the Bear's Place instead and tell them that he had told me to call them.

Shred was my ace in the hole. Not only for David's solo show but also for Drop Kick Jesus. I refused to get discouraged. So I took his advice and went to T.T. the Bear's Place next.

I sent them an email too. However, this email was a little bit more professional than the one I had sent to Shred. I used his name as a reference so the request wouldn't appear unsolicited.

If no one wanted the show, I was determined enough to host it in my own backyard and not charge anyone any admission. I lived close enough to Boston. Fans would come, if it was advertised. I refused to let anything get in the way.

Jenny worked on the flyer already. She found a great picture of David to use. He was leaning forward and singing into a microphone. She imported it into Photoshop and removed all the background, so it was just him. She moved him onto the left side of the flyer and used the mantis logo to fill up the right side. The rest of the background was left blank.

We brainstormed together the wording of how to advertise the show. After going through a few phrases like: *David Reilly solo acoustic show featuring God Lives Underwater songs*, and *God Lives Underwater unplugged featuring David Reilly*, and some others, we decided to keep it simple. We used *David Reilly of God Lives Underwater* as the heading. All that was left to fill in was the venue, date, and time.

I received a reply from T.T. the Bear's Place, and they had agreed to put on the show! In the email, they had asked a slew of questions that I couldn't answer without conversing with David first. They wanted to know if there was going to be a contract, how much money he wanted, does he want to pick the opening bands, etc.

I called David and told him that T.T. the Bear's Place agreed to put on the show. He told me to email them back and tell them that he didn't care if it was Friday or Saturday night, nor did he care who the opening bands were either. The only stipulation was that he got a cut of the door. He wanted at least one dollar for every person who paid to get in.

I emailed my reply to T.T. the Bear's Place. They agreed to David's stipulations. Friday night, August 31, was available. David could headline. He would get forty minutes, and he would play around midnight. I thanked them profusely on David's behalf.

I gave Jenny the details, and we finished making the flyer.

We also added the tagline, *Playing all the God Lives Underwater songs and new ones you haven't heard…* to get fans excited about hearing some *Up off the Floor* songs too.

After we printed out five hundred flyers, we were ready to hit the local music stores and clubs in Boston. We also decided to bring them to every concert we attended to hand out to people as they left the venue.

I figured that it would be a huge push to get people to the show if I tried to book a radio interview, or at least an advertisement, on a Boston radio station. Three different Boston radio stations had been large supporters of God Lives Underwater over the last six years. I didn't think I would have a problem getting on the air with at least one of them to advertise that David was coming back to Boston.

WBCN had booked them to play the River Rave and two different Xmas Raves. WAAF had asked them to headline the first-ever Locobazooka. WFNX had never really dropped them from their rotation of alternative music during the 1990s.

Because the WFNX station was literally a mile from where I attended college in Lynn, I decided to start there.

I called them to ask how to go about getting a deejay to announce a show or even how to get on the radio to announce a show myself. I spoke to their secretary. I explained the story to her of what happened with God Lives Underwater and how David was going to be performing his solo show. She said she remembered them and the hits they had on the radio. She advised me to come by the radio station.

I intended to swing by after my next day of classes.

I called David to update him on everything going on. I told him about the flyer. He wanted Jenny to email it to him so that he could approve it. I also told him about trying to get on the radio to advertise the show.

"Rocky, I don't think that's going to go over as well as you think. None of the Boston stations are very happy with God Lives Underwater. WBCN felt like we owed them something after booking us at the River Rave, two Xmas Raves in a row, and that first show with Maids of Gravity where we first met. They weren't thrilled at all when we played the WAAF Locobazooka show. They felt like it was a stab in the back, because WAAF was their rival. Then WAAF said they would never have anything to do with us ever again, after we headlined the second stage of WBCN's River Rave. They basically pulled us from their rotation."

"Well, what about WFNX?" I asked. I realized then that I hadn't heard God Lives Underwater on WAAF at all since that River Rave show.

"That might be the hardest station of all. They tried to get us to play their sponsored shows every year. Every year we had to turn them down because we were always playing the other stations' festivals. Out of the three stations, they got shit on the most by us not playing for them."

All of a sudden, my heart sank. I realized that this business wasn't all fun and games. There really was a mob mentality if there was treason, or even worse, loyalty to a specific station.

"Okay. Well, I'm still going to try WFNX tomorrow. If that doesn't work, then I promise not to waste my time with the other ones."

"I think that's probably smart. Let word of mouth and the flyers be the push. I've been pumping the show online with emails and message boards."

"Jenny and I have plans to go into Boston this Saturday.

We're going to spend the entire day hanging flyers. We have also been taking a stack of flyers to all the different concerts we attend to pass them out as people leave the venue."

"Sounds like you got everything under control!"

He made a joke about hiring me as his manager if the show was a success. Whether it was a joke or not, it sure felt good that he put so much faith in me.

A few days later, I nervously made the short drive over to WFNX. I silently rehearsed what I was going to say. I realized that I only had one real shot. If WFNX had felt so shunted, like David had warned, perhaps they would agree to sponsor his show, in order to make it an official WFNX show.

Right on the spot, I decided this would be the approach that I needed to use. I was going to present them with a business proposition.

I was greeted by a very pleasant secretary. I explained why I was here. I gave her the person's name who I was instructed to speak to. I told her that I was David's Boston manager. She told me to have a seat on the plush couch that was in the waiting room.

She disappeared into the back of the station. When she returned, she told me that she had informed my contact that I was here. I hoped that it wasn't going to take long. I didn't think my nerves would be able to handle the anticipation.

I watched what felt like a hundred people come and go. Some of them looked at me curiously and others paid me no mind. Time stretched out indefinitely. I might as well have been at a God Lives Underwater concert, waiting for them to show up.

After about an hour of not even being acknowledged, the secretary told me that she was going to go see what the holdup was. She disappeared into the back again. This time, she returned with a man dressed in a suit.

I stood up.

I tried to be as professional and courteous as I possibly could. I extended my hand for a handshake and introduced myself. He didn't extend his hand and, instead, left me embarrassingly holding out my hand.

"My name is Brian Paone," I said awkwardly. "I was hoping to discuss the possibility of WFNX sponsoring a show. It's David Reilly of God Lives Underwater at T.T. the Bear's Place. He's playing his very first solo acoustic show of old songs and debuting new songs from the new God Lives Underwater album that hasn't even come out yet—"

"No. I don't think so," he suddenly interrupted.

I was stunned. "Excuse me?"

"I don't think so. God Lives Underwater has never done anything for us over the years. To be quite frank with you, I don't think we should do anything for them. If that is all, I was in the middle of a meeting. Excuse me."

The man walked away without saying anything else to me. Even though I was disappointed, at least I could finally tell what David had warned me about.

Over the weekend, Jenny and I took a backpack full of flyers to Newbury Comics in Peabody and Saugus, Guitar Center in Danvers, Sam Goody in Peabody, and the Record Exchange in Salem. Then we headed into Boston.

We taped flyers around telephone poles outside major

clubs, left stacks of flyers at Newbury Comics, visited random tattoo and piercing shops, and alternative clothing stores along Newbury Street.

We spent the better part of eight hours just plastering the North Shore, Boston, and Cambridge with flyers for the show.

David called my cell phone about a week later.

"Jenny and I have blanketed most of the area with flyers for the show," I stated.

"That's great, me-han. That's what I want to talk to you about."

Uh-oh. "What? Is everything okay?"

"I don't know how to tell you this. I feel awful. I'll make it up to you somehow… I don't think I can come."

"Why not?" I felt my stomach erupt.

"I got robbed."

"What do you mean, you got robbed?!"

"I fell asleep with my backpack that I take with me everywhere. The money for the train ticket was in the backpack. Someone stole the backpack. My clothes were stolen. A checkbook for an account that Gretchen had just set up for me was stolen. All I have left is my Pennsylvania ID card. There's no way I can afford another train ticket."

"Aw, man! There's no way that you're not coming here, especially with a show booked now and everything. I get paid on Wednesday. I'll go to Western Union and send you the money again."

"Rocky, you really don't have to do that! I feel awful. I'll pay you back with the cash I make from the show."

"No way, man! I'm doing this because we're friends. I'm

not looking for any restitution. You need the money more than I do. I can afford another ticket for you, but, this time, don't keep it in your backpack! Let Gretchen hold onto it or something."

"I promise!"

I felt a little better.

"I'll drive out to Ambler and get you myself if I have to," I said. "You're not cancelling this show!"

Drop Kick Jesus had band practice that night. During one of our breaks, I vented to my bass player, Eric, about David being robbed.

"And you believe that story?" Eric asked me as he took a drag of his cigarette.

"Well, yeah. I know David well enough to know if he was lying or not."

"Think about it, Brian. You sent him cash. He mysteriously got robbed?"

"So?"

"He's a junkie, man!"

I was speechless. I wanted to defend David and tell Eric that he was wrong. David wasn't a stereotypical junkie! Eric just didn't know the type of person David really was.

"Sometimes you can be so naive," Eric finished.

"He's not even using anymore," I defended. "Plus, I really think I would be the last person David would steal from."

"Once a junkie, always a junkie. That's what they do! All I'm saying is, watch your stuff when he's here."

It was true that David was a struggling drug addict. Never for a second did I ever think of him as a junkie or of all the connotations that came along with that stigma. My eyes were opened once again to how other people, including fans, often viewed David.

It was time to prove them wrong.

MANTIS FIVE

"I hope you finally feel at home up there."
Fluzee: "Take Good Care" - 7

After David sent me a short list of equipment that he needed to play the show, I called Daddy's Junky Music. I reserved two acoustic guitars that David had specifically asked for.

I woke up with such a complete range of emotions the morning of the show. I was excited that I had pulled off David's very first solo show somehow. I was also nervous that David was going to spend the whole weekend with me.

Jenny and I had to get the equipment by two o'clock so we could get into Boston and pick up David from the train station in time. While we were at the store, I had a conversation with the clerk who was helping us. He asked what the gear was for, so I told him about the show. He said that he had been a God Lives Underwater fan back in the 1990s and wanted to come too.

We also engaged in a heated discussion about the Peter Gabriel–era Genesis being far superior to Phil Collins–era Genesis. This included my opinion that *The Lamb Lies Down on Broadway* by Genesis was possibly one of the top ten best albums ever recorded.

For only fifty dollars I rented the gear for twenty-four hours. We put the guitars in the backseat of my car and drove back to my house to wait for David's arrival.

On the way he called my cell phone. I was so sure that the whole thing was about to be called off.

"Rocky!" It was difficult to hear him because there was a lot of wind rushing through the phone. "Just so you know, I'm coming out there with some friends. They're driving me. I'll just meet you at the club instead of the Amtrak station. I'll call when I get there. Is that okay?"

"That's fine. Are they staying at my house too?"

"No. They're getting a hotel room and then going back to Philly. I only bought a train ticket back home for Monday, so I can give you half of your money back."

"It's okay, David. Keep it. Use it for food or something."

"Okay, me-han! Thanks! I'll see you in a few hours. I do want to go back to your place to drop off my bag and practice the set. I haven't actually practiced any of the songs yet, since I don't have a guitar anymore. Do you think we'll have time?"

"I'm sure we will. We'll check in, so the club knows you made it, and then we'll head to my place. I'll have you back at the club before you go on."

"How far away from the club do you live?"

"A little under twenty miles, but it's all highway so it takes about fifteen minutes without traffic."

"Perfect."

"What time do you want me to meet you there?"

"What time do you think we'll be there?" David asked the driver. Then he told me, "We should be there around six."

I hung up, and Jenny wanted to know what was going on. I told her the plan. Then I called Dann. He was going to meet us at my place after we got David from Cambridge. We dropped the guitars off at my place and then took Jenny's car into Cambridge when it was finally time to meet up with David.

The anticipation was killing me throughout the day. The drive into Cambridge wasn't any better. We decided to park in the garage down the street. Jenny didn't want to take a chance finding a metered parking spot.

Everything was going as planned, but there was something nagging me the whole time. Even with all the work, time, and effort that Jenny had put into promoting this show, she would still be denied entry unless David could pull some serious strings. T.T. the Bear's Place was a twenty-one-plus club, and Jenny wasn't twenty-one yet. Since David had a history of getting Dogboy and me into T.T. the Bear's Place at the first WBCN Xmas Rave, we were hopeful. However, that was a much different time for God Lives Underwater in 1995. In 2001, I doubted that David had that kind of ability anymore.

As we walked from the parking garage to the club, we passed the very same corner the tour van had gotten a parking ticket six years earlier.

I saw David outside the club with some other people. All our work and excitement had led us to this moment. Jenny was just as nervous as I was, only she was meeting him for the first time. She had never been able to see God Lives Underwater live or David in person before.

David turned and saw us approach. My face lit up with a smile. It was so good to see him again. It had been at least three years. He appeared rested, healthy, and happy.

I held out my hand for a shake. He put his arms around me and gave me a big hug.

"Brothers don't shake hands," he said.

David was dressed in his usual style. Shorts with longjohns underneath, an auto mechanic's work shirt, the chain of his wallet down almost to his knees. His hair was a lot shorter than it was the last time I saw him. It looked groomed and clean.

He introduced me to the people he was here with, the person who drove him from Philadelphia and also two other people who would record tonight's show. They were going to capture both the audio from the soundboard and some video for a DVD.

"So you're the one who has helped out with all of this!" he said to Jenny after I introduced her. His bag was on the ground against the club and he tossed it over his shoulder. "Let's go inside and check in so we can get back to your place. I really need to practice what I'm going to be playing tonight."

"Before we go in, I need to discuss pulling a big favor for us," I said. "T.T. the Bear's Place, as you probably remember, is a twenty-one-plus venue. Jenny's not twenty-one yet."

"I see."

"Remember back when you guys played here for the WBCN Xmas Rave, you got Dogboy and me in when we were underage? I was hoping you could talk to someone now and let them know the situation."

"Okay, let me see what I can do."

He opened the front door and went inside. Since it was still so early, it looked like only the bartender and the person who would be working the doors were here. The door closed behind David. We were left standing outside.

A few moments went by, and David came back out with the guy who was probably going to be working the door. The guy kept the door open with the heel of his foot as he talked with us.

"I'm sorry, but these are the club rules," he said as he looked at Jenny.

I could see her face finally understand that, despite all the hard work she had done for the show, all the hours spent making a flyer, printing copies, all the places we had visited to advertise, all the time she had been a God Lives Underwater fan, all the excitement she had for this show, she wasn't going to see any of it.

"What if you put big black Xs on her hands so you know she won't drink?" David suggested.

"I can't afford to have someone notice her in the club. I could lose my job. We could get shut down."

"What if she stays with me the entire time, never leaves my side, and while I'm playing she will just sit on the stage?"

"I really wish I could give you a different answer. I just can't let her in."

At this point David knew that he wasn't going to win. The days of pulling some tricks were obviously over.

"Okay. I understand your position."

"She can always stand outside and listen to the show," the guy suggested.

"Yeah, right. That will be fun. Thanks!" Jenny said sarcastically. She walked away with tears in her eyes.

"Thanks anyway," David said apologetically. He followed behind us toward the garage. He put his arm around Jenny's shoulders and said, "There just wasn't much more I could do."

"I know," she said. "I'm just gonna drop you guys off and head home."

"Are you sure? You don't want to hang out with us and go home when it's time to leave?" I asked.

"Nah. I just want to go home now. If you guys decide to do anything after the show, give me a call, and I'll come meet you."

I felt guilty that she had spent so much time helping with the show, and yet all she could do was leave. I felt like it was somehow my fault.

During the car ride back to my house, we talked about everything. We discussed God Lives Underwater, music, movies, and other random subjects. I called Dann and told him that we that were on our way back. If he wanted to head over, we would be there soon.

Jenny dropped us off. I told her that I would call her later. I asked if she wanted me to call her during the show so she could hear it, but she said no.

We went inside the house that I was renting with K.J. and Mike. K.J.'s and Mike's bedrooms were on the first floor, and my bedroom and bathroom were on the second.

David and I walked up the stairs to my bedroom, and he put his bag on the floor. I showed him the guitars that we had rented, and he inspected them.

"You have a refrigerator in your room!"

"Yeah. Did you want to go get some stuff for the weekend?"

"How close is your nearest liquor store?"

"Literally across the street next to that gas station."

"Can we go and pick some stuff up for the weekend before I run through the songs?"

"Sure . . ." I said hesitantly.

I didn't know if I should question him about still being clean. I also didn't know where alcohol fell in his perception of sobriety. He could tell that I was mulling it over in my head.

"Don't worry, Rock. It's the only thing I didn't quit. I don't even get drunk. I just like to have a drink."

"That's fine, man. You know that I worry about you. That's all."

"I know, Rock. You don't have to anymore. I really feel great about everything this time. I'm here with you for the weekend. I'm playing a show tonight. I'm healthy. I even wrote some songs by myself. I feel like everything is falling into place."

"You have no idea how happy it makes me to hear you say that!"

"I'm gonna go change," he said.

"Go ahead. The bathroom is right there."

He grabbed his bag and noticed my fifty-five-gallon aquarium. He bent down to try to find whatever was inside.

"What's in there?"

"That's just my turtle, Wilma," I said. "She's probably sleeping in one of the tunnels."

"Yeah! I think I see her."

"I hope she doesn't wake you up in the morning. When the sun comes up, she runs around the tank and her shell clicks against the glass. Sometimes it's loud enough to even wake me up."

"I'm a light sleeper, but I can't sleep past four. It's like my body won't allow me to, no matter what time I go to bed," he confessed. He pulled some clothes out of his bag, held them up, and added, "I'm gonna play in my pajamas tonight. You don't think anyone would mind, right?"

"I think people would prefer that you do," I replied, laughing.

"They're just so comfortable. I want the show to be as intimate as possible."

He went into the bathroom and closed the door.

I heard Dann's car door slam outside. I ran down the stairs to let him in. As we walked up the stairs, I told him David was in the bathroom changing into his pajamas. Dann chuckled. I closed my bedroom door, and David came out of the bathroom.

"Hey, me-han!" David said to Dann.

"How's it going?" Dann asked.

They shook hands.

"Alright. It's been a long time, huh?"

"Yeah! Since Avalon in 1995."

David walked over and picked up one of the guitars. He started fiddling with the strings.

"I use weird tunings, so I need two guitars. One in regular tune and the other in my tune. If I used only one guitar for both, there would be way too much time between songs while I tuned," he said as he reached in his bag and pulled out a handful of loose papers with writing on them. "I don't remember a lot of my lyrics. It's been so long since I've played any of these songs. Actually what I don't have are the lyrics to *Empty* and *GLU*. Do you guys have those albums around here? I don't even have a copy of them anymore."

"Really?" I asked and walked over to my CD collection. "I can burn them for you."

"Okay, that would be awesome. I'll go through your albums and pick out some stuff I want. I haven't had a copy of these in years. I think I may have traded them for drugs or something, back in the day," he added. He took them from me, opened up the inserts, and laid them flat on my bed where he was sitting. "I'm going to be playing some songs tonight that the band never played live."

I glanced at Dann, and we were both very excited.

"I'm going to play 'Scared' and 'Medicated to the One I Love'."

"Oh man!" I said. "You can do that acoustically by yourself?"

"Yeah. I wrote the song on piano. It can't be that hard to transpose it to guitar. I haven't actually tried it yet though. This will be my first time. You guys tell me if I should do it or not. I'm also going to be playing one of the first songs I ever wrote, called 'Lost.' It's a song Jeff and I recorded as Heavy. You guys know about those two Heavy songs, right?"

Only true God Lives Underwater fans knew of the two songs that David wrote with Jeff years ago called "Lost" and "Someone Else." They recorded them while God Lives Underwater was recording *Empty*. According to David, the project was called Heavy due to the songs not being heavy enough to be God Lives Underwater songs. It was both a pun and a play on words. Very few people had actually heard them. We only knew that they existed.

Dann and I couldn't believe that we were going to be hearing one of them live in my bedroom.

"Hey, do you mind if I call Jenny? Maybe I can talk her into coming back here to watch you play the set. I mean, you're practically giving us a private version of the show itself. It's better than nothing. She only lives a few miles away in Danvers."

"Yeah, okay. While we're waiting for her, we can run across the street for the beer."

"Works for me."

I called Jenny, and she answered the phone. "What are you doing?" I asked.

"Talking online with Reena. I just told her about what happened."

"Well, David is going to be playing the entire show for us in my bedroom right now to practice. Why don't you come back here and watch him rehearse? It sucks that you can't get into the show, but at least this way you'll still be able to see him play."

"I don't know. I'm already settled in."

"C'mon, Jenny! Come back!" David yelled behind me.

"See, even David wants you to come!"

"Okay, fine. I'll leave in a few minutes."

"She's coming!" I said and hung up my phone.

"Great! Let's go get some alcohol!" David suggested.

"I'll stay here in case Jenny shows up while you're gone," Dann offered.

We ran across Lynnfield Street and went inside South Peabody Liquors. David went to the back of the store and looked through the coolers for a specific beer.

"You're gonna have to buy it for me. I don't have any ID on me," he said.

"That's fine."

After searching for a few minutes, he found what he was looking for. "It's raspberry beer from Belgium. It's called Belgian Lambic Ale."

He handed it to me, and we walked to the counter. I put

the beer on the counter and pulled out my license for the clerk.

She took it and looked at David. "I need to see his ID also."

"I don't have any on me."

"I can't sell alcohol to you if you don't have any ID, and you're together," she said.

"I just came from Pennsylvania today on vacation. I don't have any ID on me."

"I'm sorry. I can't sell you any beer," she said.

"Tell me. Do I look like I'm under twenty-one to you!?" David said agitatedly. "This is ridiculous! I'm thirty years old, and you're telling me that I can't even be in the store while someone with a valid ID buys beer?"

"Look, I'm not selling you this beer."

He stood there in silence with his lips curled. Then David ripped the beer off the counter and went to the back of the store. I followed him.

"I'm gonna put the beer here," he whispered. "Let's go back to your place, and have Dann come and buy it by himself. He'd do that, right? If I told him where I put it?"

"I'm sure," I said. I just wanted to get David out of the store. We headed for the door.

As David opened the door, he said, "This is bullshit!"

We walked across the street back to my place, went upstairs, and told Dann the story.

"I hid the beer in the back right corner cooler. It's Belgium beer. You can't miss it."

I tried to give Dann some money.

"Don't worry about it. I got it," he said.

"You have ID on you, right?" David teased.

"Yeah," Dann replied, laughing.

We watched Dann run across the street from my bedroom window.

"That really was bullshit," David said.

"Yeah. It was."

He grabbed a guitar and tuned it some more while he looked over his handwritten lyrics of the songs that he was going to play.

"Jenny should be here any minute," I said.

David strummed the guitar and tried to match his voice to the right key. At that moment I got the chills. I realized that we were going to be hearing God Lives Underwater songs again live. Not to mention, in my bedroom of all places.

Dann came back with the beer and handed David the bag.

"Did she say anything?"

"She gave me a funny look. She probably knew exactly what I was doing. How could she stop me? I was by myself, and I had positive ID," Dann said.

David took the bag and put it in my fridge.

There was something oddly comical about David wearing pajamas in my bedroom with an acoustic guitar in one hand and beer in the other. He sat at the foot of my bed. Dann and I sat on the floor directly in front of him.

"Do you want to wait for Jenny?" I asked. I didn't want her to miss anything since this was the only show she was going to get.

"How about I just practice for a bit? When she shows up, I'll just start over from the beginning. I need as much practice as possible. I haven't even tried to play some of these songs yet, since I don't have a guitar at home. You're going to be hearing them as I try them for the first time."

I leaned back on my palms to support my weight. I still couldn't believe what we were about to see. David placed the pieces of paper with the lyrics all over my bed so he could read them from where he sat.

"Okay, since I've never attempted 'Medicated to the One I Love,' I'll start with that one."

He played the very electronic song on acoustic guitar for the first time. His guitar and his voice filled my room. He had to keep looking at the lyrics. When he hit the second verse, he stopped and laughed.

"I gotta look this up. I can't believe I completely forgot the words."

He found where he was in the song and continued playing. I couldn't believe how different the song sounded. Somehow it still sounded just as powerful.

"I think I'll try something easier to boost my confidence. That was a little rough." He strummed the air and counted to four. Then he hit the strings, and sang, "*I can see / See the signs / I've been waiting here for you . . .*"

David was able to get through "No More Love" flawlessly.

During this song it really hit me. He was really here in my bedroom and in his pajamas. We were really listening to him play these songs. I would never get anything like this ever again. I needed to focus on every moment of what was happening before it was lost to me forever.

Although David looked healthier than I had ever seen him, he still seemed fragile—almost as if he had transformed back to the time when these songs had been written.

He was at the beginning of "Whatever You've Got" when we heard Jenny's car outside. I opened my bedroom door to let her in.

David stopped playing. "We were waiting for you," he joked.

"He only played three songs so far," I said.

"I'm gonna start from the beginning, anyway."

Jenny sat on the other side of me and said hello to Dann.

"Okay. I'm going to play as if this was the show. When I'm done, we'll figure out if anything went wrong or needs work."

That was my personal reward for all the hard work we had put into his show. It wasn't the show itself, but that private practice performed in my bedroom. That moment, right then, made everything worth it.

David even played "Scared," which was one of the only God Lives Underwater songs never played live during their entire career. He also got through "Medicated to the One I Love" with much less difficulty than before.

I looked at Jenny and Dann, and I could see the complete concentration on their faces. They knew we were witnessing something very special. The audience was going to get a show that would be talked about for years to come.

"Okay. I think I'm going to end the set with a Heavy song. I'm gonna play it for you now. This is called 'Lost.'"

Dann and I looked at each other. We understood just how important this was. The Heavy tracks were always the rarest of them all. David was probably the only person who actually had a copy of them. The thought of God Lives Underwater fans coming to the show tonight, unaware that they were going to get a Heavy song in the set, made my stomach flip in excitement.

"What do you think? That runs about forty minutes, right?"

"Yeah, I'd say so. Your choice of songs is perfect. I can't believe how amazing they sound acoustically. To hear 'Scared' like that, after listening to it for so long the original way, was awesome."

"Okay! So now I gotta make up some sort of set list order. I'm going to wing it for the most part. I'd still like to have them written down, so I don't forget one while I'm up there. Am I playing enough songs from *Up off the Floor*?"

"You only get forty minutes, David. If you saturate the set with songs that people don't know, they may walk away wishing that you had played older stuff. Giving them a taste of songs from the new album is good, but sticking to what everyone knows is the way to go."

"I agree," Dann added.

"I think we should head back to the club. The first band is probably playing by now," I said.

"Who else is playing?" Dann asked.

"I don't know. The club booked some local bands. David is going on at midnight."

"I should get going," Jenny said. "David, it was a pleasure to finally meet you. I'll see you tomorrow. Thanks for playing for me."

"Sorry, kiddo, that I couldn't get you in."

"That's okay. What I just saw makes up for it."

"I don't think we're going to be able to fit both the guitars and all of us in my car," I said to Dann.

"We can take my car. I'll drive," Dann suggested.

"You don't mind?" I asked him.

"Not at all."

We carried the guitars to Dann's car.

"I'll sit in the back so David can ride shotgun," I offered.

As music filled the inside of the car, Dann asked me, "Have you heard the new Primitive Radio Gods album yet?"

"I didn't even know they had a new album out!"

"Yeah! It's called *White Hot Peach*."

Dann pulled his car out of my street.

"Do you mind if we shut off the music?" David asked. "I'd like to ride to the show without any music playing."

"That's fine," Dann said.

We spent the ride talking about *Up off the Floor* and Seven's death. When we got to the show, there were only about forty people or so inside. I really wanted a good crowd here to prove to David that people really did still care about his music.

I could see the video camera by the soundboard as we walked into the back room to drop off the guitars. We were in the very same room where Dogboy had almost gotten into a fight with Lou Barlow once during a sold-out show. How times have changed.

We went to the bar, and David ordered a drink. One of the local bands was playing. We sat and waited. It felt like an eternity. It would be even longer if people didn't show up. I tried to tell myself that it was okay either way. Maybe people would be coming later since it was such a late show.

Some people did filter in about an hour later. A few fans were even wearing God Lives Underwater T-shirts. A handful of people recognized David at the bar. Others recognized him but didn't approach him. I supposed that he could even be intimidating in the pajamas he wore.

My friend Mike and his girlfriend Hanna came. They arrived just as the last opening band got off the stage.

Right when it was time for David to play, it felt like the floodgates had opened. People arrived in droves.

"Do you mind setting up the stage for me and doing my soundcheck?" he asked.

"Not at all."

"Just grab a chair from the bar, and I'll use that. Also get a music stand to keep the lyrics on. Thanks."

I grabbed a chair from one of the tables and waited for the last band to get all their equipment off the stage. When the stage was clear, I placed the chair in the middle and grabbed a music stand that the club had provided. I placed the music stand next to the chair.

I went into the back room and grabbed both guitars. I sat in the chair with a guitar and looked at the soundman. He told me to say something into the microphone. I pulled the microphone close to my mouth and spoke into it.

The soundman asked me to play David's guitars to get his levels right. This was going to be a very straightforward mix. I played the only thing I knew on guitar, my old Yellow #1 songs. I didn't know how to play anything else.

I made a quick mental count of how many people were here. Club capacity at T.T. the Bear's Place was three hundred people. Based on the limited available standing room, there were a good 270 fans here.

Although the soundcheck was over, I still held one of the

guitars by its neck. We only had one guitar stand, and I didn't want to put it on the floor in case it threw off his odd tuning somehow.

The back door opened. David came out and headed straight for the stage. A round of applause erupted when the audience realized that the show was starting. I handed him the guitar and jumped off the stage.

He sat down and addressed the crowd as the soundman turned off the overhead music.

"How you guys doing?" David asked.

"Alright!" someone yelled.

"I'm David from God Lives Underwater. This is gonna be mellow, just so you know what you're expecting. I know you've been at our other shows where people get pushed around and stuff. This is gonna be real mellow. So, if you wanna sit down and stuff, that's cool too."

I laughed because I could see this was David being self-conscious and unsure of himself. He didn't know exactly how the fans were going to react to what he had planned. His speech was a way of providing a disclaimer, so no one could be disappointed.

"The song I'm gonna start off with is on an album that didn't come out yet. It's called 'Miss You More Than Anything.'"

There was a round of applause. I didn't know if the fans were happy that they were going to hear new songs, or if they were just supporting the show.

He played "Miss You More Than Anything" from *Up off the Floor* perfectly. The crowd was completely silent during his performance. It felt like people were almost afraid to breathe. David's voice sounded warm and strong. As the song progressed, I could hear him get his confidence back. He pushed more power into his voice as he hit the middle of the song.

The song ended. There was only a split second of silence. Not only did the fans clap, they cheered!

"Thanks," he said as he tuned his guitar. "This is gonna be a patient show because I tune my guitar for every song. I'm a prick like that."

There were a few laughs from the audience.

"I mean, I tune it to different tunings. It would be one thing if I had it tuned regular. Then I could just have someone else do that."

There was a period of David tuning the guitar and not saying anything else. The crowd had fallen silent.

"You still there? Alright!"

He played "Can't Come Down" from " from *Life in the So-Called Space Age*. Although his voice cracked a few times, that kind of frailty was welcomed. It was just so intimate. There weren't any barriers between him and the audience. If his voice hadn't cracked at all, it wouldn't have been as powerful of a show.

Halfway through the song, some ladies in the audience got too loud. Without stopping the song, David yelled, "No talking louder than the performer!" He kept the guitar riff going for a few more bars, and his voiced changed. Then he said, "It's cool, baby. I'm just kidding."

I had never seen his humor so apparent during a show before. His other shows were always so serious. The fact that even his eyes laughed made me realize that he was having the time of his life. He was stripped down. He was just so raw. This was good for his soul.

When the song ended, he received an even louder applause. "Thanks!"

Then he went right into "Happy?" from *Life in the So-Called Space Age*. When "Happy?" was finished, the clapping seemed to go on even longer than before.

"Thanks. This song, the name changes every year," David said as he looked around the club. "So I guess that's the bar over there, and then this is the show." David chuckled. "You guys are interested, right?"

Claps and cheers erupted from the crowd.

"Okay. They're probably like, 'What a sappy motherfucker up there onstage!'"

David looked at the people at the bar who were clearly not God Lives Underwater fans. They had probably never heard of him and had just stumbled in for a random drink. Most of the audience at the front looked back at the bar and laughed.

"Paaaaarty!" David added in a frat-boy voice.

He went right into "23" from *Empty*. When he got to the lyric, *I've spent twenty-three years now trying to get by*, he changed it to, "I've spent *thirty* years now trying to get by."

The song ended, and David let the applause die down.

"Thanks. Let's see . . ." he mumbled. He flipped through the sheets of lyrics. "Did you ever see that episode of *Tom and Jerry* where Jerry's uncle was over? He's the guy from Texas, and he plays the guitar? He's like"—David put on his best cartoon voice and imitated the dialogue from *Tom and Jerry*, which got everyone laughing—"'Froggy went a-courting, and he did ride c-c-c-Crambone! Froggy went a-courting, and he did ride . . .' and he's like *Boing*! Then he goes after Jerry to pluck one of his whiskers to use as a guitar string, and he goes 'You know I can't play my g-g-g-guitar without my g-g-g-guitar strings!' You know that episode I'm talking about?"

"That's my favorite episode!" someone from the crowd yelled.

"That's mine too! Everyone's. Every time I tune my guitar, I think of that," David said and, with his voice, mimicked a guitar being down tuned. "Froggy went a-courting and he did ride Crambone. Alright. This is from my first record ever."

He played "Lonely Again" from *GLU*. He got through the first bar or two, and then he had to stop to retune the guitar and look at the lyrics. There was a long silence from David.

"Whew! This is what happens to you when you get old, me-han. Gotta have cheat sheets. Alright, ready?"

He started "Lonely Again" from the first verse and cut out the intro. When he finished, he received a rowdy set of applause despite the pause in the song. It was such a fan favorite.

"You guys doing alright?" he asked after the applause had died down. "This is my favorite title of any of the songs I have. This is 'Medicated to the One I Love.'"

"Aw, that's cute!" someone said.

David played "Medicated to the One I Love" from *Life in the So-Called Space Age* for the third time in the last four hours. Right at the end, he went into the final chorus wrong. He stopped and collected himself. Eventually he finished the song.

That moment really drove home how unscripted and uncalculated the show really was.

"That was rough, I know," he apologized.

The crowd laughed. Then everyone burst into applause to show that no matter what mistakes he made, they were really with him through all of it.

"I only played it once before on guitar. But I couldn't get a piano here. It wasn't part of the budget, ya know?"

"Don't worry about it!" someone yelled.

"Alright. I'll just go right for the goods."

He played "No More Love" from *GLU* with almost as much energy and emotion in his voice as if the rest of the band was right behind him and everyone was plugged in.

"Sometimes I just get tired of playing guitar. Could you tell? I'm so used to having people rocking around me, I can kinda just grab the mic and jump around and have fun. You guys are very patient. I'll give you that much. This is called 'Whatever You've Got.' It's from the still-to-be-unreleased-record *Up off the Floor*. Which incidentally is not coming out because of legal bullshit and the record industry."

The crowd booed.

"Yeah. They went bankrupt, and now they want their money back that they gave me to record the album. They said, 'Here's the money. Record an album. We're out of business. Can we have the money back? And then we'll give you the rights to your record back.' So, you know what I've been doing? I've just been dubbing it and giving it to people."

Someone yelled, "Yeah!"

The whole place clapped and cheered.

"Fuck 'em, right? If I'm gonna get evicted anyway, you guys might as well have my music. So this is called 'Whatever You've Got,' and some people are misled because there are some train references in the song—about the train. It's because I was riding the train, and I thought of the song. It's not about the death of my girlfriend, because she died by train, like in November."

My heart sank. I couldn't believe he was going to talk about Monica in front of all these people.

"It's not about that, because I'm not gonna write a song about that." David then sang, "*I feel the train changing tracks / The sound of that / I reminisce . . .*"

I knew the song probably better than anyone else in that club. I was practically the only person in the audience who had even heard it before. David had already gone past where his next line of lyrics should've been and instead he just kept strumming the guitar. His strumming became weaker by the second. It was apparent to me that he wasn't going to be able to even sing the next line.

Suddenly he stopped altogether, and there was a deafening silence in the club. I could actually feel the air we were breathing become as heavy as a brick. Then tears welled up in his eyes.

He looked away from the audience. He took a moment to collect himself.

"Started talking about the girlfriend. Give me a minute," he apologized without looking at the audience.

"It's alright, man!" someone shouted.

"It's been a rough year," David replied. His voice trembled.

It was the most honest and sincere moment I had ever experienced with David. I could hear some of his fans try to choke back their own tears. If he had just stood up and walked away, no one would have cared. This moment transcended far beyond just seeing the singer of God Lives Underwater play a solo acoustic show. I could feel whatever remained of the wall crumble, and the lines disappear. We all became David's support system. David had let an entire room of strangers into his heart. It made continuing a little less scary for him.

"Let it out!" someone yelled from the back.

"No. I'm not into that kind of therapy, me-han," David chuckled subtly. "I've had that kind of therapy this year, and you can see the lines on my face. It added a few years."

He strummed his guitar once.

"It's all good!" someone said.

"Alright, I'll get it this time." David started the song over from the beginning. "*I feel the train changing tracks / The sound of that / I reminisce . . .*" He stumbled and tried to continue. "*I tried so hard.*"

He just stopped right at the end of the word He had clearly started to cry again. He could barely even get out, "*I tried so hard.*"

"I'm just gonna move on," he said. His voice sounded exhausted and strained. "It's a little too much for me to handle right now. I'm gonna do something lighthearted. I'll get back to it. Do I have any lighthearted tunes?" he joked. "My gosh. I know what I'll play ya!"

He took a moment to fiddle with the guitar.

"Yeah. I'm not about to start crying onstage. Can't do it, me-han. Alright. This is called 'Ordinary Man.' I wrote this when I was sixteen."

I had never heard of the song before. I shot a glance at Dann, and he gave me a nod as if to say, "Oh, yeah!" David completely surprised everyone by playing something we had never heard of. I wondered if this was going to replace the Heavy song.

"Alright. I'm gonna try that other song again." He sighed

when "Ordinary Man" was finished. "Something about it just doesn't want me to get through like the first verse."

I held my breath. David began "Whatever You've Got" for the third time.

"I feel the train changing tracks / The sound of that / I reminisce"

This time, it was perfect all the way to the very last word. The crowd gave him a lengthy applause when he fell silent at the end of the song.

"I got a couple left," he said. "Wow! This has never been played live, for sure!"

He then played "Scared" from *Empty*. When the song was over, he flipped through his lyrics sheets.

"I know I really only got one left, I just . . . Let's see here. I want to make it the right one, ya know?" he said quietly. It sounded as if he was talking more to himself than the audience.

"Last call!" the female bartender screamed as loud as she could. Her voice was almost louder than David's, even with his microphone.

David paused for a moment as he realized that this was the last song of the night. He decided not to play the Heavy song or to play any of the God Lives Underwater songs that hadn't been played yet, not even another song from the unreleased new album.

He strummed his guitar as he sang the first line of lyrics to "Stripped." I looked at Mike and Dann. I smiled and almost cried from excitement.

David had decided to close his solo show with the song that I had watched God Lives Underwater physically learn how to play on the *Empty* tour at Axis during a soundcheck.

I thought it was very fitting that David closed his show with a Depeche Mode cover. They were his favorite band and the reason why he started playing music in the first place.

Because he played "Ordinary Man," there was no real reason to play a Heavy song. At least a cover was something people would know. Especially a cover that God Lives Underwater was known for.

The crowd went crazy when he finished. He waved to everyone as he got up and headed for the back room. People yelled, "Encore!" but the show was over.

After David came out of the back room a few minutes later, we hung around so he could talk with everyone who wanted to chat with him. Some people wanted to discuss *Up off the Floor* while others wanted to ask David if he remembered them at some of his shows. Nobody mentioned anything about Monica or his breakdowns during the show.

David was humble and appreciative toward everyone who approached him. He signed some autographs and joked with almost everybody. A few people wanted their pictures taken with him. A lot of people told him how happy they were that he had played the show.

We were the last ones to leave the club. David was soaring with confidence and a newfound motivation for his music. When we got into the car, he asked Dann if he could look through his music collection to pick an album out. David grabbed the latest Slipknot album, *Iowa* and we blasted it on the ride home.

While on Route 1 North over the Tobin Bridge as we left Boston, we passed a speed limit sign that read *15 Miles Per Hour.*

"You have got to be kidding me! They expect people to go that slow on this road?"

We tried to explain that it was just because of the Big Dig. No one actually obeyed that speed limit!

After Dann dropped us off at my house, we went upstairs to my room and got ready for bed. Since David was already in his pajamas, he didn't really have to change. I put an extra twin-size mattress on the floor for him. I positioned it right next to my bed in front of the television in case he wanted to watch something or talk before falling asleep.

He was on the mattress and I put on MTV2, so we could hear some music. We discussed how amazing the show was and what our plans for the next day would be. Since it was Labor Day weekend, we had a few barbecues scheduled with some friends of mine. When I noticed he had stopped talking, I quietly shut off the television.

I lay still and listened. The only sound in the room was David's breathing. It was very deep and almost on the verge of a snore. I finally drifted off to sleep. I was thankful that he was healthy and happy again.

His breathing assured me of that with every exhale.

The sun was already shining through my bedroom windows as Wilma made her early morning run up and down her tank. She banged her shell loudly on the tank's glass as she waddled into her water dish. The immediate realization that David was sleeping on my floor suddenly jolted me out of sleep.

When I looked at the extra mattress on the floor, it was empty. David was at my computer desk doing absolutely nothing but looking out the window at the sunrise. His body was relaxed, and he appeared tranquil but somber. His face was turned away from me.

I had no idea how long he had been like that. He had probably spent the entire time just sitting there. It was a very peaceful moment.

He finally noticed I was awake and turned toward me.

"I hope I didn't wake you."

"Nah, man. Wilma woke me up."

"I can't sleep past four, no matter what time I go to bed. It's physically impossible. I don't know why."

"Have you been just sitting there the whole time?" I asked.

"I used your computer and went online for a bit. I had a few emails to send. I'm still trying to get someone to release *Up off the Floor*. It seems like the only label even remotely talking to me about it is Metal Blade. They want to do a multi album deal to make it worth their while. Honestly I just don't know if God Lives Underwater has that much of a future anymore."

"Last night's performance should show you that people still care."

"Yeah. I'm not talking about the fans. I'm talking about the people in the band. Last night also proved to me that maybe there's enough interest in my music to try to pull off a solo career." He laughed.

What he had said probably sounded too pretentious, even for him.

"The good news is, it looks like I might be doing a collaboration with Aaron Lewis from the band Staind. His manager contacted me. Aaron is actually a huge God Lives Underwater fan. He wants me to lay down some vocal tracks on something he's working on. If that happens, it would be great to just get my name out there again."

"That would be awesome," I concurred.

I turned on the television, and MTV2 was on. David sat on my bed, and we wasted a few hours just watching videos.

He looked through my music collection and picked out a handful of albums he wanted me to burn for him. One of them was *Tea for the Tillerman* by Cat Stevens.

"What are our plans for today?" he asked.

"Well, we're having a barbecue here at the house. Then we can go to my friend Mike's house later for another cookout there."

"That sounds great. It's been a while since I've been to a barbecue where I can just eat, relax, and not worry about anything."

"Tonight's barbecue here is where you can meet all the guys in my band and some of my other friends."

"What are we doing until then?"

"Well, my keyboard player, Justin, isn't coming to the barbecue, and he really wants to meet you. God Lives Underwater is one of his favorite bands. He's working right now. I thought we could drive up there, just so he can meet you. We'll make it short. Other than that, no real plans until later."

"Do you mind if I jump in the shower?" he asked.

"Of course not. There are towels in the bathroom. I'm gonna call Jenny and see if she's up yet."

David went into the bathroom, and I heard him turn on the water. I sat at my desk and called Jenny. I told her our plans for the day. She said that she would be over soon so that she could go with us to see Justin.

I hung up the phone and checked my email. David's singing voice traveled through the bathroom door into my room. It took me a moment to make out which song he was singing.

I laughed when I realized that David was in my shower and, at the top of his lungs, was belting out Nelly Furtado's "Turn off the Light." After a few minutes, he stopped the water and came out dressed in the same clothes he was wearing the day before.

"Was that Nelly Furtado?" I laughed.

"Yeah, me-han! That's an infectious song. It's probably my favorite song to sing in the shower."

"That's so funny. Jenny is going to be here soon, so we'll leave when she gets here."

After I showered and got ready, we got into my 1990 Chrysler LeBaron convertible. Unfortunately the convertible top had broken on a trip to see the band Yes in Boston just two days earlier. Yes was touring on the *Magnification* album. In the parking garage, I had tried to put the top down after the show, when something snapped, and the motor broke.

Of course, David immediately said, "Put the top down!"

"It actually broke just two nights ago!"

David sat in the passenger seat, and Jenny was in the back. She had to lean forward into the middle console just to hear and be part of the conversation.

Justin was working as an assistant manager at Cambridge Sound Works in Nashua, New Hampshire. On the ride up, I put on Tool's *Undertow* album. "Sober" came on.

"Is this Tool?" David asked.

"Yeah! I have all of their albums in here. If you want, I can change it. *Undertow* has always been my favorite."

"Nah. It's cool. God Lives Underwater was actually asked

to be on a Tool tribute album that's supposed to be coming out."

"Really? That would be so cool," Jenny said.

"Yeah. We aren't really big Tool fans though. We don't know enough songs to make a good choice. Someone had this album on recently, and some song came on, you know, about the carrots, and I was just like 'That's the song we're doing!'"

"You mean 'Disgustipated'?"

"Yeah! That one. I worked on it a bit. I made it shorter than the original song because, it's, like, what? Sixteen minutes long? I made it really electronic. I thought it would be fun to do vocals on that song too."

"What happened?"

"I don't know. We never heard back from the label that was going to be releasing it, so I stopped working on the track. Then the whole band's legal and label problems started. It was just forgotten."

"Wow! God Lives Underwater covering 'Disgustipated' by Tool. Now that would have been an awesome song!"

I flicked through the tracks to the last song on *Undertow*.

As soon as it started, David said, "Yeah! This song! This whole thing just cracks me up. That's why I wanted to do it."

After about an hour, we reached Nashua. I found Justin's store pretty easily. Justin had always held David as one of his personal idols. He had no idea that we were actually going to his store. He did know that David was staying with me for the weekend, but this visit was going to be a complete surprise.

I parked the car, and we walked inside. Justin was waiting on a customer. When he looked up and saw us, he looked confused until he noticed David looking at one of the stereo systems. I saw his knees practically buckle from the excitement.

Justin asked the other employee he was working with to finish with his customer. I introduced David to Justin. Justin always had a unique habit when he was nervous. He just laughs uncontrollably. To make it worse, they were belly laughs, not just little giggles. Upon this introduction, Justin bent over and hysterically laughed.

"David Reilly is in my store!" he exclaimed.

He laughed until tears came out of his eyes. He had to take his glasses off to wipe them dry. He apologized. Nonetheless, every time his laughs subsided, they started again.

Eventually he got a hold of his composure and was able to have an intelligent conversation with David.

When I could tell that David had run out of things to say, I said, "Okay, let's get going."

They shook hands. When we walked out of the store, I saw Justin mouth the words *Thank you!* to me.

"Do you think we can stop at the nearest store to get some ice cream?" David asked as we pulled out of the parking lot.

"Sure. You feel like ice cream this early in the morning?"

"Not really, but it's just the only thing that really stops the heroin withdrawal. I'm having really bad cravings right now."

"Ice cream! Really?"

"Chocolate ice cream specifically. There's just something about the chemical makeup of chocolate that blankets the urge inside my brain when I withdraw. If I don't feed that urge, either with the ice cream or a drug, I can get very sick."

"Really? Wow!"

"It's not forever. It's just the stage of recovery I'm in right now. It'll pass soon, and then I'll be in the clear."

"Would you rather just get a big tub of chocolate ice cream and leave it in my fridge?"

"Actually that would be a good idea. Sometimes I go a full day without needing it, but some days I could eat five bowls. Depends on the day." He shrugged.

"Can you make it until we get back to my place, or do you need to get some now?" I asked as we pulled onto the highway.

"I can make it, but I don't want to go too long. I might start to get very sleepy, cranky, and I'll probably feel sick."

It dawned on me that Dogboy hadn't seen David since the last God Lives Underwater show he had attended back in December 1996 during the *Empty* tour. Even though Dogboy had only been to three God Lives Underwater shows, he had become close enough with David that I thought it would be an awesome surprise to swing by Dogboy's apartment. I knew David would love to see him again too.

"Hey, do you want to see if Dogboy is home?"

"No shit? Absolutely! I haven't seen that kid in forever! How is he?"

"He's okay, I guess. We actually had a falling out right after Sue and I broke up, and we aren't nearly as close as we used to be. I only occasionally talk to him."

"He was with you the night we all met."

"Yep."

"Remember when he almost had to fight Lou Barlow?" David asked.

"I sure do! I thought that we were going to have a brawl in the back room."

I pulled off the highway near Dogboy's apartment in

Danvers. We stopped at a CVS, and David bought the largest tub of the most generic chocolate ice cream they had.

"It doesn't have to be a brand name. It just has to be chocolate," he said, laughing.

The ice cream sat on David's lap as we continued driving. I pulled into Dogboy's long driveway, and we went around the back of the house.

"I don't even know if he's home or not," I said as I knocked on his door.

"You should have called," Jenny suggested.

"Nah. The element of surprise is so much more interesting!"

Dogboy opened the door. "Holy shit!"

They shook hands, and Dogboy invited us in. We sat on the couch.

"Hey, me-han, do you have a spoon?"

Dogboy gave him a spoon. David opened up his tub of ice cream and ate it right out of the container.

"So, how are you doing, man?" Dogboy asked.

"Great! I'm clean and healthy."

"It's been a while, huh?" I said to Dogboy.

"Yeah, it has. I always felt bad not going to any more shows. But with college and some other stuff going on, it was always difficult."

"Don't worry about it," David said.

We sat and chatted for almost an hour. David was more relaxed than he had been with Justin. It also probably helped that he had a half tub of chocolate ice cream in his system.

As we said good-bye, I invited Dogboy to my barbecue, but he declined. He said that he already had plans.

We made our way back to Peabody.

"David, if you don't want to talk about it, that's cool, but what exactly happened with Monica's death?"

I didn't know how to bring it up, but I still wanted to ask.

"She was buying me a Christmas present when she crossed a street with train tracks in Philly. She didn't look both ways. She didn't even see the train. They said that she was dead the moment it hit her. At least there wasn't any suffering."

"I'm sorry. Really. We don't have to talk about it."

I was nervous about the barbecue. We were having at least fifteen people over. I knew David's personality enough to know how he would usually react to being around that big of a group of people who he didn't know. David was always an introvert with strangers. He might become too awkward and maybe even remove himself from the event altogether.

When we got home, my roommates were already getting the backyard and the house ready. Jenny and I decided to help set the tables.

"I'm gonna go upstairs and lay down for a bit, okay?" David said.

"Yeah. That's fine. Are you feeling okay?"

"I just get tired really easy. If I fall asleep, come up and wake me when people are here."

"Sure thing. If you want to put the television on, just use the remote that's on top of the cable box."

"Okay."

My bass player, Eric, and his fiancée, Kristen, arrived with drinks and a ton of meat. Kristen asked immediately where David was. I told her that he was upstairs taking a nap. I didn't think it was wise to go wake him just yet. More of our friends arrived. After two hours of David's absence,

I thought it was time to go wake him.

He was passed out on the mattress with the television on Mute.

"David?" I asked quietly. "People are here. Do you wanna come and get something to eat?"

"Sure." He stood up, went into my bathroom, and splashed water on his face. "I'm sorry about that, Rocky."

"Why are you apologizing?"

"I don't mean to be a party pooper."

"No one thinks that! Especially me."

We went downstairs together and into my backyard. There were tables set up with food and drinks. A bunch of patio chairs were arranged in a big circle. I introduced everyone to David. There were about twenty people here. I knew that some folks were only here because they knew that David was staying at my house.

David grabbed some chicken and inspected some of the food. "Who made this potato salad?"

"I did," Kristen said.

"This is exactly how I like my potato salad. Hardly anyone knows how to make it like this! This is real Philadelphia potato salad. It even has Italian dressing in it!"

"That's how I always make it," Kristen replied.

I could tell that David was impressed. His plate almost toppled over with heaping spoonfuls.

There was a small stereo on the windowsill next to a collection of music from old school metal and thrash bands. David looked through the collection and got pretty excited about some of the rarer albums.

"Who's music is this?" he asked.

Eric said that it was his. They shared their tastes in metal for quite a while. I smiled. David was getting along so well with my friends, and he was being sociable with people he had just met. He really looked like he was truly enjoying himself.

Then the most embarrassing moment of the day happened when David took his food and beer to a patio chair. Unbeknownst to him, he chose the one chair that was broken. The seat just wasn't attached to the frame of the chair. When his butt hit the seat, it fell out from underneath. He immediately found himself with his ass on the ground, his knees around his chin, and his entire plate of food dumped onto his chest and stomach.

Eric and I both witnessed the disaster and were the first ones to help. We each grabbed a hand and pulled him out of the collapsed chair. I was so embarrassed. I was also terrified about his reaction. Kristen asked if he was okay. He replied that he was. He politely excused himself and said that he was going upstairs to get cleaned up.

I was mortified. I was also extremely nervous that we had lost David for the night. He was someone who hated to be the center of attention. Especially when it was something embarrassing. I was scared that his level of comfort had been ruined.

After some time had passed, I said to Jenny, "I better go check on him."

I went upstairs, opened the door, and saw him on the mattress watching television.

"You okay?" I asked.

"Yeah. I just needed some alone time after that."

"I understand. That's why I didn't come up right away."

"I'm good. I just needed to decompress. Is there any food left?"

"Absolutely."

He got up, shut off the television, and we walked back outside together. Nobody even mentioned a single thing about it.

After he filled up his plate again, he went inside and sat at the kitchen table to eat instead. He didn't do this to escape my friends. People had migrated inside anyway. Not to mention, David probably wanted to make sure that he sat in a stable chair this time.

"So you're in Rocky's band?" he asked K.J.

"Yeah."

"You guys don't sound anything like his last band, Yellow #1, do you?"

"No. Not at all." K.J. laughed.

"Good!"

"What do you mean?" I teased.

"Rocky gave me a copy of that album. We put it on in the tour bus and turned it up loud. It freaked us out so much that someone actually screamed, took it out of the stereo, and threw it out of the bus window onto the highway."

Jenny burst into laughter.

"I can't believe you did that!" I said.

"That's awesome!" K.J. laughed too.

"Have you even heard that stuff?" David asked.

"Do you want another copy?" I joked.

"No way! Maybe we were just high, but, damn, that shit was scary!"

"Thanks a lot!"

"You really threw it out the window?" Jenny asked.

"Yep. It's somewhere on the side of the road in the Midwest."

"Well, this band sounds nothing like that one," K.J. reaffirmed.

"In Rocky's defense," David said, "I probably know what that feels like. Back when American Records were looking to sign us, they booked us to open for Slayer in Florida. They were touring on the *Divine Intervention* album, if I remember correctly. Rick Rubin was there. He wanted to see our live show, and he was curious about the crowd's reaction."

Slayer was K.J.'s all-time favorite band. I saw his eyes light up.

"We only made it through a few songs before we feared for our safety. Let's just say, Slayer fans did not get what we were all about. They definitely let us know!"

"I didn't know you opened for Slayer!" I exclaimed.

"Just for that one show, if you can even call it that!"

My friends came in and out of the house. David was very generous with his old God Lives Underwater war stories. Once people realized that it was okay to ask about the band, he would tell stories to anyone who wanted to hear them.

It was about nine o'clock when people left to go home. Since I had promised Mike that we would make an appearance at his cookout in Needham, it was just about time to head over there. Eric and Kristen were also invited, and they said that they would follow us to Mike's house. Jenny, David, and I took my car.

There were a handful of people in Mike's backyard when we got there. Mike approached us, shook David's hand, and offered us some food. Surprisingly we were still hungry. Mike threw some chicken on the grill.

We safely sat in chairs in a semicircle. However, the mosquitoes were out in full force. I knew that we weren't going to stay long. It was getting late, we were being eaten alive, and we were tired.

Halfway through his chicken, David noticed that it wasn't cooked all the way through.

"Hey, what are you trying to do, kill us?!" David said.

"What do you mean?"

"The chicken's undercooked!"

"No, it isn't!"

Mike poked at the chicken with a fork and tried to convince us that it was fine. We just smiled and nodded. When he turned away from us, we both tossed our plates in the trash. We hung around for a little while longer until it was time to head home.

Jenny was going to spend the night at my place too. David made a joke about how funny it was that both of us could sleep comfortably in a twin-size bed because of how small we both were.

The food we had eaten acted as natural sleep aids. We were passed out before any of us could even say good-night to each other.

Sunday was our day to relax. David wanted to see *Jay & Silent Bob Strike Back*, so we made plans to go to a matinee at the Liberty Tree Mall AMC Theatre in Danvers with Dann.

David was awake again before Jenny and me, but this time, he was using the computer for email and business when we woke up.

After we all took showers, we met Dann at the theatre. Before the movie, there was a trailer for *The Royal Tenenbaums*. At the end of the trailer, the announcer said, "From the team that brought you *Rushmore*!" and David was really excited.

"That's one of my favorite movies!" he said loudly.

After the movie, we left the mall, said good-bye to Dann, and drove Jenny back to her car which was at my house. She had already made plans and couldn't spend the rest of the day with us.

When we pulled down my dead-end street, I saw my mother by my house in her car. She waved as she got out.

"Hi! I'm Brian's mom!"

David shook her hand.

"I've heard so much about you over the last six years, I figured this might be my only chance to meet you. Brian talks about you all the time. So are you enjoying it here on your vacation so far?"

"Yeah! We've really just been hanging out and meeting all of his friends."

"How did the show go?"

"It was really great."

"What are your plans for the rest of the day?" she asked.

He looked at me quizzically.

"I'm taking him to the Willows."

"It's definitely a nice day for that!" she said.

Salem Willows was a park in Salem surrounded by the ocean with beaches and a pier that had huge arcades, rides, miniature golf, and a boardwalk with food stands.

We chatted outside the house, and then she said that she didn't want to keep us, so she said good-bye. After we also said good-bye to Jenny, we ran inside to grab sweatshirts in case there was a breeze blowing off the water.

I took the long way so David could see the Salem tourist attractions. We passed by the Witch Museum, Pickering Wharf, House of Seven Gables, Peabody Essex Museum, and the Salem Commons.

Once we parked at the Willows, I could see that it was pretty busy. When I asked if he wanted to play any video games, I was immediately reminded of the time I saw the God Lives Underwater interview on Much Music when David and Jeff never took their eyes off the skiing game, as much as the guy was trying to talk to them.

David said that he was hungry, so we picked one of the food stands and ordered some lunch. I suggested that we sit on the rocks at the water's edge to eat. We took our food and climbed onto the rocks. We sat right where the water splashed below us.

"I'm sorry if you were bored this weekend," I said.

"Nah, me-han. Not at all."

"I really wanted us to have a jam-packed, fun-filled weekend. It just turned into one big meet-and-greet with my friends."

"Don't worry about it, Rock. Seriously, I had a far better time than you think."

"Seriously?"

"Yeah." He started to poke something with a stick and looked into the water. "This weekend has been really good for me. It taught me something really valuable too. I finally learned that I can be happy without all that shit inside me. You have a great group of friends who made me feel really welcomed without making me feel uncomfortable."

"Thanks."

"It was good to see Dann and Dogboy again too. I also had the opportunity to see the area in person and not from the window of a tour bus."

"I know that Dann and Dogboy wished they saw you more during the touring days."

"I really like it here. I don't feel any pressure like the other places where I've lived. You've kept me so busy that I haven't even thought about the struggles of staying clean. I feel safe here. That says a lot."

"That means more to me than you know. I worry about you, David."

"No need to worry about me, Rock."

"But I do. Sometimes I feel more like a big brother than a friend."

"I feel like you really have been a big brother to me too. Like this weekend for example."

A warm breeze came off the water. It was a clear and gorgeous day. The sun was out. There were families on the beach. The boardwalk was packed. David made me believe that he really was going to be okay.

"I actually have been thinking," he began. He paused as he stared over the water. "I really like it here. I like what I've seen. I've enjoyed not having any temptations. I might want to move here."

"Are you serious?"

"Well, yeah. I love the way this area is laid out. I really like all of your friends. I would want to get my own apartment, and it would have to be cheap, but I could find some work around here, right? I mean, this is a pretty populated area."

"Wow. I can't believe we're even discussing this!"

"I just haven't felt this comfortable anywhere in a really long time. I'm not very good with temptation. You do realize that you're one of my very few friends who is still around, right? Other than my band and some friends I had before God Lives Underwater, that is. I never felt like you were just a fan."

"Neither did I."

"I may not have always had enough time to hang out with you. Sometimes we would even go months without talking, but I always thought of you as one of my best bros."

"That means a lot to me. Sometimes I thought I was just the annoying kid, who showed up at all the shows and tried to tag along."

"Oh, c'mon! You should have known better than that. I knew who was there for me because they truly cared about me and who was only there for me because I was the singer of God Lives Underwater."

"You mean like Kerrie?"

"I don't care what you think of Kerrie," he said. "She's a good kid."

"I never liked her. I just think we rubbed each other the wrong way right from the beginning. I mean, I hadn't seen her in two years, and the first thing she did was brag about being in the studio with you guys during *Life in the So-Called Space Age*."

"She told you that?"

"Yeah."

"She wasn't even there! Me-han, I wish I had heard her say that! I would have said something. That was definitely something I didn't like about her."

"Yeah. She told me at the Middle East show when we were

all sitting around the table. That was the night I met Scott, and you met Sue."

"I remember. I really wish I had heard that!"

"No biggie. Over, done with, gone."

"Do you think you could look for a place for me here when I go back home?"

"You really are serious about this?"

"Yes. It would be good for me, even if it was for a year. Maybe I could use that time to write a solo album. Weirder things have happened."

"Would you ever even consider writing one? And I don't mean the Robot Teen America album."

"Well, I don't know. I really like being in a band, but I have been so wrapped up in all the legal bullshit of *Up off the Floor* that I don't know if I have the ambition anymore. The Robot Teen America album was really my tribute to Seven and an excuse to fiddle around with a new computer program I had."

"Would it be like God Lives Underwater?"

"Nah. Have you ever actually heard my two Heavy songs?"

"No, sorry."

"I think it would be more like that. Maybe a little lo-fi and indie sounding, but with some Radiohead and Spiritualized influences mixed in. Probably less Depeche Mode sounding than God Lives Underwater."

"That sounds awesome."

"Eh. Maybe I'll invest in an acoustic guitar and write again. Or I could always just make a hip hop album with big fat beats. Friday night's acoustic show really showed me that I enjoy the singer-songwriter atmosphere. That was a lot of fun."

"That was a great show."

"I could live here for a while. If I can just settle this crap with the label, I could work on some new God Lives Underwater songs. Or maybe I'll just keep the songs for myself and start a solo career."

"If you wanted to jump on it now, I'm sure it wouldn't be a problem with K.J. and Mike if you moved in with us at the house until we found you your own place. I wouldn't even charge you rent. It would be my contribution to get you back into writing again."

"Thanks, Rock! I would only want that for a month or so. Then I would want my own place."

"Of course. Hey, so what has Jeff been up to these last few years?"

"He's been producing. Do you like Neil Diamond?"

"I love Neil Diamond!" I replied. "Why? Don't tell me that Jeff—"

"Neil released a new album in July called *Three Chord Opera*," he said, interrupting me.

"I know. I bought it the week it came out!"

"Wow! You are hardcore!" He laughed. "I did see a bunch of Neil Diamond albums in your collection, now that I think about it. If you ever met him, would you feel the need to tell him what your favorite song on the album was?" he asked cheekily. When I refused to answer him, he asked, "You know the song 'At the Movies' on the new album?"

"I certainly do. It's track four," I said, flaunting my Neil Diamond geekdom.

"Jeff programmed the percussion on that song. Neil actually hired him as a studio musician for the album, but 'At the Movies' is the only track that he actually played on."

"That's crazy! I really love that album."

"Do you want to get going?"

"Sure."

We walked back to the car and drove to my house. We went upstairs and spent the rest of the day just watching television and listening to albums that David wanted me to burn for him.

I pulled out my copy of *Three Chord Opera* and opened up the insert. Sure enough, Jeff Turzo was listed in the credits as percussion programmer, just as David had said.

On Monday morning, we swung by Bagel World in Peabody to grab bagel sandwiches for breakfast at Jenny's house. After we got our sandwiches, we drove to Jenny's. Her mother and her younger brother were home. Jenny's brother had become a God Lives Underwater fan through constantly hearing their songs from Jenny, so it was really exciting for him that there was a rock star in his house.

As soon as we walked through the door, Jenny's dog, Lady, greeted us by barking, running around, jumping, and being excited all at the same time. David flinched. Jenny's mother grabbed Lady by the collar and apologized.

"It's okay," David said. "I just don't do well with dogs."

It wasn't fear. It was just *get it away because I don't like it*. Lady settled down a bit when we sat down at the kitchen table.

Jenny's mother offered us plates, but we declined. The big wrapper the bagels came in would be sufficient.

Lady hunkered down on the floor right next to David and stared at him. David didn't seem to even notice her at all. He unwrapped his bagel sandwich which was overflowing with food. When he leaned forward to grab a napkin, Lady saw her chance. She jumped up by putting her two front paws on David's thighs. In one swift swoop, she grabbed his entire bagel sandwich off the table and took off.

"LADY!" Jenny's mother yelled, but David's sandwich was completely gone.

I was mortified for the second time. First, David falls through a chair at my cookout with a full plate of food. Now, a dog—and he hates dogs—stole his entire breakfast that he had been drooling over for the last half an hour. I looked at Jenny, and she was beet red. I didn't even know how to begin to apologize.

Jenny's mom came back in the kitchen and offered to make David breakfast. "I can make you a real breakfast. Eggs, bacon, pancakes."

"That's okay."

"I am so sorry, but she's so crazy with food."

"If you turn your back even for a second, it's gone," Jenny reaffirmed.

"Why don't we do this? Here, give me half of your bagel," I said to Jenny.

The good thing about Bagel World was that they cut their bagel sandwiches into halves. I took half of mine and half of Jenny's and put it on David's plate. David tried to refuse, but we insisted. He finally accepted.

Of all the people Lady could have stolen food from, it had to have been David. I couldn't believe it.

After breakfast, we decided to head to South Station and hang out there until it was time for David to go. David wanted to find new sunglasses before he got on the train. We took Jenny's car and headed down Route 1 South in Saugus to Newbury Comics. They sold sunglasses, and it was a cool place to kill some time.

"Hey, David, look at this!" I said as soon as we entered the store.

I pointed at the flyer that Jenny had made for his show. It was still hanging on the wall next to the front door where we left it.

"I think this can come down now," he said as he took it off the wall. He crumpled it up and handed it to the clerk behind the desk to throw away.

The clerk looked at him suspiciously. He was probably trying to figure out who David was.

I wanted new sunglasses too. David and I spent a good amount of time trying them on. We laughed as we tried on the goofiest-looking pairs. After we found the right sunglasses, we checked out and continued our way to Wonderland Station in Revere.

From the view of the traffic circle just prior to the entrance of Wonderland Station, there was a very large apartment complex.

"Find out how much those apartments go for," David said, pointing to the apartment building.

"Seriously?"

"Yeah. I think those would be perfect. I would be within walking distance from the subway. I wouldn't need to buy a car or anything. It seemed like it only took fifteen minutes to get here from your place, so I would still be close to all you guys. How far is Boston on the train from this station?"

"About twenty minutes."

"See? Perfect."

"Okay. I'll make some phone calls."

I was ecstatic David was still serious about moving so close to us. Those apartments did make sense.

We arrived at the station, purchased our tokens, and made the ride from Wonderland into South Station. We still had about an hour to kill before David's Amtrak train would board.

We grabbed a table, had a few deli sandwiches for lunch, and discussed the plan of attack for getting David an apartment in the area.

When it was time for David to leave, he hugged Jenny and told her that it was good to meet her. He thanked her for all of the work that she did for the show. David apologized again for not being able to get her in to the actual show.

He then turned toward me, and he hugged me. "Thanks, Rocky. For everything."

"Don't mention it," I said.

He slung his backpack around his shoulder and smiled at us. We didn't turn away until he disappeared into the train.

When David returned home, the plans for moving to Massachusetts fell apart. I had looked into the apartments in Revere, but I had been informed that they weren't the right atmosphere for someone trying to stay clean. I also had a hard time finding an apartment within David's price range that wasn't seedy. After multiple conversations about a potential move and an offer to live with me for the year, we realized it just wasn't feasible enough to pan out.

A few weeks later, Drop Kick Jesus had a show in Albany, New York. David called me on my cell phone while we were in our tour van traveling through the mountains of western Massachusetts into New York. He wanted to discuss coming back for a visit. Maybe even stay a full week this time.

"Why don't we try to book another show for me in Boston? If you want, your band could play too. We'll coheadline. I could either play before you guys, or I could play after. That might be a good way to get some of my fans into your band and some of your fans into some God Lives Underwater stuff."

As we discussed plans for a second solo Boston show, along with a weeklong stay at my place, I eventually lost signal when our tour van traveled farther into the mountains. Sadly this idea was never mentioned again.

Shortly after that David started his Fluzee project.

Even though he had been bitten by the bug to write again, his idea for a solo album took a backseat. David was ready to move on from his God Lives Underwater days. *Up off the Floor* still didn't have a release date in sight. He also wasn't comfortable enough to go headfirst into a solo career. Instead, David started a brand-new band with Patrick Haslup, and the original drummer of God Lives Underwater, Adam Kary. They were called Fluzee.

Over a six month period, David wrote new songs. For the first time in almost a decade, he was writing songs for a band other than God Lives Underwater. Fluzee had a full EP's worth of material. They even self-recorded their debut album called 7. Once again, it was another tribute to Monica.

During the recording of 7, I had many phone conversations with David.

"Rocky, I swear I think I have the best group of songs I have ever written."

"Really? That's saying a lot, since you said *Up off the Floor* was the best album you ever wrote."

"I know! But for the first time, I am writing in a good place. I'm healthy. I feel good, and my head isn't in the clouds. I'm happy."

"What are your plans for the Fluzee album?"

"We have a record-release party booked at a local music store in Philly on July 13. We recorded and duplicated the album ourselves."

"That sounds awesome."

"You should come to the show! It would be great to see you, and get your opinion on the new band and the new songs!"

I wrote down July 13, 2002, into my daily planner with a question mark. As I wrote down the date, I noticed the odd coincidence that it was exactly two years to the day of the very last God Lives Underwater show on July 13, 2000.

"I'll see what I can do. Jenny and I might be able to make the trip out there for the show."

"That would be fantastic. The new songs are much less electronic than God Lives Underwater, but they still rock just as hard."

"Sounds like you are really proud of this new band."

"I am! It feels good to play with Adam again, even after all the shit that went down with God Lives Underwater after the *Empty* tour."

It would be good to see Adam again, I thought.

Unfortunately July 13 arrived too quickly. Between our jobs and Drop Kick Jesus desperately trying to write a third album,

Jenny and I just couldn't seem to organize the trip. I felt guilty that we were missing the release party, so I made sure that we called the store that was hosting the Fluzee show.

Someone who worked for the store answered.

"Hello?" I said.

I could hear a lot of noise in the background and what sounded like a large group of people. It really made me yearn to be there.

"Can I help you?" the man asked.

"Yeah. Tonight is the Fluzee show, right?"

"Yeah." He practically had to yell to be heard over the noise behind him.

"Listen, I know this is going to sound weird. I'm calling from Massachusetts. I'm really good friends with David, the singer for Fluzee. I was supposed to be at the show, but I couldn't make it. Is there any way that you could get him to come to the phone?"

"How will he know who you are?"

"Tell him Rocky is on the phone. He'll accept the call."

"Hold on."

I heard him put the phone down. A few minutes went by. I listened to the background noise of the room. Eventually the phone picked up.

"Hey, me-han!"

"David!"

"What's going on, Rock? I wish you could be here!"

"Yeah! Us too. Jenny and I just wanted to call and wish you good luck. Not just with the show and the album, but with the new band in general."

"Thanks, me-han."

"I bet it's gonna feel good to play in front of people with a full band backing you again! Not just a chair and an acoustic guitar," I teased.

"Hey, don't you ever talk shit about that show! You said Jenny's there?"

"Yeah. She's sitting next to me."

"Let me talk to her."

I looked at Jenny, handed her the phone, and said, "David wants to talk to you."

"To me?" she asked.

She was flattered that he would go out of his way to speak to her. She put the phone to her ear. I could only hear her side of the conversation. It was filled with varieties of "cool" and "awesome" and a few laughs. She handed the phone back to me when she was done.

David and I finished the call. When I hung up, I looked at Jenny, and she had a huge smile on her face.

"What?" I asked.

"He called me 'kiddo'!"

"Really?" I asked, chuckling.

"Yeah! Do you think that means that he really does like me?"

"I'm sure. Especially, since he gave you a nickname. I've honestly never heard him call anyone *kiddo* in the seven years I've known him."

"David gave me a nickname!" she said, giggling.

"He sounds so happy and healthy, right?"

"Yeah! He seemed so excited about these new songs and the way he's been writing. He can't wait for us to hear the new band," Jenny said.

"You could tell how strong his voice was, just by speaking to him."

"That makes you feel good, huh?"

"Yeah. It makes me feel like he may actually make it."

My concern for David's health had finally turned into faith and confidence.

The following was printed inside Fluzee's album insert in David's handwriting:

> *I was engaged and madly in love with Seven (Monica) Young. A passenger train she was rushing to catch in order to replace the nose ring I lost that day killed her. I still wear the engagement ring she gave me. It's inscribed with the word "Slave" on the outside of the band. I buried her with the engagement ring I bought her and dressed her in what she would have worn to a Ramones show. She didn't care for the music I made, but she loved me, the person. I will never be the same Seven.*
>
> *rest in peace,*
> *David.*

MANTIS SIX

*"I've only just woke up from years and years of dreams. /
My life was passing me by so fast it was obscene."
David Reilly: "Stay" - Inside*

I had gone back to school and had finally finished my degree in Criminal Justice. I got a job with the Peabody Police Department as a dispatcher in July 2002.

My band, Drop Kick Jesus, had some personnel difficulties and creative differences while we were writing our third album. We officially called it quits in the fall of 2002.

Eric, the bass player from Drop Kick Jesus, a guitarist named Pete, and I started a brand-new band in February 2003 called The Grave Machine. The very next month after The Grave Machine formed, Jenny and I ended our relationship in order to save a friendship.

David and I had been friends through the rise of all three of my bands: Yellow #1, Drop Kick Jesus, and now The Grave Machine. He had also witnessed the demise of all three of my serious relationships: Christine, Sue, and Jenny.

Fluzee released their only album, *7*. They played a handful of local shows in Pennsylvania to promote it. Fluzee eventually broke up in 2003. They never even got the chance to write a second album or find a commercial avenue to get the songs to God Lives Underwater fans. The 7 album did fairly well, considering its limited release and very little promotion. Die-hard God Lives Underwater fans had followed the news of a new band and bought the album blindly. Other than that, it just didn't get the legs that it should have.

Although I didn't speak with David much between Fall 2003 and Spring 2004, I did send him some emails keeping him updated on my life. He never sent any replies.

However, during the first week of March 2004, I got the following email in my in-box:

Hey man,

Sorry I havent spoken with you in so long, things were on hold for about 6 months so i could get clean, and goto jail, and pay fines and tickets. All is good now. I gained about 60 pounds, got my drivers lisense back, bought a car, got a new manager, and now im booking a tour, and probably gonna make a solo record. Sorry to hear about you and yer girl, but thats life pretty much in a nutshell. Youve beaten the odds tho, by remaining friends. I have a hard time doing that, well i guess the old girlfriends have a hard time too. Im gonna be rehearsing and writing and doing some minor studio gigs to make dat cash, but i will prolly see you in may. or maybe even late April. My number is 215-237-7322. its a mobile, and my rates are outrageous, but you can certainly call.

your bro
David

I replied to his email with generic questions about the solo material. I asked him where he was living. I commented on the fact that he had disappeared from me for six months.

About a week later, I had this response waiting for me:

Hey Rock,

Whats up? Things are good here. Im still staying with my sister and babysitting. Im almost 7 months clean now, and life is good. My manager Thomas or as I like to refer to him "the rooster", is doing a pretty good job booking shows, and working on the website. You should get in touch with him, he could prolly use some input from you since your a GLU fan and along time friend of mine. I hope all is well with you, and drop me an email when you get the chance.

David

With the demise of Fluzee, David decided to do what he had been contemplating for three years since staying at my place. He wrote his first solo album in 2004.

The difference between Fluzee's album and his solo album was that he had a label interested in signing him. Corporate Punishment Records negotiated with David to release the album and got him on the road for a handful of national shows.

The first solo album had a release date of June 17, 2004. Two members of the band Everything Ends from New York—David Trusso on guitar and Benjamin Juul on drums—joined him on a tour of only seven shows in May 2004. Once again the number seven found its way into everything David had done since Monica's death. The tour spanned five states: Ohio, Michigan, Pennsylvania, Massachusetts, and New York. The shows featured songs from the solo album, *Inside*, and some God Lives Underwater songs. David was back. God Lives Underwater fans finally had something to cheer about again.

David mailed me a burned disc that had four of the new songs that were going to be on *Inside*: "Keep Dreaming," "Stay," "Far from Home," and "Blaming the Truth."

We spoke a few times on the phone leading up to the tour that would come to Boston. There was a six-day gap in between the Philadelphia and Boston shows. David suggested making it a long weekend vacation again.

We made plans for him to come Wednesday night, the nineteenth of May. He would leave the morning after the show that following Saturday. That would be the last night of the tour. It would be a short drive to New York City.

The last weekend in April, I received a mass email from David. This was an email that he had sent out to everyone in his address book to update us on what was happening.

> *Hey everyone.*
>
> *So im leaving this weekend to start rehearsals for this little tour, and hope to see you. I also figured i'd let you know that theres more music and updates on my site. My E.P. "inside" is now turning into a full album to be released to some degree soon. Spread the word, the team welcomes everyone.*
>
> *regards,*
> *David*

My cell phone rang one night about a week before the Boston show.

"Will you be able to put up Ben and Trusso the night after the show?" David asked me.

"Sure! If they don't mind sleeping on my floor in sleeping bags."

"Nah. I'm sure they have slept on worse. I'll come Wednesday night by myself, and then Ben and Trusso will meet us at the club on Friday. We'll all leave for New York on Saturday morning."

"That sounds like a great plan! The only problem though is, I have tickets to see The Who at Great Woods on Thursday night with Kristen, my bass player's wife."

"Wasn't she the one who made that kick-ass potato salad at the barbecue?"

"Yeah, that's her."

"Okay. Well, that actually works out perfectly because there's a friend of mine who I'd like to visit while I'm there. Maybe I'll just crash at her place and meet up with you Friday morning in Boston."

"Whatever's easiest."

"Will we be hanging out with Jenny at all?"

"Yep! She pretty much freed up her whole weekend for your visit."

"It'll be great to see her again. What about Dann and Mike?"

"Yeah. They'll all be there. Jenny has her own apartment now in Allston. We can probably go there Friday before the show to hang out."

"Rocky, this is the first time that I'll see you in ten years that you don't actually have a girlfriend."

"What's that supposed to be mean?"

"I don't know. You always seem like the type that needs a girlfriend. Don't take that the wrong way. I'm just saying."

I couldn't really argue because most of that statement was true.

"I bought a car," he added.

"No shit! Really?"

"Yeah! I cleared up all my outstanding warrants, spent some time in jail for them, got my own checking account, got my driver's license, and bought my first car."

"That's awesome, David."

"Yeah. I'm pretty stoked about it. I'll be driving by myself from Ambler to your house."

"What type of car did you get?"

"It's a beat-up Volkswagen, but I love it."

"That's awesome! Not only are you coming back to Boston for a show but you have a backup band, and you wrote your first solo album!"

"I know, right? Things are falling into place. It looks like *Up off the Floor* is finally going to be released by the end of the year too."

"Whoa!"

"Yep. I have a label working with me on the master tapes. I've been going back and forth with Jeff over all the details. Our attitude, at this point, is to just get it in the fans' hands. This album was recorded over four years ago."

"I know. I've had my copy now for over three years. Do you think the band might get back together since the album is finally coming out?"

"Seriously, Rocky, I don't know. Jeff got married and lives in Los Angeles. I put so much energy into my *Inside* album, and I have so many new ideas for my next solo album, that I don't think any of our heads are in God Lives Underwater. I don't mean forever, but who knows? So anyway I'll call you from my cell when I'm getting off the highway near your house."

"Sounds good!"

I was at The Grave Machine practice in Danvers, just waiting for David's call the whole time. I didn't know what time he was going to arrive at my house, but I just had a feeling that it was going to be during rehearsal. My phone was on vibrate so I would be able to feel it when it rang.

I was so excited to see David again that I could hardly focus on practice. The rehearsal space where we practiced was only about ten minutes from my house. When I told Jenny that David was coming to stay with me, she said she wanted to be there when he arrived. I told her I would call her when David called me so she could meet us.

Sure enough, in the middle of practicing one of our songs, my cell phone vibrated. It was David. When the song was over, I went into the hallway to call him back.

"Hey, me-han! I'm at your house. I parked on the side of your driveway in front of the fence. I hope that's okay."

"Yeah, not a problem. Give me ten minutes. I'm leaving now."

I went back into the jam room, told my band that I had to leave, grabbed my stuff, and called Jenny.

As I turned onto my street, I could see that Jenny and

her friend Erin were already out front with David. When I saw David standing next to his little brown car, it made me so proud that he had driven all the way here on his own. It was a testament to how far he had come with getting his life together.

I parked in my driveway and got out of my car. David gave me a hug. Jenny had already introduced David to Erin. We went inside and into my room.

I set up the same mattress in the same spot on the floor next to my bed where it had been when David had stayed with me back in 2001. He placed his bag in front of Wilma's tank.

"She's still alive and kicking, huh?"

"Yep. Still waking me up in the morning too."

He laughed. David not only seemed like he was in good spirits but he looked fantastic. He had filled out. His face was full, and he had gained a lot of weight. He looked like a normal human being. I had witnessed so many of David's different sizes and shapes. This was the healthiest and strongest I had ever seen him.

Jenny and Erin sat on my floor while David unpacked his stuff. He asked if we had ever heard of the band Elbow. When we said that we hadn't, he asked if he could play them. He put in Elbow's *Cast of Thousands* album, which we all really liked a lot.

"That's really cool that you guys can still be such good friends after breaking up, having been together for so long," David said to Jenny.

"Yeah," Jenny replied with a smirk. "He can't get rid of me that easily."

"Do we have plans tonight, or are we just gonna stay in and hang out? It doesn't matter to me. Either way is cool. I haven't seen you guys in so long, I could care less what we do," he said.

"I thought that maybe we could just keep it low-key and get something to eat in a bit," I said.

"I'm always down for Denny's," Jenny said. "Since I moved out of the North Shore, I miss the late-night Denny's runs."

"Rocky was telling me. You moved somewhere closer to Boston, right?"

"Yeah. I have an apartment in Allston, walking distance from the Paradise."

David finished getting all of his toiletries out of his bag and into my bathroom. It seemed like he had settled in. "I'd like to hang here for a bit, if you don't mind. I just drove, like, eight hours, and it would be nice to kick back and relax before we go out again."

"Not a problem," I replied.

David looked at my bed.

"That isn't the same bed you had last time I was here."

"Nope. I bought a Tempur-Pedic bed last year."

"Is that the one that has the commercial with the girl jumping next to a glass of wine that doesn't spill?"

"Yep."

"Oh, I gotta try this!"

"I hate it," Jenny muttered under her breath.

David crawled on top and scooted himself so he was half sitting on my bed.

"Now this I could get used to," he said.

I sat next to him while Jenny and Erin stayed on the floor. We remained in my room chatting and getting caught up with all our lives.

"Well, I'm hungry," David announced.

That was our cue to go get something to eat.

We piled into Jenny's car and drove to the Denny's in Danvers. We had no problem getting a table since it was around midnight on a Wednesday evening. We ordered as much disgusting, greasy, breakfast food found on Denny's menu as we could.

David told us all about his *Inside* album, as well as a batch of new songs that he was working on. He told us about how much he liked the two guys that he was touring with, and his manager, the Rooster. *Up off the Floor*, after all these years, was finally going to get a proper commercial release. We also went over the demise of Drop Kick Jesus and how The Grave Machine was formed.

After we ate our midnight breakfast, we paid our tab, and Jenny drove David and I back to my house. I invited her and Erin upstairs again to hang out some more, but she declined and said they would see us on Friday instead. We made plans to go to Jenny's early on Friday so we could hang out before the show.

David and I climbed the stairs to my bedroom. I asked him if he wanted to watch television or just go to bed.

"Nah. I'm not that tired yet. Do you have BET?"

"As in, Black Entertainment Television?" I asked.

"Yeah."

"I'm sure I do," I replied suspiciously. "I have digital cable."

"That's my favorite channel to have on in the background."

"Are you serious?"

"Yeah. Some of the beats that are in those new songs are just brilliant. I wouldn't mind getting into producing and making beats for some hip hop artists."

I flipped through the channels and found BET's all-night video marathon.

"Perfect," David said.

BET was actually the only channel that we watched the entire weekend he was here.

David went into my bathroom and changed into his pajamas. He lay on my bed with his head on one of the pillows where he could see the television. I was at the foot of my bed, half sitting up so I could see both the television and David while we talked.

"So tomorrow night I'm going to see The Who with my friend Kristen. You can either stay here for the three hours I'll be gone or do whatever," I reiterated.

"That's the good thing about having a car. I won't know until tomorrow, but I have a friend in Boston that I might stay with. I'll come back here in the morning."

"That's fine. Whatever you want to do."

"Do we have plans tomorrow?"

"My friend Nick, the singer of the industrial band Tragedie Ann, wants to hang out during the day. I thought we could all go to lunch together."

"Yeah. That sounds good."

"Have you ever been to the Rainforest Café?" I asked him.

"I have heard of it, and I know what it is."

"We have one in Burlington, which is like twenty minutes away. I thought we could go there. You know, something different."

"That sounds okay," he mumbled. After a few minutes of watching rap videos on BET, he remembered, "Hey, did you hear about the girl's album that I might produce in New York?"

"Nope."

"Yeah. Brittany Garrison. She's a teenage pop singer. They might hire me to work on her album. They sent me some of her demos so I could hear her. I remixed one of her songs."

"Wow. I had no idea. What type of stuff is it?"

"It's pop, but it's the perfect stuff for me to put my fingerprints all over to get into the production world. I think she's very talented. Her original demos needed a lot of work. I have the one I remixed with me if you want to hear it."

"Sure."

David slid off the bed, rummaged through his bag, and found the disc he was looking for. "Here, put this in."

I put the television on Mute and turned on my disc changer. I put the disc in.

"Okay, the first track is the original version."

I pressed Play. What I heard was raw, simple pop music with a female singer who had a pretty good voice. The music behind her voice was very generic.

"Okay. Now go to the next track. That's my remix."

What I heard almost made me fall over. I hadn't realized, until that moment, how long it had been since I had heard anything that even remotely sounded like God Lives Underwater. The music was so signature God Lives Underwater that I was surprised. The intro could have easily been from their *Life in the So-Called Space Age* album. It made me yearn for what used to be. David was right. His fingerprints were definitely all over that song.

The vocals were almost exactly the same. The music was just very David. The marriage between his vision and sound was perfect for Brittany's tone and melody. It really sounded like God Lives Underwater, but with a female singer.

"I can't believe that's the same song!" I said.

"I know, right?"

"What are you doing with her?"

"They want me to spend some time in upstate New York to work on the rest of her album. I decided to go ahead with it after how happy I was with the way that song turned out. Heck, if she takes off, this could be the start of my producing career."

"Honestly I hate that genre. But even if I didn't know you and I heard this, I would consider buying it."

"Thanks, Rock!"

"Make sure you bring this to Jenny's on Friday. I know she'd be interested in hearing what you did with that song."

"Right on!"

He put the disc back in his bag and lay once more on my bed.

We watched a little more BET, and he explained that he thought the new Britney Spears song "Toxic" had some of the best programming he had heard in years.

"Are you serious?" I asked. I never really could tell when David was joking.

"For sure. I listen to the programming on that song, and it just kills me. It's so good, it's brilliant. I'm not talking about Britney Spears on that song. I'm talking about the production and the programming of the strings."

I realized that he was being serious. He had the ability to listen beyond the surface of a song and instead listen with producer ears. For that I respected him even more.

We sat in silence through a few more videos. David looked very relaxed on my bed. The only light in the room was the glare from the television and the soft glow from Wilma's nighttime thermal lamp.

"Have I told you about my theory on dreams?" David asked.

"Nope." I looked at him.

"Well," he said, propping himself up on one elbow. "I have done some serious thinking about this lately. I came to the conclusion that I know exactly what dreams are."

"Okay. What are they?"

"Dreams are unfinished thoughts."

"And by that you mean . . ."

"Alright, Rock. Follow me here. How many times throughout the day do you have a thought, but you never follow through or finish it? Maybe because something else distracts you, or you don't have time to really think about it. I know it happens to me all the time. My theory is that, when we dream, we're actually finishing all the thoughts we had during the day that we didn't get to."

"Makes sense, I guess."

"Seriously. I've been thinking of all the dreams I've had at night. I realized that I could trace them back to a moment in the day where I was thinking about something and never completed the thought. Our brains finish the thought for us while we sleep."

"Dreams are unfinished thoughts," I repeated.

"Exactly. I don't think that's an angle that's been investigated in dream theory yet. I'm hoping I can get it out there and become the person who solves the riddle of what dreams are. If you think about a hot girl you saw on the street or try to figure out your bills or whatever, but then you get distracted, you never get the opportunity to go back and finish the thought. Your brain stores the thought and finishes it for you when you sleep."

"Very interesting," I said. "I could buy into that theory."

"See, that's what I'm talking about! We just gotta get everyone else on board, and then I can be a millionaire and write books and go on talk shows to discuss how I cracked the dream code. You laugh, but I'm being serious. I totally have a new view on a lot of things, Rock."

"I believe it," I said. I was just so happy to hear David sound so healthy and in such good spirits.

"Did I tell you that I've been asked to be a drug counselor at a rehab program in Philadelphia?"

"What? No!"

"Yep! One of the hospitals that runs a rehab program got in contact with me and asked if I'd want to be a counselor."

"That's great! What did you say?"

"I told them that I would think about it."

"How did they even think to approach you in the first place?"

"How much do you know about detox or rehabs?"

"Not a lot," I admitted.

"Well, a junkie will take an ex-junkie a lot more seriously than some counselor who just has a college degree. Junkies want to hear from their own kind. The fact that I'm clean, but still battling my addiction every day, gives me so much more clout. Plus how awesome would it be to help other people like me?"

"Yeah. Remember how you used to feel when people would tell you that you helped them with your lyrics?"

"I don't really want to talk about that, but, yeah, you're right. This would make me feel like I could understand their appreciation. It'll be a place where people wouldn't give a shit about the band I was in. They would listen to me because of what I would say and what I have lived through. I never really had that."

"I see your point. I think that it's amazing, David. I think you should do it."

"It's on a volunteer basis. I wouldn't get paid for it, but I wouldn't be doing it for the money anyway."

"Of course not."

"I think it would be good for me to share the stories that I hate to tell. Shit you don't even know about, Rock."

"David, do you have any idea of how little I know about that part of your life?"

"That's true. I never wanted you to be a part of that life. There was always something very dirty about letting you see any of that. Do you remember the show way back on *Empty*, outside at that festival?"

"The WAAF Locobazooka show?"

"Yeah, I think that's what it was. The show where we had to sign autographs for Strawberries, and you stood behind us."

"Yep, that was the show."

"Do you know that every time I excused myself, I was leaving to snort shit up my nose to stay high throughout the day?"

"Are you serious? I had no idea."

"I just couldn't bring you into that world and let you see me like that."

"Well, thanks for hiding that from me, I guess."

"That's why I think this gig will be really good. Not just for the people I'll be helping, but also for myself."

"I completely agree."

"Maybe I can even push my dream theory on them," he said with a smirk. Then David flip-flopped his body around my bed. "You know, one thing that sucks is this antidepressant they got me on."

I sat up and looked at him. "Yeah. Last October my doctor put me on Effexor XR for depression," I admitted. "I took myself off of it after ten weeks because it was fucking me up."

"Tell me about it. I am on Trazodone, and I can't sleep. It's like my dick stopped working. I know that's supposed to happen with heroin, but since I've been on this stuff, I can't seem to get hard."

I was shocked that David was sharing that with me.

"I know exactly what you mean. When I was on Effexor, my sex drive went down below zero."

"Fucked up, huh? They put you on something to stop making you sad, yet it takes away the one thing that makes most of us really happy."

We eventually fell asleep while BET was still playing on the television. David never moved from my bed to the mattress on the floor.

I wasn't sure if I had any unfinished thoughts that I dreamed about that night. I drifted off to sleep more proud of him than I had ever been during any of the times I had seen him giving the world his music.

We weren't going to have a full day to spend together on Thursday, due to the fact that I would be leaving around five o'clock to see The Who. They were touring on the *Endless Wire* album.

I called my friend Nick, and we set up a time to meet for

lunch at the Rainforest Café. Nick had been a fan of David's programming and was very interested in talking shop with David. I figured lunch would be comfortable for David, even to be with someone he didn't know, if that person knew almost as much about gear as David did.

We met Nick at the Burlington Mall around noon. Almost immediately after we sat down, I realized that this was one of the biggest mistakes I had ever made with David.

The Rainforest Café might have been exciting for a small child. Inside, it contained simulated thunderstorms, mechanical wild animals, bright murals of trees and leaves, and random bursts of sounds and wails. But for David, it was hell in the form of sensory overload. I could tell as we walked to our table, which was in the very back of the restaurant, that just being there was already making him anxious.

"Are you okay?" I whispered to him as we passed underneath the simulated night sky, complete with shooting stars and lightning strobe lights.

"I already don't like this place."

"We can leave and go somewhere else."

"I don't know. I'll try it out. But I might have to leave."

The hostess sat us at our table. I took a seat next to Nick, across from David.

The elephants roared, the monkeys screamed, and the birds squawked loudly. I realized that this was the most anti-David place I possibly could have picked. What the hell was I thinking? He wasn't the type of person who ever enjoyed being surrounded by bursts of animal noises and mechanical moving creatures.

"I'm so sorry! I didn't even think about how you might react to this kind of a place."

"It's just a little too much stimulation for me."

"It's kinda freaking me out too," Nick cowered.

"Well, you say the word, and we're gone."

"Nah. We'll eat and leave. It's fine, really."

However, I could tell that David was totally claustrophobic among the novelty and attraction that had made the café famous.

"Shit! There's no cell phone signal in here! I'm waiting for a text message from the rest of the band about when they're leaving, and I can't miss it!"

"Seriously we can leave."

"Don't worry about it. I'll just check my messages when we leave."

I looked at my cell phone, and it also read No Service on my display screen.

David was extremely uncomfortable. The restaurant was so much of an overload for him that I thought that he might just freak out. It made me wish that he would either let me take him somewhere else to eat or that the food would arrive quickly so that we could get out of here.

Then everything changed.

Nick was talking about his band, Tragedie Ann, and the programs that he used in their songs which were almost identical to the program that David had used to make the Robot Teen America album. The conversation was off and running. The more detailed they got in the conversation, the more I saw David loosen up and forget how uncomfortable he was in the restaurant. Nick kept right up with David about his knowledge of gear and music programs. It turned into one of the most fluid exchanges I had ever seen involving David and someone he didn't know.

David talked about the Robot Teen America album, and how he had written and recorded all four tracks with a program called Orion. Nick stated he had never heard of it, so that just led David down a path of being a salesman for the Orion program.

I told Nick that I would play him the Robot Teen America album sometime so he could hear what David was talking about. Nick did actually investigate the program later and used it in some of Tragedie Ann's songs that appeared on their debut album, *Corruption of Reason*.

As we ate our lunch and the discussion continued, the motif of the café faded into the background. David even forgot that he didn't have a cell phone signal or that he was terrified of the mechanical animals around the tables.

Nick told David that he would send him some of his band's music. David gave Nick his email address and said to contact him if he ever had a question, or a problem, with any of the programs he used.

As we paid for our lunch and walked out, David found a cell phone signal, and he had some messages from his band. He called Trusso back. They made arrangements for load-in at the club, and David gave Trusso directions to the show.

After he hung up, I felt the need to apologize again as we walked out of the mall. "I'm sorry for bringing you there."

"It's cool. It was just a little too much for me."

"Yeah. You freaked out a little when we walked in, and I thought, *oh, shit*."

"I just don't do well with that much stuff going on around me."

"I really should have known that. You would never survive at Disney," I joked.

"No way! That's my worst nightmare."

We said good-bye to Nick and made the drive back to my house.

David packed an overnight bag and left his main bag at my place. We hung around in my room and watched more BET while I waited for Kristen's call to tell me that she was ready to be picked up for the show. When Kristen called, David and I left the house.

Later that night, after The Who show was over, it was gridlock in the parking lot trying to get home. Kristen and I had a conversation about David and how good he was doing. We reminisced about that cookout years earlier when he had praised her for her potato salad and then had fallen through the chair in front of everyone. She told me how embarrassed she was for him. I told her how embarrassed I was just a few hours earlier when I had brought him to the Rainforest Café and didn't even think about how he couldn't handle overstimulation.

Kristen admitted that she really didn't know much about God Lives Underwater or David's music. Conveniently I had my copy of *Life in the So-Called Space Age* in the car. While we waited for the parking lot to empty, we listened to the album. I gave her a brief history of the band and how I knew David.

Kristen commented about his voice. We listened to the entire album before we could vacate the parking lot. She could absolutely see why they had such a cult following.

Life in the So-Called Space Age ends with an untitled track. It's an instrumental that becomes almost too repetitive and borderline irritating. When the music finally ends, there are only six seconds left of the track. The final six seconds of the album concludes with Jeff saying, "That was awesome!" and David answering, "Thanks, me-han!" Having his signature "*Thanks, me-han!*" hidden at the end of one of their albums seems very fitting.

It was hard to believe that their most popular album had been out for seven years already. It still managed to sound fresh, groundbreaking, and exciting to someone who hadn't heard it yet.

I was dragged out of slumber, not by the sunlight coming through the windows, or Wilma running back and forth in her tank, but by the sound of my cell phone ringing.

After clearing my throat, I managed to muster, "'Ello?"

"Rocky! What's the plan, me-han?"

"Hey, David."

"How was The Who?"

"Amazing," I answered. I cleared the cobwebs from my head. "What time is it?"

"Um, I think a little after ten. I'd like to leave my car at your place tonight. Can I just drive back now and then we can take your car into Boston?"

"Yeah, totally. Come over whenever you're ready."

We hung up, and I got ready for the day with fervor. David was at my house in less than an hour. He must have left immediately after he had hung up the phone.

Our plan for the day was simple. We would go to Jenny's apartment in Allston, get something to eat, wait at the club for David's backup band to arrive, and then wait for the show to begin.

David left his little beige Volkswagen in front of my house, and we made the drive from Peabody to Allston. I hadn't been to Jenny's new apartment yet, so I used MapQuest for directions. David held the printout, and I must have taken the wrong exit somewhere.

At one point, he tossed the directions in the backseat and said, "Looks like we're winging it!"

After a few turns, and a phone call to Jenny, we finally made it. We parked on the street, and she came out to meet us. We then followed her up the single flight of stairs.

After being in a relationship with Jenny for the past three years, it was weird to be in her first apartment, which was really big for the area. It had two floors and more rooms than I expected.

When the tour of her apartment was over, we went into the living room and sat on her couch.

"You guys aren't hungry for lunch yet, are you?" she asked.

"Nah, I'm not," I said.

"I'm good," David replied.

"Okay. When we get hungry, there's an awesome wrap place I want to take you guys to."

"Sounds good to me," David said.

"Hey," I said, turning to David, "Did you bring the Brittany Garrison disc?"

"Yeah, it's in your car."

"Run down and get it."

"What's this?" Jenny asked with an apprehensive chuckle.

David left the room with my car keys.

I explained to her that David was hired to help write a female singer's album. I also explained that he had a copy of the original song how it was sent to him and then the new version that he had remixed.

"Jenny, I swear to you, it's God Lives Underwater with a female singer. It gave me goose bumps. Wait until you hear the original. Not that it's bad, but the difference of having David work on it is astronomical!"

I heard David trot back up the stairs. He handed Jenny the disc. "The first track is Brittany before I was hired."

We listened to roughly two minutes of the five-minute track.

"You get the picture," David said. He crouched on the floor with the remote to the disc player and pressed the Track-Up button. Then we listened to the David Reilly version of the song.

"If he doesn't have a career singing his own songs, he has a career in producing," I said to Jenny, over the music.

"Yeah, wow! I can't believe the difference!"

He let the song play all the way through before he took the disc out of the player and put it back in its slim-line case.

"David, tell her about your theory on dreams."

"Dreams?" she asked.

"Are you sure she wants to hear this?"

"Yeah, it's very interesting," I said to him. Then I turned to Jenny. "David came up with a theory on what dreams are that's very enlightening."

"Okay," she said.

"Dreams are unfinished thoughts. All of our dreams are thoughts we had during the day that we didn't finish. They have to play themselves out somewhere. So we make up a dream to finish the thought, whatever it is."

"Okay. I can buy that," she said.

We went into her bedroom to look through her music collection.

"I'm getting hungry," I said.

"Yeah. I could go for one of those wraps," David said.

"We can take my car since I know exactly where we're going," Jenny said.

We got into her new car. Her Toyota Corolla that she had during David's last visit had been totaled on Storrow Drive when she hit a guardrail during a torrential rainstorm.

We drove to a quaint sandwich shop where everything was made to order. I got a chicken, bean, and rice wrap, but tried to make it resemble a burrito as much as I could. David said that it looked good. He then proceeded to tell the lady to make him the same thing but to load his up. There was so much food, I thought it was going to explode! Jenny put her vegetarian wrap together, and we grabbed a table by the window.

"Hey, remember when Jenny's dog ate your bagel sandwich?" I asked.

"Thanks for bringing that up!" Jenny said, turning red.

"Yeah, I was more embarrassed that your mom was going to cook me breakfast after that happened than anything else," David replied.

We ate our wraps. We discussed new bands we had discovered, movies, and everything else. As we finished our food, Jenny asked if we wanted to do anything else. We still had a lot of time to kill.

"Is Newbury Street anywhere close to here? I'd really like to look in some of the shops while I'm here. Last time I was on

Newbury Street, I didn't have too much time to shop."

I couldn't tell if he was looking at me to see if I remembered that awful afternoon before the Stabbing Westward show when Sue, Kerrie, and I were with him on Newbury Street.

Jenny drove us to Newbury Street. Remarkably we were able to find a parking space. We went into the Virgin Records store, Newbury Comics, Allston Beat, and, oh, yes, Condom World. It was a beautiful day out, and it felt so good to be shopping with David the day of a show.

He spent a good portion of our time there text messaging Trusso and Ben, trying to give them directions from New York to the show.

We went into an army surplus store because I had been looking for a plain green T-shirt to wear onstage at The Grave Machine shows. Luckily I found the perfect color and size. I was debating whether or not to buy it. When I showed it to David, he told me that he thought it was the perfect material for moving around onstage. This was the only purchase that any of us made.

When it was time to go, Jenny drove us back to her apartment.

"Erin, who went with us to Denny's Wednesday night, is coming over. She wants to take photos of tonight's show, if that's okay," Jenny asked.

"Absolutely," David replied.

Jenny called Erin when we got inside, and we waited for her to arrive. The clock was ticking closer to the time when David wanted to leave for the club as well as when Trusso and Ben would be getting there. When Erin arrived, we made sure we had everything, and we left the apartment to walk to the club.

The Paradise was a short distance from Jenny's apartment. It was the same club where I saw God Lives Underwater for the first time, back in June 1995. It was the club that had brought our entire friendship full circle.

The Paradise was the very first club, and unbeknownst to me, also the very last club where I would see David perform live.

As we walked down Commonwealth Avenue, David spent most of the time on his cell phone with Trusso and Ben, still trying to give them directions. All of the equipment was in the van with them.

When we got there, David introduced himself to a man standing outside, who brought us into the venue.

The show was being held in the Paradise Lounge, which was the smaller room next to the main concert area. Although the lounge had tables and chairs, it didn't have an open area in front of the stage to stand. I thought it would be just fine, with this new chapter of David's music. A sit-down performance was exactly what David's fans needed.

The stage was only a few inches from the floor, and the room had a very open-mic-night feel to it. Two small speakers sat on either side of the stage. But then again, this was not going to be the plugged-in, megajuice of God Lives Underwater. This was David Reilly, singer and songwriter.

We were treated like royalty by the club. It felt like a payoff for so many years of being stressed out about getting into shows. They gave us food and drinks, and treated us like we were in the band.

Dann was driving to the show and would be here sometime right after doors opened. Mike was coming from work and would be here before David hit the stage.

After about an hour of waiting outside by the front of the Paradise—next to the McDonald's where David had spilled his chocolate milkshake all over the table, so many years ago—the van pulled up with Trusso, Ben, and all of the equipment.

They parked right in front of the club and jumped out. They explained to David that they had gotten lost and that was why they were late. Other than that, it was all coming together perfectly. They opened the back of the van while David introduced us. Jenny, Erin, and I helped David, Trusso, and Ben bring in the gear for the show.

We got to hang out inside the club before doors opened. We sat at one of the large round tables. We ordered our alcoholic beverages at a reduced price and waited.

As the doors opened and people filed in, some recognized David, and came over to say hi and to shake his hand. He was in great spirits and welcomed every exchange. When Dann showed up, David stood and gave him a hug.

There were two opening acts. David was at the bar a lot, talking to people. He was just making himself available to everyone. This was one of the few times I had ever seen him like this at a show. Even at the last show at T.T. the Bear's Place, he was somewhat of a recluse. For the first time, he looked and sounded so happy.

It was finally time for David to go on. Mike had shown up with two of his friends. There was a level of excitement in the air. While Ben was building his drum kit, I was thinking how great it was going to be to hear some of the *Inside* songs along with old God Lives Underwater songs again.

David and Trusso spent the show sitting down. David was on the right side of the drum set and Trusso to the left. The show was amazing, both in texture and atmosphere.

David's voice sounded strong and rehearsed, the voice of confidence.

Ben and Trusso were in perfect time with David and added a level of subtle backbone to each song. The audience sat with all eyes on the stage. Everyone cheered excitedly when a song was played and laughed at David's anecdotes.

The audience was smaller than expected, but every person here focused on what was happening. If this was the true start of his solo career, it wasn't a shabby start at all.

Erin took pictures from the table where we sat. Dann was on my right, and Jenny was on my left. I could see that Jenny was happy too. She was finally able to see David perform at an actual venue.

The set list for the show consisted of six God Lives Underwater songs, five solo songs from *Inside*, and a Depeche Mode cover: 23 / Tortoise / Can't Come Down / Happy? / Whatever You've Got / Miss You More Than Anything / Keep Dreaming / Stay / Spinning / Blaming the Truth / Far from Home / Stripped.

There were no surprises this time. It was great to see "Tortoise" from *Empty* for the first time. It felt much more like how a show set list should have been and not so off-the-cuff like David's last show.

As soon as the show was finished, Dann, Mike, and I helped break down the equipment. Since David's band had headlined, there was no immediate rush.

"What's the plan for the rest of the night?" Ben asked as he disassembled his drum set. "Do you know where we're staying?"

"You guys are more than welcome to crash at my place," I said.

"Yeah. There's more than enough room at Rocky's place," David added.

"Is that where you're staying?" Ben asked David.

"Yeah. I sleep on the floor on a mattress." He laughed.

"Well, we brought our sleeping bags."

"What's this?" Trusso inquired.

"Brian said we could crash at his place tonight."

"Are you sure? That won't be a problem?"

"Not a problem at all. In fact I think it would be fun! We can stay up and watch BET all night," I said sarcastically, glancing at David.

He just shook his head. "Hey, me-han. There's some dope shit on that channel."

"Is there a safe place to store the van with all the gear?" Ben asked.

"Yeah. I live on a dead-end street that only has two houses on it. My backyard butts up against an elementary school. No one goes near my street."

"I could go for some food," Trusso said.

"Yeah. I'm starving too."

"Why don't we hit an IHOP or something on the way back to my place?"

"Sounds good," David said.

"What are we doing?" Mike asked from behind me.

"We're going to pack up and head to IHOP. Then back to my place for the night. You're more than welcome to stay with me if you want to hang out," I offered.

"Alright. I might just do that. Which IHOP?"

"Jenny, which IHOP is around here that's relatively on the way back to my place?" I asked her.

"The one in Brighton"

Ben and Trusso drove the van with all the equipment. Jenny and Erin rode in Mike's car. David went with Dann. Trusso and Ben said that they needed gas for the van, so we all pulled into a gas station on Commonwealth Avenue and waited for them to fill up.

When we arrived at the International House of Pancakes, some people who had been at the show were there as well. We decided to make it one large group. They had to clear out the entire back set of tables and push them together to fit us. There was such an abundance of teasing and humorous interaction between David, Trusso, and Ben that it made sense how well everyone clicked onstage.

We were there for a few hours. Of course it took a long time for us to get all of our food. Even after the plates had been cleared and we had gone through a few pots of coffee, we stayed as a group just telling stories and joking around.

If this was to be the last group activity I ever shared with David, it was the most carefree, light, and happy I had ever seen him. We didn't want to leave. Once we got the evil eye from the waitstaff, we had to move our shindig back to my place.

Dann apologized and declined the invitation back to my place. He had to work in the morning, and it was too late already. Before Dann drove home, David gave him a hug outside in the parking lot.

"Take care of yourself," Dann said. "It was good to see you. Don't let another three years go by before you come back."

"Don't worry, me-han. I'll be back before you know it!"

Dann waved as he got into his car and drove out of the parking lot.

"I think we're gonna go home too," Jenny said suddenly.

"Are you sure?"

"Yeah," she said and turned to David. "It was great seeing you! We'll have to do this again sometime."

"Absolutely! Take care of yourself, kiddo. Let me give you my phone number. You can either text me or email me to keep in touch."

"It was nice meeting you," Erin said. "I'll make sure that either Brian or Jenny sends you a copy of the pictures I took tonight."

"That would be great."

"It looks like it's just the five of us coming back to my place," I said to David.

"That's fine with me."

"I'll shoot the girls home and just go straight to your place from there," Mike said.

"Do you know the way from Jenny's?"

"Yeah. Storrow Drive. It's the fastest way from Jenny's place to your house."

I nodded in agreement.

"I would say good-bye," Mike said to David, "but I'll be seeing you in a bit."

Jenny and Erin got into Mike's car and waved good-bye as we drove from IHOP back to my house in Peabody with Trusso and Ben following behind in the van.

Once we got there and I showed them where it was safe to leave the van, we all quietly went upstairs so we wouldn't wake my roommates.

"Wow, I guess you have a lot of room up here!" Ben exclaimed.

"I told you! You can put your sleeping bags anywhere."

"I'm putting mine right in front of the fridge," Trusso said. He sprawled out underneath the windows in front of the refrigerator.

David dove onto his mattress in front of the television and clicked on BET.

I laughed and shook my head.

My cell phone rang, and it was Mike. He was more upset than I had ever heard him.

"I'm still on Storrow Drive, stuck in all this construction traffic. I've been at a standstill this entire time, and no one is moving. I'm just going to turn around and go home."

"Are you sure? We're not going anywhere. I don't care what time you get here."

"I'm more pissed off than anything. I don't think I would be any fun. This sucks!"

"Yeah, it does."

"Tell David that I'm sorry and apologize for me. Tell him that it was great seeing him again. I'll catch him next time around."

"Will do."

We hung up, and I turned to David.

"Mike is caught in Boston traffic. He's not going to make it, but he says he's sorry, and it was good to see you."

"Next time you talk to Mike, tell him that he owes me one for blowing me off!" he said with a smile.

After Ben and Trusso snuggled into their sleeping bags, David and I continued to joke and tease each other with only the flicker of BET illuminating the room. David fell asleep first. I only knew this because of the very distinct sound of his breathing.

That was the last time I would ever hear David fall asleep again.

On May 22, 2004, David and the band had their final show on the tour at Arlene's Grocery in New York City. This would also be the last time David would ever perform live.

David and Trusso and Ben really wanted to get on the road as soon as possible.

"We should go for a quick breakfast and hit the highway," Trusso said. He rolled up his sleeping bag after we had been woken up by his girlfriend calling his cell phone.

"There's a Dunkin' Donuts right down the street. Afterward, you could follow me to Route 95. That's how you get to New York from here."

"Sounds good to me."

David drove behind me while the guys followed in the van. We made the five-minute trip to the Dunkin' Donuts on Washington Street in Peabody and went inside.

There was a window that had a small counter with three stools to the left of the front door. I told David to sit there so no one else would take our seats while I placed our order.

While I was in line with Trusso and Ben, I looked at David. He sat on the stool and just kept spinning around. His chain wallet clinked the steel pole of the counter every time he made a full circle. David had the unique ability to be so childlike and yet so serious at the same time.

I ordered his bagel and orange juice, and my coffee, and

walked back to the counter. I sat next to him. We looked at the parking lot and could see the line of cars waiting to be served in the drive-through. Trusso and Ben got their food and joined us at the counter.

We mostly ate in silence. David looked out the window and wore his big sunglasses. This wasn't the glamour of the big God Lives Underwater tours, but I truly believed that he was really happy.

We finished our breakfast and threw away the empty wrappers. As we exited the building, David held the door open for an old lady, and she thanked him. He didn't say anything in reply, but he didn't have to. Sometimes his body language said more than his words ever could.

Outside in the parking lot, Trusso and Ben thanked me again for letting them stay at my place. I told them that, anytime they were in the Boston area and needed a place to stay, either with David or with their own band, my place was always open to them.

"Just follow me to the highway. I'll pull over and wave my hand for you to keep going. The road in front of you will be Route 95 South."

"Well, Rocky. This is it again. Until next time," David said.

"Alright, man. Give me a call, or shoot me an email when you get home, so I know you're back okay."

"Will do. And thanks, me-han, for everything."

"You know, you've always been like a brother who I only see on holidays."

He laughed. "Give everyone a hug from me and tell them I said good-bye."

"I will."

David's much larger frame, and loosely-fitted work shirt, consumed me for a moment while he hugged me, and then he pulled away.

"Take care, Rock."

"You too. You better!"

Once inside my car, I waited at the entrance of the parking lot to make sure they were all behind me so I wouldn't lose any of them on the way to the highway. We pulled out onto Washington Street, made a right onto Lynnfield Street, took a right onto Summit Street, and then made a quick left onto Centennial Drive where the highway started.

I pulled over, rolled down my window, and flagged them in the direction of the ramp.

David drove by my car first. He waved as he went past. I watched the two vehicles enter the ramp for the interstate. The sight of their taillights finally disappeared out of my vision.

And that was it. I would never see David again.

Only three weeks later would be the ten-year anniversary of when Dogboy and I stood outside the Paradise, waiting for the doors to open, and . . .

"I think that's God Lives Underwater. That guy is David Reilly, the singer," I said to Dogboy.

"If you think it is, go say something," Dogboy replied.

I moved off the wall. I did a fast trot to catch up with the band. I opened my mouth and asked, "Excuse me. Are you David from God Lives Underwater?"

He looked at me.

It may have taken him only a second to reply, but it was almost a second too long. It made me want to apologize. I almost wanted to go back to the wall.

"Yes, I am," he finally answered.

Hey dude,

thanks for putting me and the boys up over the weekend. I had a good time hanging as usual. I am about to sign a new deal this week, and should be in better shape soon. As of now i got no gas, and no phone minutes, so contact me via email.

late
David

This was what was in my in-box a few days later. I replied to the email and checked the God Lives Underwater website that remained functional, and still very active with news and a message board. People were posting pictures from the solo shows they had attended.

The biggest news on the forum was that *Up off the Floor* finally had a release date! According to the news flash on the website, the final God Lives Underwater album was actually going to hit stores on September 28, 2004.

There was a discussion thread of people talking about a rumor that "Choir Boy" and "Fame" were going to be omitted from the album. I couldn't believe this. I had been listening to the album with twelve tracks on it. Even though I knew I wasn't listening to the songs in the correct order, I never imagined I was listening to a version of the album that would have more songs on it than the official release. This did not seem right to me, plus it made me feel bad for their fans! "Choir Boy" was as great of a God Lives Underwater song, even better in my opinion, than some of the other songs that were staying on the final cut.

I sent David an email. I hoped that all of this was just a rumor or Internet gossip and that the official release of *Up off the Floor* would be the complete twelve tracks that were recorded for the album.

David's response was very disheartening and very disappointing.

> *choir boy and fame omitted due to votes. i voted keep em, gary and jeff voted, nix em. the end. i actually dont feel one way or the other at this point. Perhaps they can get released later in some other format.*
> *peace*

David had been outvoted. After almost five full years of the songs being finished, he was just content to have the album released, even if it was missing two of the tracks. That was a much smaller battle to fight than the war he had just won, getting the album released at all.

David traveled to upstate New York to start work on Brittany Garrison's album. Her family put David up, all expenses paid. He was working in the studio with her on a daily basis, trying to get tracks down for her album.

While he was working on her solo material, David recorded a duet with Brittany called "Love Will Complicate." At the time, he was unsure if it would be a track on Brittany's upcoming album, or tucked away to be included on a future solo album of his. I only got bits and pieces of what he was doing through email.

I was at work one day when my cell phone vibrated. It

was David. I looked at Jamie, the other dispatcher, and asked if he could handle the control room so I could take the call. I left the dispatch center of the Peabody Police Department and went outside.

"Hello?"

"Hey, me-han."

"What's up, David?"

"Nothing much! Just chillin' up here in New York with Brittany."

"How's that going?" I asked.

"Slow, but really good. The only problem is that there isn't much to do here when I'm not working. It's kind of in the middle of nowhere. It's easy to get really bored, but the good side of that is that there's no temptation to fall back into my bad habits. I'm almost forced to stay focused."

"Well, that's good."

"Yeah. I broke up with my new girlfriend this weekend."

"I didn't even know you had a new girlfriend!" I said.

"It was pretty new. I didn't know if it would last anyway," he replied.

"I'm sorry to hear that."

We talked for a bit longer. I was nervous that the guys in the control room were going to be upset, but this was an important call to me, so I kept talking.

"Hey, why don't you come up here and spend a weekend with me?" he suggested.

"I guess I could do that."

"I'm having a great time here producing and stuff. But seriously, sometimes during my downtime, I'm just so bored. It would be rad if you could come up just for a weekend. We could hang out. I'll show you what I've been working on with her."

"I could definitely get a weekend off," I said, "if you're serious."

"I'm totally serious. If you can pull it off, I would love to have you here. I'm sure that Brittany's family wouldn't mind a guest for the weekend. They're really awesome people."

"Okay. I'll see what I can do." My brain was already planning.

"Hey, me-han, when I'm finished with this album, I could really use another vacation. I'd love to come back and stay with you and hang with your friends again. For a full week this time. No show booked, nothing. I don't want that added pressure hanging out with you. Just two bros for a week."

"Absolutely! I have a bunch of vacation time saved up. You know, *mi casa es su casa*."

"It will be like in a month or something. Now that I have my own wheels, it's much easier to get around and take trips. We could just go and hang out at that beach place you took me to."

"Salem Willows."

"Yeah."

"And watch BET?" I said teasingly.

"Of course."

"Sounds good, man. You take care. I gotta get back inside to work. Keep me posted on when you want to come visit for a week, and I'll put in a vacation request."

"Alright, Rock. Take care."

After I hung up, I went back inside to finish my shift. I was psyched that David had invited me up to New York to hang with him for a weekend and that he wanted to stay with me again.

I sat at my computer, and sent both Mike and Dann an email to update them on the conversation I just had with David.

> *Hey guys, david (reilly) just called me. we had a long talk. He's holed up in upstate New York right now producing that girl's album and he's bored out of his mind. He's so bored he wanted me to come stay with him for a few days, lol. Anyway, when he is finished with the album he said he wants to get away from Pennsylvania for a bit. Him and his new gfriend broke up this weekend and it wasnt a pleasant one. So he said he is gonna probably come stay with me next month for a while. No gig or anything, no pressure to play, he just wants to come and stay with me and hang out with all of us for a week or so like he was just part of the gang.*

Just after that, David's debut solo album, *Inside*, was finally released. It was phenomenal, powerful, and emotional. That's all we ever asked from David as an artist anyway, and he didn't fail to deliver.

His solo album didn't sound too much like a God Lives Underwater album. He left the God Lives Underwater sound to God Lives Underwater but took the emotion and energy that he had in that band and added his own flavor to make it his own sound.

I was in my kitchen cooking some pasta when my cell phone rang. It was David. I could hear people screaming in the background.

"Hey, Rock! What's up?"

Unfortunately I didn't go to New York to stay with him for the weekend as he worked on Brittany's album. We didn't even speak again until he returned home to Ambler. Although the trip to stay with me for a week hadn't been forgotten, it just wasn't first-priority anymore.

"I'm at Billy's T-ball game."

Billy was David's seven-year-old nephew. David had recently become a major part of his life. David always spoke of his nephew with such love and admiration. I knew how proud David was of Billy and how much love he had to give him. Also Billy seemed to look up to David the same way.

I could hear the game in the background.

"Just watching a group of seven-year-olds run around," he added, laughing.

"Cool! What's going on?" I asked.

"Nothing much. Just sitting here in the stands. I had some minutes on my cell, so I thought I'd call."

I could hear the cheers and boos from the parents in the background.

Although David and I chatted for a short amount of time, what struck me the most about this phone call was how mature and responsible David had become. David had come along way.

It made me wonder if there was a family man trapped under all the touring, record contracts, albums, heroin, cocaine, suicide threats, and personal struggles. Maybe David was finally just growing up.

All of the doubts and worries that I have had concerning him over the last decade were fading away.

It was September 2004, I was forced to move out of my house in Peabody that I had rented since April 1997, due to the landlord putting it on the market. Since I didn't have a new place to live yet, my grandmother let me move into the family room in her basement until I could find a new place to call home. I moved into her house in Saugus while she spent the winter in West Palm Beach, Florida.

Up off the Floor had come out the same month that I moved into her basement. I bought it the day it was available. The album was old news to most God Lives Underwater fans, especially to those like me who had a version of it already. I still went out and bought the album to support David, plus for the artwork, the correct order of the tracks, and mastered versions of the songs. Until I owned the official copy, I had still been listening to the version where all of the tracks were different in volume.

Even from the beginning, David publicly made the fans aware that he wasn't happy with the way the album sounded when it was released. The burned copy of the album that he had been handing out for years was actually a better-sounding version than the album in the stores.

Most God Lives Underwater fans agreed. Even though we bought the album, we would still only listen to the burned version of it.

"Completely unlistenable" was how David referred to it in an interview.

October 2004 was the month after I was forced to move into my grandmother's house in Saugus and also the month after *Up off the Floor* was released. It was also four months after David's solo album, *Inside*, had been released.

Most important, that month I met the woman I would eventually marry.

The Grave Machine played a show in Nashua, New Hampshire, on October 30, opening for a band called Coven of 13. They were promoting their debut album, *Out of the Fire, Into the Pit*.

The singer of Coven of 13 was the most beautiful woman I had ever seen in my life. I spent the entire time during The Grave Machine's soundcheck just staring at her. I knew it was meant to be when, during our set, I asked if anyone in the audience could get me a glass of water. She was the only one who took my request seriously and handed me a glass of water from the bar. I spent the entire time Coven of 13 was performing just staring at her as well.

Our running joke through our marriage has always been that it was love-at-first-soundcheck. I was twenty-seven years old when I knew I had laid eyes on the woman I was meant to be with forever. Stephanie.

Somehow I had gotten her email address before the night was over. Our first date was lunch at Uno Pizzeria & Grill in Boston and then the movie *Saw*.

David had been with me through my relationships with Christine, Sue, and Jenny, but I really wanted to tell him about Stephanie. She was different. She wasn't a girlfriend. She was a woman who I could spend the rest of my life with.

Shortly after meeting Stephanie, Mike sent me an email at work saying that he had been reading David's blogs online, particularly a post about how David's girlfriend had overdosed and had died on David's couch. I immediately called him.

David answered the phone, and I told him that I just gotten word about his girlfriend.

"Yeah, me-han. She just killed herself on my couch," he said matter-of-factly.

Much later I would get the full story of how Amy had died on his couch after shooting up heroin. He seemed shaken but not completely irrational. He probably just didn't want to talk about it too much. I could hear something in his voice. Was it guilt?

"What's up with you, Rocky?" he asked, clearly wanting to change the subject.

"My new band has finally started playing shows again. I met this amazing girl that I swear, David, between you and me, I could marry and be happy with forever."

"Wow, me-han! That's saying a lot from the guy who has had three separate three-year relationships in the last ten years."

"I know. I know," I said, slightly ashamed.

"Okay. I've always been supportive. What's her name?"

"Stephanie."

"Does she know that you and Jenny are still close friends?"

"Yeah. I told her that right up front. She's an officer in the navy and, on our first date, she said soon she'll be stationed somewhere else."

"And you stuck around?"

"David, this girl makes me feel like no other."

"I had that, once."

I winced at the thought that he brought up Seven and compared her to Stephanie.

"She's amazing. I can't wait for you to meet her."

"I'm sure I will," he replied with confidence.

I wish I had known then that David would never get to meet my wife.

Stephanie and I jumped into our relationship full-force. We were so sure that it was right for both of us that it didn't matter how fast we moved. David would have definitely agree with me.

In February 2005, five months after moving into my grandmother's basement, and four months after meeting Stephanie, I found an apartment in the same city where I grew up: Lynn. Even weirder was that the apartment I was moving into was the same apartment I had lived in with my parents when I was in middle school. Funny how that worked out.

The very next month, Stephanie moved in with me. This was the first time a girlfriend had ever lived with me. The Navy gave Stephanie her orders, though, right at the same time she moved in.

In June 2005, she would be stationed in Jacksonville, Florida. This left so many problems. What would happen with my band? Would Stephanie and I have a long-distance relationship and just hope it survived? Would I move with her?

We still had three months to figure all of that out.

Stephanie and I were driving back to our apartment from Boston to Lynn via Route 1 South on May 5, 2005, and it dawned on me that it was David's birthday. I had yet to miss a birthday correspondence in almost a decade. I wasn't going to start now.

I opened my cell phone to call David and clicked on his name in my address book. Immediately I got a message stating the number I had dialed was out of service, and to check the number and dial again.

When we took the exit for Revere, which would bring us to our apartment in Lynn, I called Jenny.

"Hey, it's me," I said.

"What's going on?"

"Do you know what's up with David's cell phone? Today's his birthday, and I can't get through. Did he change it? Do you know?"

Jenny said she had the same number I did. I had to accept the fact that I would have to send him a birthday email this year instead.

David picked up some new fans with the release of *Inside*. The die-hard God Lives Underwater fans had returned and purchased his first new piece of music since the Fluzee album came out back in 2002.

David launched his official website where he made himself available to fans who left messages. On his website was posted the biggest announcement of David's career. Universal Records had signed David for his future solo albums!

David immediately worked on his second solo album with producer Walt Bass at the helm. David's personal webpage became the central mecca for news and updates on the upcoming album. The album was going to have an early 2006 release date. It was going to be titled *How Humans R(x)*.

God Lives Underwater and David Reilly fans had something to look forward to again. David announced a tour to support the album after its release. It would be the first real tour David would do since God Lives Underwater toured on *Life in the So-Called Space Age* back in 1998.

On May 15, 2005, I asked Stephanie to marry me.

We were outside Axis on Lansdowne Street in Boston on our way see the band Dredg. They were touring on the *Catch Without Arms* album. She said yes and made me the happiest person in the world.

The Navy sent her to Jacksonville, Florida, for her first duty station in June 2005. She moved to Saint Marys, Georgia, on the Georgia/Florida border. She commuted every day to the naval base in Jacksonville.

At first we decided that I should move with her. I had to announce to my band, The Grave Machine, that in July I was going to move south to be with Stephanie. Unfortunately, because of that decision, my band broke up in July 2005 just months after we had recorded our self-titled debut album in Albany, New York.

I decided that it was time to take my first real break from the music world. After recording a total of four albums with three bands and playing close to one hundred shows, I felt musically burned-out.

After much deliberation and many hours of discussion, Stephanie and I decided that I should wait after all and not move until 2006, so I could work at the police department a bit longer and save some much-needed money. I spent the next ten months just working at the Peabody Police Department, helping to plan the wedding, and just trying to keep myself occupied so far away from Stephanie.

We set a wedding date of October 21, 2006. The wedding would be in Derry, New Hampshire. With the joy of getting married to the most beautiful and wonderful woman I had ever met also came the sadness of the last time I would ever hear David's voice.

In September 2005, I decided to call David from work after reading one of his blogs on his website.

"Hey, me-han."

"I read that you were doing another solo tour."

"Yeah. I think I'm coming to Massachusetts, but it's more west than you are."

"The Compound in Fitchburg," I said.

"Right."

"That's farther away than Boston, but only by about half an hour."

"What would a show in Massachusetts be without staying at your place?" he asked.

"Does the schedule allow you to stay with me again?"

"I honestly don't know, Rock. It would help me out if I could stay at your place though. The night after the show at least."

"That's fine. I don't live in the same house anymore. I have an apartment in Lynn next to my mother's house."

"What's going on with your woman?"

"Stephanie? Actually I wanted to talk to you about that. The wedding date is October 21, next year."

"I can't believe my little Rocky is getting married!"

"I know, right?"

"What did you want to ask me?"

Here it was. I had always imagined that David would be at my wedding one day.

"If Stephanie and I got you to Massachusetts, and paid for your gas or whatever, would you come to the wedding? I know you've never met her, but it's my wedding."

"You know I'm not good with crowds."

"What?" I asked, disappointed.

"I'm just kidding, Rock! I would even be in the wedding if you asked me. But I'm hoping you don't," he said, laughing.

"Nah. It would mean a lot to me if you were there."

"Would I have a place to stay?"

"Of course."

"I'm there!"

Tragically only David's memory would make it to my wedding. His enthusiasm to share in one of the most important days of my life was the last thing I ever heard from David Reilly's mouth.

David passed away less than one month later.

The following was David's very last blog he ever posted online before his death:

> *im healthy, making my record, and i got a new roommate. you will ALL be invited to the wedding. promise.* How Humans R(x), *will be completed in 3 weeks, and im making flyers for the three shows. the compound in MA, Don Hills in NYC, and Grapestreet*

in Philly (manayunk). i got my band in place, my girl in my apartment, and YOU. im fucking happy goddamnit.

David finished *How Humans R(x)* the same month he passed away.

MANTIS SEVEN

> *"I've got to leave this lonely and scary world back here on Earth. / It's not your fault / I flicker out."*
> David Reilly: "Crazier Than Me" - How Humans Rx)

The Philadelphia Inquirer – October 19, 2005

David F. Reilly, 34, of Northern Liberties, multitalented musician, songwriter and vocalist, recording artist, cofounder of the pseudo-industrial electro-rock band God Lives Underwater, died of a bleeding ulcer Sunday, October 16, 2005, at Temple University Hospital, Philadelphia. He was formerly of Ambler. He was born in Washington, DC, May 5, 1971. Mr. Reilly battled substance abuse for years. "David lived the hard rock-and-roll lifestyle, and it took its toll on his health," said his producer, Walter Bass. "When he recently took pain medication for an abscessed tooth, it was too much for his liver."

His father, Francis, said, "He struggled with his ongoing addiction problem. He was in and out of rehab hospitals." He had been clean for six months, his father said. Mr. Reilly started playing the piano at age five and eventually taught himself to play drums and guitar and to sing, his father said.

"He never wanted formal lessons." The thin young man with tousled blond curls was consumed with making music during his years at Lansdale Catholic High School. "He was not a good student. He spent his time playing with several neighborhood bands," his father said. Mr. Reilly graduated Lansdale Catholic High School in 1989.

After high school, Mr. Reilly moved to Los Angeles and cofounded God Lives Underwater with partner Jeff Turzo in 1994. The song "No More Love" was used in the 1995 film *Johnny Mnemonic*, starring Keanu Reeves. Another of the band's songs, a cover of the David Bowie hit "Fame," was used in the 2001 film *15 Minutes*.

The four-piece band toured nationally and internationally with some success, his producer said. In 1995, *The Inquirer* called the band "an unholy marriage of punk/metal and industrial/techno, plus Beatlesque melodies. This flavor of chaotic and weirdly beautiful icing is new."

The band broke up in 2000, and Mr. Reilly moved back to the Philadelphia area, settling in Ambler with his fiancée, Monica Young. Later that year, Young was struck and killed by a SEPTA train while running across the tracks in Roslyn. "After Monica's death, David's music became very dark and brooding," his father said.

He eventually moved to Northern Liberties, signed with the Philadelphia label RuffNation, and began performing as a solo artist. Mr. Reilly was close to finishing a full-length album at the time of his death, his producer said.

Mr. Reilly is also survived by his parents, Linda L. Bechtel of Lancaster and Francis X. Reilly of North Whales; a sister, Gretchen M. Runner of Ambler; a nephew, Billy Runner of

Ambler; a grandmother, Helen R. Bechtel of Hanover; and his fiancé Rachel Shirley of Philadelphia, formerly of Jacksonville, FL.

Visitation 9:00–10:30 a.m. for relatives and friends today at Emil J. Ciavarelli Family Funeral Homes, 951 E. Butler Pike, Ambler. Funeral will be held Fri., Oct. 21, 2005, at 11:00 in St. Anthony of Padua Church, 259 Forest Ave., Ambler. Burial will follow in Holy Sepulchre Cemetery, Cheltenham. Memorial contributions in David's name can be sent to a charity of one's choice.

On the morning of October 17, 2005, a day after Mike's birthday, I sat at my computer at the Peabody Police Department. Before checking my email, I went to my favorite music website to get my news on all the bands that I followed.

I had always imagined that, if David had ever died, Jeff would give me a call. He would magically just know my phone number. We would have a good laugh about how David pulled one over on us, and then we would have a drink. I secretly hoped that I would be told in a very intimate and personal way. This wouldn't be further from the truth.

I was ready for a normal workweek of taking 9-1-1 calls and dispatching officers. I ordered my coffee as I loaded up the Internet to check what Thursday, Placebo, Ministry, or Neurosis were doing that week.

Then I saw everything that I had always feared. The statement was void of any candy-coated introduction. I was paralyzed.

R.I.P David Reilly
(11:34 PM PST 10/16/2005)
Former God Lives Underwater frontman David Reilly passed away this morning as a result of complications from a stomach problem.

That was it. Ten years of friendship was over within that twenty-word statement. It was the worst possible way to find out. I stared at the words and kept thinking that there just had to be an update that it was only a false report. I hoped that it was just another rumor like the one spread by the soundman in Rhode Island back in 1996.

This time, though, there wouldn't be any amendments of the news. There wouldn't by any retractions of or apologies for the mistake.

I stood in the middle of the control room of the police department as my heart sank. It was just business as usual for everyone else.

"Can you handle the radio for a few minutes?" I asked Jamie. "I have to make a few phone calls."

I grabbed my cell phone. I didn't quite know who I was calling yet. I just knew that I had to call somebody!

I went outside without a jacket and walked around the corner of the building to get some privacy and stay out of the October Massachusetts wind. Dann! Dann was always in touch with music-related current events. He would tell me that he heard an update. It was just a hoax, a prank. It was a stomachache, not death.

When he answered, my statement was very calculated and direct. "David died yesterday." I heard myself say the words but I still didn't believe them.

I told him what I knew, which was very little. He said that he would try to find out more. He asked if I was okay. I told him that I was just . . . numb.

I called Mike, who was on his way to work. I told him that it was only fair that he heard it from me instead of reading gossip about it online. He took it hard almost immediately. There didn't seem to be any denial. He told me later that he almost couldn't even bring himself to go into work that morning when he reached his building.

I called Jenny next, but I got her voicemail.

"Jenny, it's Brian. I don't know if you've heard yet, but I thought you should hear it from me before finding out the way I did. David passed away over the weekend. Give me a call if you want to talk about it."

Although David was dead, it was somehow comforting to know that he had died from something that wasn't drug-related. It warmed my heart in a cold way, all things considered.

I went back inside to my captain's office. I told him that I just found out that one of my best friends passed away, and I needed a few moments before working again. He offered to give me the whole day off, but going back to an empty apartment probably wasn't the best thing for me.

I went to the back of the station, stood next to an empty cell block, and called Stephanie. When she let me vent, I finally lost composure. Although she comforted me the best she could, it was hard to accept it completely, because I still didn't have all the facts yet. It felt like such a mystery.

I was supposed to go see the band Crisis that night at the Palladium in Worcester. They were touring on the *Like Sheep Led to Slaughter* album. Drop Kick Jesus had toured with Crisis many times. In fact Drop Kick Jesus's show at

CBGB's was when we were on tour with them. Because of my involvement with them over the years, they had me on the guest list. I just knew I wouldn't be able to enjoy a concert or be able to be social.

I sent an email to the guitarist of Crisis explaining what had happened and why I wouldn't be there. Unfortunately that was the last time Crisis would ever play Massachusetts, as they broke up shortly after the conclusion of that tour.

I called Dann and Mike, and asked if they wanted to come to my apartment that night to have a memorial for David. I didn't want to be alone. I suggested that we get a pizza, play all the God Lives Underwater albums, and reminisce about the times we hung out with David. Both Dann and Mike agreed.

When I got back to my console, I thanked Jamie for covering for me and logged onto the God Lives Underwater website. There, posted at the top of the discussion forum, was a message from David's cousin.

> *Hey, this is Kristine. David was completely clean. No doubt about it. We are all proud of him. However, his body like his Uncle's, (who was a heavy drug addict), was like that of a 93 year old and his body just gave up.*

She said it best. *We are all proud of him.*
David would be forever clean. How could we not celebrate that?

Dann and Mike arrived at my apartment almost at the same time. Mike even brought a present with him. He had collected all of the songs that David had posted online that were going to be on his second solo album, *How Humans R(x)*, and had burned them onto a disc. We had an unofficial version of David's posthumous album, albeit with no official track order.

I added *How Humans R(x)* to my disc player already loaded with the God Lives Underwater albums, David's *Inside* album, the Robot Teen America *Living in Syn* album, and Fluzee's *7* album.

We ordered a pizza and a bottle of Coke from Giovanni's sub shop, and sat on the floor of my bedroom.

The disc changer made a very distinct whirling noise as it spun the collection of discs around in random order. A faint beep was audible just before each song began.

The very first song, out of more than seventy, struck us as odd. When it started, we just looked at each other. There was a definite eerie connection between the lyrics of "Take Good Care" and our tribute. David had written the song as a letter to someone who had passed away.

I hope you finally feel at home up there. / I know when you arrived / You were unaware. / I get the feeling that you're okay... / If you care / Could you try again to contact me? / And say everything will be alright.

We talked about the first time we saw God Lives Underwater live and how we found out about the band in the first place. Dann spoke about that first night I had introduced him to David. Mike spoke about his barbecue.

Although my disc changer never, ever played two tracks in a row from the same album on Random mode, in the middle of our God Lives Underwater memorial, it not only played a track from the same album twice but it was the same song too! I had that changer for three years. It had never done anything remotely close to that before. We looked at each other in shock. Of all songs to play twice in a row, it was "Happy?" from *Life in the So-Called Space Age*.

After we had been in my room for a few hours, I mentioned that the changer hadn't picked anything from *Up off the Floor* yet. We agreed that this was odd since there were only eight discs for the player to choose from.

Our palaver continued, and we occasionally laughed at our memories. I talked about the time when David had fallen through the chair at my cookout, when Lady had eaten his breakfast at Jenny's house, and when he had spilled his chocolate milkshake all over the McDonald's table. Mike mentioned when he had almost killed David with undercooked chicken. Dann brought up when he had to buy the beer that David had hid in the store across the street from me.

Other stories we told through tear-stained eyes. Mike talked about how he regretted taking Storrow Drive and never making it back to my house. Dann described how he saw God Lives Underwater on their *Life in the So-Called Space Age* tour in Pittsburgh while he was in college at Carnegie Mellon.

The hardest part for me to talk about, and to come to grips with, was when I thought about how David would never sleep on my floor again. I would never fall asleep to the sound of his heavy breathing. I would never hear him sing Nelly Furtado in my shower. He would never meet the woman I was about to marry.

The mystery of a repeat playing of "Happy?" twice in a row returned, when, this time, my disc changer played "Take Good Care" twice in a row.

When the pizza was gone, the soda had somehow been mixed with rum. Four hours had fallen off the clock. Since

Dann and Mike both had to work in the morning, they got ready to leave.

My disc changer had still completely ignored *Up off the Floor*. I thought that there might be something wrong with the disc itself, which would explain why the changer had skipped over it so many times. I also noticed that it hadn't played "Vapors," my favorite song from *Life in the So-Called Space Age*. It had played probably every other song from that album.

I walked Dann and Mike to their cars, and left the stereo playing. I ran back up the stairs to clean up the mess we had left behind. My disc changer finally landed on "Miss You More Than Anything" from *Up off the Floor*. I felt weak.

Hey, me-han! Thought you'd pick up on my way of saying, Hi, Rocky.

I called Dann. "Guess what album the next song was from after you guys left?"

He guessed right. If that wasn't enough, the next song after that played was "Vapors."

I decided to skip the funeral for the sake of David's family and their privacy. I would say good-bye on my own time, in my own way, at his grave site.

Other than the tracks that my disc changer had randomly played during David's tribute, I hadn't really had the chance to sit down and listen to *How Humans R(x)* yet.

David had been posting the songs for the new album on his website as he had finished them. He left them up for only a few days at a time so fans could get a taste of what *How Humans R(x)* was going to sound like. Mike had luckily downloaded each song to his computer as David had posted them.

David had also emailed me some of the songs when he had finished them. I had been waiting to hear the album as a whole when it was released. The copy of *How Humans R(x)* that Mike left me was the closest I would ever get to hearing it.

I put my headphones on and listened to the last album of David's career. Possibly the best one.

At this point in time, Stephanie had been stationed in Florida for five months. We had planned our wedding as best we could under the circumstances.

David had died three weeks ago. Many thoughts and unanswered questions ate away at my brain. Another two months would pass before I would even begin the process of writing this book as an outlet for my grief.

I was also not in a band for the first time since 1995.

Of course I missed Stephanie. I missed David. I missed being in a band. I missed writing short stories. I missed creating. I drank more to help fill in those empty spaces. I also drank alone, which was something I had never done before.

My need to send David an email outweighed the reality that it would go unread. I sent David a very drunken email to Fluzee33@yahoo.com at 10:06 p.m. on November 10, 2005.

> *You know how proud I am of you. You didn't let me down, you didn't let any of us down more importantly. It's been a long hard road man. You know that my place is ALWAYS your place, whether it's to visit me and my family or if you need a place to stay, even if it is on my floor!*

Remember those mornings I woke up with you sleeping so I could listen to your breathing to make sure you were ok? You finally are ok. I gotta be honest; you weren't the easiest person to love. You left behind a lot of people that will never understand, but you also left behind a small handful of people that DO *understand. And those people care about you more than you could ever have known while you were here. Do you think that Mike and Dann loved you because you were the singer of God Lives Underwater? Fuck that man, you had the ability to blur that line with them between fan and friend. Christ I hope all your pain is gone. Even knowing how this ended I would do it all again, I would never trade all those hours and days we spent together even if I knew you were leaving and going home to Heaven. David, I tell you . . . I would never have forgiven you if you went out the "bad" way and that's why so many of us are so proud of you. Heh, have you heard the new Depeche Mode album? I think you'll like it a lot. I'll play it for you sometime; it's a cross between* Violator *and* Music for the Masses, *but with a little more raw feeling. I know how you were disappointed with* Ultra *and* Exciter, *but you would have liked the new album. Anyway, the save the date cards for my wedding are going out soon. Can you believe I'm getting married? Was Monica waiting for you when you went Home? Man, I have never seen you love someone like you loved her. Jenny won't talk about your death, I think it freaks her out a little bit. I'm sorry I keep crying for you, I cry because I know you fucking made it and that makes me so proud and happy. Have you seen Stephanie and my invite list for the wedding?*

Ya, Stephanie came up with a great idea. Stephanie and I, and Mike and Dann are gonna take your seating card and we are gonna put you with us at the head table. Fuck you, if you don't make an appearance at my wedding!!! I will be VERY pissed off the next time I see you if you don't celebrate the greatest day of my life with us! Dann and Mike are both groomsman. If I thought you would want to be, I would have asked you too. If you miss my fucking wedding I will kick your ass when I see you next, and you know I will!!! Please David, you have no idea how this is eating me up inside that you don't know my wife in the flesh. So ya, we are saving a spot for you in my wedding, and it's going to be a great day and a day I need you to be there with us. I love you, you bitch. Heh So, I thought this was funny. The girl that always takes my order at Dunkin Donuts noticed something was wrong the day after your death. Her name is Nilza and I told her on the side that you had passed away, and when I described you she remembered you!!! And then I remembered the last time I saw you was at that Dunkin Donuts and she cooked us our breakfast sandwiches and I said good-bye to you from that Dunks as you followed me to the highway to go to NYC. I remember that so vividly. You sitting at the counter eating your sandwich. I NEVER thought that was the last time I was going to see you. I now understand that you said goodbye because you had to, but that doesn't mean you have to actually say goodbye. Man, I wish I knew why I was having such a hard time with your death. I don't know if you know this, but your bday is the same bday as Sean's, (my best man in my wedding and best friend) and you left us on Mike's bday and you told me about Monica dying on my bday. I'm trying so hard to celebrate your life and not mourn your death. Fuck I miss you. But thank you for the subtle signs already that you are still with me. Believe me, they don't go unnoticed!! We are so proud of you David, at least your friends are. Thank you for making me sooooo proud to be your brother.

In November 2005, Front 242 played a gig in New York City to promote their latest album, *Pulse*. Mike and I decided to make the four-hour trip from Boston in my new Scion, named the Bantha-Mobile.

Mike wore a God Lives Underwater T-shirt with the mantis logo on the front that day. After doors opened, we went into the club and found a great spot for the show. Some random guys in front of us noticed Mike's T-shirt and turned to talk to us.

"Hey, nice shirt. Didn't I just read somewhere that the singer recently died?"

Mike noticed how uncomfortable I had become. He saved me from having to talk about David and explained what we knew about the circumstances surrounding David's death.

Even though it was nice to know that there were still people who cared, I just had to remove myself from the conversation before it even really began. I wasn't ready to talk to strangers about David yet.

I flew to Georgia to spend New Year's Eve 2006 with Stephanie.

One night, during that trip, I fell asleep for what felt like only a few seconds, before I startled myself awake. I had the most vivid dream.

In my dream I introduced David to my late grandfather, Anthony Paone, who had passed away in 1990 from cancer. We were in a field of green that looked like the field in the film adaptation of Pink Floyd's *The Wall* when Pink, as a child, ran through the grass to meet the adult version of himself.

After I introduced David to my grandfather, they shook hands and walked away.

They both looked great!

It had been three months since David had died. I spent every night thinking of him. Some nights I spent with a little too much alcohol in my body while *How Humans R(x)* blared in my headphones.

Just like that, I realized my time of grieving was over. It was time for me to do something about it. I had to put all my memories of him on paper. I didn't care who wanted to read it. I was doing it for myself. I needed a way to move on.

At 9:32 p.m. on January 29, 2006, I opened up Microsoft Word to start writing this book and begin my healing process. Just as soon as I began typing did I realize that it would never really be complete unless I got in touch with David's sister, Gretchen, and visit his grave.

Fortunately Gretchen contacted me herself through a website that I had launched designed for updates, advertisements, and promotions of this book. Eventually we even spoke on the phone. After so many years of hearing things about her, it was surreal to be talking to her. David had even told me at one point "If there's ever an emergency, call my sister."

After some discussion, Gretchen realized that she had known about me as well. She gave me her full blessing to write and publish this book. We also discussed a trip for Mike and me to go to Ambler to stay with her and David's nephew, Billy, for a weekend.

Many emails and phone calls later, Gretchen quickly transformed from a contact to a friend. We used each other to lean on. Although she knew about me through David, she had become very guarded about who she opened up to. There were some stalkers who had made her life difficult and deceived her around every corner.

As I was still a stranger to her, Gretchen wanted to find confirmation that I was who I said I was, since we had made plans for me to say at her apartment for three days. She found the proof on David's laptop in his email contacts.

I received an email from Gretchen shortly after we discussed the visit.

His address book in Yahoo, very few people in there, yet you are one of them. It says "Rocky."

That was so nice to hear. I don't know which part of the email comforted me the most, but just the fact that he actually had me listed as Rocky in his address book was enough.

It was the proof Gretchen needed.

Mike and I vigorously planned the weekend trip that would bring us to David's grave as well as the privilege of staying with

Gretchen and Billy in their house, the same address where all those packages and mailings I had sent to David over the years were delivered. David also lived there, off and on, since 1997. Most notably it was where the Robot Teen America debacle had happened.

I finally felt like everything was coming full circle. I was also working on this book almost every night.

I was so wrapped up in the planning of the trip to Ambler that I didn't really grasp the fact that I was traveling almost four hundred miles to visit a tombstone with David's name on it. Talking with Gretchen on almost a daily basis was actually candy-coating the real reason for our trip.

We originally wanted to visit the grave on David's birthday, May 5, but then my plans to move to Georgia were expedited. It looked like I would already be gone by then.

At the beginning of March, Gretchen and I agreed that the weekend after St. Patrick's Day 2006 would be best. Mike made sure that he didn't have any preexisting plans either, so we confirmed the trip. We would arrive around midnight on Friday night and leave sometime around noon on Sunday. I had about thirty-six hours to visit with David's family, stay at his old place, see some of the sights, and visit the grave. Hopefully it would be enough time to say good-bye.

I had been working on this book for two months, and the website's visitor traffic increased daily. I was receiving hordes of messages from people all over the world who knew David and wanted to get in touch with me. I had been talking with Suzanne, a friend of David's, who lived in Philadelphia. When I announced that I was going to spend a weekend visiting the grave, she contacted me. She wanted to know if Mike and I would meet her for lunch on our way home. I told her, if time permitted, we would. We made tentative plans.

I made a list of items to pack for the trip in the same notebook that I was using to work on my book outlines, so I wouldn't forget anything. Sleeping bag, toothbrush, toothpaste, shampoo, contact solution, glasses, cell phone charger, raincoat. Stuff like that.

Gretchen told us that we would be sleeping in Billy's room, and he would sleep in her bed. There were bunk beds in his room.

Mike and I could pretend that we were kids again.

March 24, 2006, the day of our trip, had arrived. We left Mike's apartment in Beverly for Ambler at 5:53 p.m. We made one quick detour to Stop & Shop where we purchased disposable cameras and snacks for the ride.

Mike and I had been on many road trips together to see bands in other states. Mike had also been Drop Kick Jesus's tour manager for most of the five years we were together.

I loaded up my car disc changer with all four God Lives Underwater albums (including their six non-album tracks), both David Reilly albums, the Robot Teen America album, the Fluzee album, the two Heavy songs, and a bunch of remixes and live tracks. I put the changer on Shuffle for the entire ride.

We also had a copy of the Armada Sound System's interview for the trip.

On October 5, 2005, a mere eleven days before David died, he did a podcast interview online with Jeff Cavanaugh for Jeff's multimedia company Creative Armada. The podcast was the last spoken interview David ever recorded before he passed away.

David had originally hired Jeff to design the cover art for *How Humans R(x)*. After Jeff found out that I was writing a book about David, he reached out to me and offered to design the front cover art for this book as well. I hired him. He incorporated unused pieces of the *How Humans R(x)* artwork into the cover of this book as his own montage as a homage to David.

Mike and I had been on the road for a few hours, and we decided to stop in Connecticut at a mall to get some dinner, which unfortunately turned into a fiasco. We entered the mall only fifteen minutes before they closed. We spent the entire time running from restaurant to restaurant to find someone who would serve us. Finally we found something in the Food Court.

We got back on the road with the disc changer in my car playing all of David's music. I calculated that we had about two hours left on Route 95. We were somewhere between New Jersey and Pennsylvania.

I asked Mike if he was ready to hear the Armada Sound System's interview. Mike took a moment to think about it. What was going through his mind was probably the same thing going through mine. Did we really want to hear David's voice knowing that was the last time it had ever been captured? We knew that, when the interview finished, we would never again hear his voice say something that we hadn't already heard. Like me, Mike understood that this was what this whole trip was about. We had to say good-bye.

"Yeah. Go ahead and pop it in," he said.

As we approached the Pennsylvania border, we stopped to fill up the gas tank and use the bathroom so we could listen to the whole podcast without interruption. I slid the interview into the disc player of the Bantha-Mobile. We waited patiently as it began.

Jeff Cavanaugh: Welcome to another podcast on the Armada Sound System. We recently caught up with ex–God Lives Underwater front man David Reilly. David has been through quite a bit over the past few years, and has come back with a new lease on life and on the music business. Armed with a four-record contract, and the resources to thrive and create, David had some great things to say about what is to come. Welcome, David. How's it going?

David Reilly: Good! Working and taking a little break right now. Here with my engineer, Walter, in the other room actually engineering this conversation! Well, he's actually my best bro too. Kinda works out to have one of your best friends from fifteen years ago also be the best engineer in town. It's pretty much where it's at.

JC: It's definitely good to get along when you're caught in the studio for hours on end. That's for sure.

DR: Oh, yeah, we have a blast! Like the record that we're doing. A lot of the aspects of it are things that me and Walt have listened to. Things that we've wanted to do for years and years. We're spending a lot of time doing it. If I was working with someone that I didn't get along with, this would suck. It would really suck. We have a good time every day. The only thing we ever really disagree on is maybe a little thing here or there, like, on a vocal thing. We compromise on things, and everything works out. I've worked with other people in the past. That's the reason why God Lives Underwater never worked with anybody!

JC: How long ago did God Lives Underwater start? Let's kind of back up a little bit here and kind of talk about where you were ten years ago, and that kind of stuff. How long ago did that come together as a band? How long was it before you were actually on the road?

DR: God Lives Underwater actually started in 1992. Jeff was in another band that was signed. I was just working two jobs. He was home for Christmas vacation. He had some of the equipment for the band that he was in. We made one song, I believe. He went back on the road after we made that song. We worked together when we were younger and stuff. We made that song, and we kind of knew that we were gonna make something go of it. Probably within, I guess like a year, we acquired some management and legal, and we got a lot of interest right away. Actually there was a deejay in Philadelphia named Josh Wink who heard it. A friend of his worked at American, so it ended up getting in the hands of Rick Rubin, and that started. American kind of sat on it for a while. They didn't release our first record until '95. That's around the time that we hit the road too. Maybe '94. I think they may have put us out on the road in '94 for maybe three months or so. Then the record came out in '95. We toured for *GLU* briefly, and then they wanted us to make a full-length right away. So '95 would be when it really pretty much all happened. But we had our deal in '93.

JC: Rubin's got a big history in music, that's for sure.

DR: He was down with us from the very start.

JC: That's a good guy to have in your corner, I guess, when you're starting out. What inspired you guys to just get together and start playing? Was it just that you guys were friends for a while and both into music, or were you in music in school together?

DR: We were friends back in the day because we were both skaters. We were both a little different than everybody else. In fact the way that I met Jeff is there was a big high school rumble. This was after I had moved out of the city and was up in the suburbs. It was the punks and the metal guys were all fighting. There was a big, huge fight. Me and Jeff were the only two guys that were like, "This is ridiculous!" and so, I was like, "Hey, my name's Dave." Then we became friends. I don't know. It was weird! I was a biker, and he was a skater, and I was like, "You should come over. I'm getting a skateboard. You should teach me how to skate." You know, and he came over. He came up to my room and there was a keyboard there, and he played keyboards. By the end of the night we were working on a song. We sort of became really, really good friends and then started a little band together. We had bands on and off through high school. He was an intern at a label and ended up getting picked up by another band to tour with when he was in college, and

I was working. When he did that, eventually we both kind of figured that at some point we were going to get back together and make some music that's gonna be really great. The time was then, once he was off tour from that band, because that band was just fizzling. He had gotten all the experience, I guess, he wanted out of it. He toured and did everything like that, that I hadn't done yet. He came home, and fortunately he made some connections.

JC: You guys definitely had your own sound. That's definitely something that we saw as fans from an early time. We also noticed that it was almost exclusively the use of Nord Leads that we noticed was pretty distinctive of your sound.

DR: Actually the stuff that's on *Empty* and *GLU* was mostly an Oberheim Xpander, which is a pretty sought-after piece of gear. We had that, and we had a sampler, and that was about it. That synthesizer was pretty versatile. Then we got a Novation Bass Station. Then we got an Oberheim OB-Mx. The Nord Leads came a little bit later. We got the Nords when we started touring for *Empty*. They became part of everything we did from that point on. A lot of keyboards came out. The Nords became our live thing, and we made a lot of sounds for it for *Life in the So-Called Space Age* and stuff. But then the Access Virus came out, and we used that a lot too. We were big fans of the Nord Leads. In fact we had a little endorsement with the company back then.

JC: That's great! They still are making really, really nice equipment. A really, really cool company. So there was God Lives Underwater, and then there were a few albums, and then there was some movie licensing, and then you guys kind of went off the radar. You came back with Fluzee, and that kind of died shortly after. A lot of fans already know, and I know it's not really a secret, but what do you have to say about the demise of God Lives Underwater? And the pseudoresurgence with Fluzee? And ultimately a long sabbatical that finds us here with you and a four-record deal with Universal?

DR: The demise of God Lives Underwater, a lot of people would say, could almost all be blamed entirely on my substance-abuse problem, but it was kind of a culmination of things. The last record deal that we had was with A&M. We had a label deal through that called 1500. There was a merger where we ended up getting shifted onto Interscope. During that shift we didn't really have an ace in the company, and we were worried about not getting the attention that we wanted. We ended up getting funding for our own label again, which went through another label called Riffage that then, in turn, tanked as well. Labels and business things started going wrong. Financially the band was kind of suffering just because we were, sort of, taking it to the next level. Bigger tours. More equipment. Bigger records. Selling more records. That kind of brought that all to a grinding halt. On top of it, we lost a lot of momentum because of me and having to get clean at times. Or to have to go away for different reasons that addicts have to take leave of absences. We lost a lot of momentum like that. And then *Up off the Floor* we were making when we were technically on Interscope. We ended up leaving Interscope with those masters. Then it went to Riffage. And then it went to another company. And then it wasn't going anywhere. Around that same time, my fiancée got killed in a train accident. I think, as terrible as it sounds, that everybody around us, and the people who worked for us, didn't think I was ever going to really recover from that. So the emphasis wasn't really on getting the record out or keeping the band together. It was sad to say, but like, "Maybe we should get away from David before everything goes with him." I couldn't really blame anybody. Jeff was doing his own thing. Producing things and doing remixes. The other guys in the band were doing other things as well. Our manager who had the label, he was managing some other bigger bands. And then my addiction became what was going on with me. There was no music. I got a short period of time where I was clean, where I had Fluzee. That was short-lived. That could have been something too, if I would have kind of kept it together. Jeff wanted to work on Fluzee with us too, but I just couldn't keep it together. And then, after I did, I was clean for a year. During that time Locomotive and Megaforce bought the rights to *Up off the Floor*. They pressed it with a manufacturing flaw. They never fixed it. I refused to do any kind of promotion for the company, or for the band, as a result that album. I don't even know what it sold, but I'm guessing that it didn't do that well. And then I decided to make my own music. To make solo music.

I made some demos. A friend of mine, Thom, put out *Inside* on his little label, Corporate Punishment, which just had some demos of mine. A friend of me and Walter's, Chris, has the company RuffNation. That sort of eventually just came into play. I gave Chris the CD. "This is what me and Walt are working on." He liked it, and he offered me a deal!

JC: You guys seemed like you were just gonna blow up and just be really huge, several times over the course. We were always really into that. How does the past experience with fame and with being a hot record seller and being out on the road and all of that stuff that goes along with it influence your attitude toward maybe going that direction again with your career now?

DR: I learned a lot. I know what not to do now, and I know to not take any of it for granted. Because to have a record deal and to be doing what—it's the only thing I am good at. So I am very blessed to be able to live off of music, indeed. I'm doing everything right, now. We spend a lot of time to make things sound the way we want to so that, when the record comes out, we can't be like, "Me-han, I wish we had just did that one thing we wanted to do in the chorus." We're doing all those things. And the way that I handle business now. I have people who are around me who care about my well-being. I have a manager who is also sober. I got a support network around me this time that it's in their interest for my life and my business. I have that kind of going for me. I also know a little bit about the business now. I know about picking a single. I know about Soundscan and management and legal, and stuff like that, and publishing now more than I did before. I know what you got to do. I know they release a single, and I have got to get out on the road. I know that I've got to put on a good show. And if the sound system sucks in a club, you still got to look like you are having a great time! Like, if things suck, and then you act like a prick onstage, dude, no one's having a good time. I had an attitude back then in God Lives Underwater. I'm kind of done with that too. A lot of things you sort of figure out. I'm fortunate to have another go at it.

JC: We actually have some footage of you guys that a friend of mine, Matt Olsen, shot when you guys were in some small town in California. You guys were having some problems with the management after the show. They didn't want to pay you and all this kind of stuff. I remember your manager at the time was talking. We have a really funny dialogue piece with your manager talking to the manager of this little Podunk town club, and it's actually really hilarious. We should get that online, or something, for people to check out.

DR: Can you send that to me?

JC: Yeah, I can. It's on a VHS, as a matter of fact, but, yeah, we can. We can get a copy of that to you.

DR: So you actually have video of my manager arguing with a club manager?

JC: Yeah, it's really hilarious! He even goes on when the guy walks away. He's like, "Yeah, well, I'm done with Uncle Fucker's Chuckle-Hut here," or something like that. It was totally fucking hilarious, man. It was awesome.

DR: That's great! I at least want to be able to hear it, me-han. I may be able to use a clip from that audio on my album if it's good enough! Definitely hook me up with that.

JC: What's your overall goal for the term of the contract? It's four records, but what's the time frame? What's going on with the constraints of the deal and all that kind of stuff?

DR: My deal is with RuffNation. They have an exclusive deal with Universal, and my deal with RuffNation is four albums. The parameters of it are to see how all the parties feel about moving on to another record, after the life of the first one. But it's four, and, basically if all goes well, I am making four albums that'll come out on Universal! What my goals are, are kind of low. I think that the label would be ecstatic if I were to sell forty or fifty thousand records. If I were able to get this product into the hands of everybody who bought a God Lives Underwater album, then they're probably going to like it. So that is more like a hundred thousand people. The other thing is that this music is maybe even a little bit more accessible than it was back then. So there's the possibility of me having some hits on it. There is a whole other market now that we really didn't have back then. Like I have thirty thousand plays on MySpace right now. Those people on there are going to buy the record! A lot of them don't even know who God Lives Underwater is! They just found me because they were doing a search for influences. They found all the people who came up for Depeche Mode, and they were like "Oh, I'll check this out!" and they liked it! And then your service. That's another outlet. So my goal is actually to surpass everybody's expectations and just continue to be able to make a living off this for the life of my deal.

JC: Those are realistic goals. So will you be going on tour?

DR: Yeah, actually I'm doing just a few dates, coming up in November. I'm doing a Philly show, a Boston-area show, a New York City show. I'm doing, like, five total. And then I probably won't be doing any touring. Unless there's one-off shows. Like, if someone comes to me, and it's an offer that I need to take. I'll be doing that. But other than that, I'll just be finishing the album. But when the album is done, I'm hoping to get out on tour around the time that it's released, which will be February.

JC: Are the God Lives Underwater albums still available?

DR: Through all of the change-of-hands that God Lives Underwater has gone through, I can say that probably the stuff on Warner Brothers/American is probably still in print. *Empty* and *GLU* are still in print but may be hard to find. *Life in the So-Called Space-Age*, it's been a while since I've seen a copy of that. That was on A&M. I believe that *Up off the Floor* is still in stores, but I don't know how long they are going to continue printing that. I really hope that they resolve the sound and manufacturing flaw that they made because, actually, I don't even like thinking about it. It makes my blood pressure go up.

JC: I noticed that there's some strategically, and some not-so-strategically, located areas online where there's quite an extensive bit of your music available for download. Candidly I don't want to get you in trouble, but I know that you're very progressive, technically, and very into computers and modern technology and what's going on out there. What are your feelings with Internet file-sharing and that sort of stuff?

DR: I don't have a problem with Internet file-sharing! I can understand why people have an issue with it. I certainly understand if the company that I work for doesn't want the music out there. If I put something up for download, it's a demo version of the song that's not gonna be on the album and wouldn't really deter people from buying the album. But, in my opinion, people are going to rip those songs anyway, and they're gonna end up on file-sharing programs. It happens to the best of 'em. There's not much you can do. I guess, if you can stifle it in any way by, hopefully, keeping your masters, by making it online before your album comes out, then that's a pretty good idea. But once you've got a record in stores and thirteen-year-olds know how to get something off a piracy CD and get it online no problem, there's not much you can do about it. I'm guilty of downloading music online! I try and buy everything that I like. The reason why I download is to see if I like it, and sometimes I don't.

Sometimes I want a good-sounding copy, but I don't want to stream it from their website. I want to hear, at least, a good-sounding MP3 of it because I don't just buy records because I like the songs. I have done that, but there's a lot of stuff that I buy because I like the overall thing. I like the way that it's mixed. I like everything about it. I'd like to hear a good-sounding MP3 of it. If I really dig it, I'll buy the album.

JC: That's a good way to look at it, I think. I agree that a lot of times you want to hear stuff before you buy it. You don't want to stand in line at Virgin at one of those kiosks, and do all of that stuff. You just want to hear the music. The other thing is that it gets shared a lot more. People get to hear it more. You mentioned MySpace earlier. That's definitely a huge venue for musicians these days. That's all about Internet streaming and downloading. It's pretty interesting the way the climate is changing. I know yesterday, when we talked on the phone briefly, you mentioned that back in the '80s, music was being made by people who could afford the equipment, not by those that could play it. When God Lives Underwater started, you told me that musicians could purchase the equipment for producing music because it was a lot more affordable at the time.

DR: Right. It's even more affordable now. There is a couple different areas with that. There was a time when drum machines and samplers and synthesizers were out of reach because they were too expensive. People who could afford them were making terrible, terrible music. And then eventually people who knew how to write songs were able to afford that stuff, but they still had to go to studios. Even since the dawn of God Lives Underwater, the home-recording process has improved so much that the demos that I've made for my record right now are pressable! The only reason why Walter and I choose to do it at the bigger studio is because you can get a great sound out of having a console like we use. The SL 9000. Which is a really nice mixing console. It's in a room with space. It has a great live room for playing live drums and stuff. Ordinarily that would be too expensive, but the label that I'm signed to owns it. So I get to record there with minimal cost. When it comes down to it, if I could make a great-sounding record that everybody would certainly not complain about, and then be able to spend the rest of my advance on living so I don't have to landscape during the day in order to be a musician, that's when you run into "Well, would I rather spend the money at the studio?" or "Would I rather be able to spend the year touring?" Right now I'm able to do both, and that's because the label owns that studio. But, in any other position, I would probably be making my records at home.

JC: A lot of people do that these days. Even I've played with experimenting with music at home, so it's not out of reach! But you can't buy talent! That's one thing that I run into, and I'm going to be taking some lessons and stuff, so that I can at least further my understanding in the production realm.

DR: You can make music with all of that stuff, but you can't go and download the John Lennon–

songwriting aspect of it. If you could do that, when they get to that point someday, then I'm out of a job.

JC: I also wanted to ask you about that, in closing here. Where do you see music going with technology? I know that, as a content creator myself in film and video production, also in web and graphics, and even 3-D animation, I see everything coming together, sort of like a freight train with no brakes. I see it getting to a point where, how long is it really going to be until you have a music production studio in something the size of a cell phone? As far as software and connectivity is concerned, how soon is it going to be before every twelve-year-old has an indie film that they're trying to enter at the festivals? So, where do you see all of this heading, as far as the availability of technology and sort of the dumbing-down of the artistic side? Do you see that the appreciation for art is, sort of, the intellectual side of our society? Do you think they're losing grasp of really what good art is, or do you think that will ever happen?

DR: There's always a segment of society that likes music and art and different art, period, that is a little left-of-center. Some would say it's more genuine. I would have to agree that, a lot of the music that I listen to, I believe has a little bit more talented songwriting going on than what you would hear on pop radio, but it's a different format. I think, like I said before, with technology, and going the way it's going, everybody is going to have an indie film that they're shopping at the cons. It'll come full circle. Everybody won't be able to make a movie like that or an indie film like that or a record, but there's going to be some that stand out above the rest that made something look like a great movie but was also a great movie. There's still very few of those people who can make music and have the technology to make it at home and make a great-sounding record and write great songs. But now that you can afford it, everyone's at least going to enter. You know what I mean?

JC: It's gonna just meet the masses. So do you feel that we might be fortunate enough to experience some kind of artistic renaissance here in the next ten or twenty years? Where we actually have really, really amazing artists? Kind of like, maybe even as recently as the '60s coming back for us to the mainstream?

DR: Yeah, I do see that! I mention MySpace again, because there's just such instant access to all kinds of music. A friend of your friends that has an unsigned band. I hear stuff that's great all the time now because people couldn't afford to make music that sounded good enough to put up. A lot of people could write great songs, but they just didn't have the resources to do it. There's a lot of talented people out there right now that you can see and hear and have access to because of sites like MySpace, and because of technology being within their reaches. So I guess we're kind of in that right now. There's sort of a renaissance right now!

JC: That's good news. I'm sure that all of the artists listening are very happy to hear that from somebody who they respect as much as David Reilly. Well, thanks, David! I really appreciate you taking the time to give us the interview today. It's really been a pleasure talking to you and sort of catching up on where you've been and where you're headed.

We arrived at Gretchen's apartment at 12:37 a.m.

The first thing that Mike and I noticed, as we pulled into the driveway of 35 Hendricks Street, was the car parked there. Suddenly the trip became real as we saw David's crappy beige Volkswagen. There it was, all alone, unused.

When Gretchen met us at the door, it felt like we had already known each other forever. There wasn't any awkwardness at all while we brought our luggage and sleeping bags into her apartment.

Billy was already asleep in Gretchen's bedroom, and we wouldn't meet him until the next morning when they got back from his Reconciliation. Gretchen had told me that Billy was really excited to meet us. He was still devastated over David's death, so meeting some of Uncle David's friends made the grief easier. I was surprised that Gretchen was going to trust Mike and me to stay in the apartment alone, while they were at his Reconciliation, after only meeting us briefly for the first time that night.

As we entered the house that David had been living in for the past eight years off and on, it felt like I already knew the place, but only because of all of the times I had addressed packages to be mailed here.

Gretchen brought us down the hallway and into the living room. The first thing I noticed were framed pictures of David that I had never seen before.

"If you want to put down your bags, I'll give you the tour," Gretchen said.

She brought us into the den that had two couches, multiple boxes, and milk crates stacked in a corner, a guitar in front of a fireplace, and a collage of pictures on a wall.

"This is where David slept when he lived here with me," she said. She pointed to the larger of the two couches. "All that stuff behind there is David's personal belongings that I haven't gone through yet."

The stacks of boxes were overflowing with clothes and items, everything that David had left behind.

"That's his guitar that he wrote most of his new songs on," she continued, pointing to the guitar next to the fireplace. "And this is the collage I made for the funeral."

Mike and I approached the large collage of photos that hung above the fireplace. We stood there quietly while we looked over all the pictures of David that spanned his time from high school, his prom, the bands he was in, and family cookouts. I was looking at his whole life in one poster-board-size collage of one hundred photos. It was just another reminder of the realization that he was truly gone.

Gretchen then brought us into Billy's room. Apparently he was a huge Star Wars fan. We dropped off our bags before she gave us the rest of the tour. Stacked on top of all of David's stuff in the den, leaning against the wall, was a small television. On the other side of that wall was the bathroom sink. After the tour of the apartment was finished, Gretchen, Mike, and I sat in the living room and talked.

Gretchen turned on the big-screen television to no particular channel for background noise.

"So you're the one who David has talked about. The one

who set up that solo show in Boston a few years ago," she said to me.

"Yep! I convinced him to come stay with me for a few days. The show at T.T. the Bear's Place was my baby."

"I have a copy of that show here somewhere on VHS."

For a moment, I couldn't even breathe. "Are you serious? I only have a copy of that show on CD. I'd love to see that show again!"

"I haven't seen it anywhere since David and I watched it a few months ago, but it's gotta be somewhere in this apartment. Unless my ex-husband has it at his house."

I wanted nothing more than for her to find that tape. The chance to actually see that show again, and not just hear it, filled me with so much excitement.

"Do you want to know how David got a copy of the show? He found someone selling it on eBay. Even after emailing them, telling them that he was David Reilly and requesting a copy of it, they still didn't believe him. He had to bid on it like everyone else!"

"Are you serious?" Mike asked, flabbergasted.

"Yes! Thankfully he won. I told him, I don't care how much it will cost us, you make sure you win that auction."

"I can't believe he had to bid on his own show!" Mike laughed.

"Even after all that, I bet the seller still didn't believe that David was the real person when he paid them!" I added.

"He won the auction, paid about twelve bucks for it or something, and we watched it as soon as it came in the mail."

Gretchen left the living room and tore apart her bedroom for the tape as quietly as she could while Billy slept. After a few minutes she came back with something else.

"I didn't find the tape, but I found these two pictures of David that I didn't even know I had!"

She handed us the photos. They exhibited a much younger David Reilly smiling.

"I'll see if Billy's dad has that tape at his apartment tomorrow. Now you have me thinking about it!"

"Yeah. I'd really love to see that again," I said.

In the middle of our conversation, David's voice came out of the television that Gretchen had put on as background noise. Not some voice-beyond-the-grave thing. It was the God Lives Underwater song, "No More Love."

We looked up and stopped talking instantly. Credits were rolling on a movie that had been on.

"I think *Johnny Mnemonic* was just on," Gretchen said.

After she checked the channel guide, she confirmed that it was indeed *Johnny Mnemonic* that had been playing. "No More Love" was the song that played during the end credits of the movie. We all exchanged a you-gotta-be-kidding-me look.

"That show you booked for him was really the first time David was truly happy after Monica's death, you know," she said to me.

"I still don't know that much about her death. I just know the little bit David told me over the last few years, but I never really felt comfortable probing."

"Well, you know that everyone knew her as Seven?"

"Yeah, but her real name was Monica."

"Right. Seven was a nickname given to her when she was a kid, and it just stuck. She was going out to buy Christmas gifts for David. I think that's why he carried so much guilt about her death. It was cold that day, and, on the way out the door, she grabbed one of his jackets. It was the kind with a big hood."

I nodded. I could picture why David could never let her go. So far every part of this story was just guilt stacked on top of guilt. Christmas gifts for him, his jacket . . .

"She was waiting to cross the train tracks. She looked to her right and didn't see a train coming, then she looked left and didn't see a train, but the large hood of David's coat took away her peripheral vision. She never looked right again, nor did she see that a train was approaching. She stepped out to cross the tracks. She was struck and dragged. We got the call that she was in the hospital, and I drove David. He was almost catatonic during the trip. I stupidly drove across the train tracks where she had been killed. When we reached the crossing, we saw them cleaning blood off the street and the tracks."

I took a deep breath and prepared for the rest of the story.

"David reacted right away. 'You don't think that's Seven's? Oh, God!' So I had to drive with David in the passenger seat over the tracks where the emergency vehicles were still washing away her blood. We got to the hospital, and David had to identify the body. They told him that she had died the moment the train struck her. It happened so fast and was so painless that she probably didn't even know she had been hit."

"That's the part David told me."

"He was literally on suicide watch for the rest of the month. He sat right there on that couch." She pointed to the long sofa in the den. "We constantly had a family member with him. We didn't let him go anywhere or do anything without supervision."

"You know, he contacted me on my birthday, the week of the accident. I thought he was wishing me a happy birthday, but he was just telling me about Monica's death."

"I'm surprised he even did that. For that first month, he was like an empty shell."

"What's the real story about his friend who died on his couch a few months before he died?" I probed.

"That was Amy. She was his girlfriend at the time. They were both in drug counseling together. That's where they met. She moved in with him at his last apartment and started using again behind his back. When he found out and told me about it, I told him that he needed to kick her out. He was doing so well with his sobriety, he didn't need some new girlfriend to fuck that up for him. After a few fights about it, David saw where I was coming from. He went back to his apartment, and told her that she needed to pack up and leave. She was no good for him trying to stay clean. She took it really hard, and begged and pleaded to stay. David stood his ground for his own health, and she packed up and left.

"Shortly after that she returned and asked if she could just use the phone. David let her in but told her that he was going out for a bit, because he didn't want to be there with her. He told her to make the phone call but to be gone before he returned. He didn't want to see her again. When David returned, Amy was dead on his couch. She had overdosed while he was gone, all because he threw her out."

"Holy shit!"

"David carried that guilt with him like a ton of bricks. If only he didn't throw her out and had tried to help her instead. Compounded with Monica's death, Amy committing suicide on his couch because he threw her out was just too much. Thankfully he was working on his solo material, so he had an outlet."

I shivered. One of the first stories David had ever told me about Heather, his ex-girlfriend, leaving him was because he couldn't get clean. The lyrics—just like those in "No More Love"—in "Please Come Back" from *How Humans R(x)* hit me and Mike like a baseball bat.

I made you leave for doing the wrong thing / When I wasn't sure of the right thing. / I believed I'd somehow spare your life. / You came back to get your things and use the phone / That's what you told me. / Found you here / But you were gone. / I was helpless / Fucking helpless!

"But with all that shit going on, you know David had been asked to be a drug counselor at a hospital," Gretchen said.

"Yeah. David had actually discussed that with me. I thought that was one of the greatest things I had heard. He told me that junkies would be more likely to listen to other junkies than someone who just had a wall full of diplomas."

"We all encouraged him to do it. I really think that's what helped him stay clean. He didn't want to let those people down. They were people who could have cared less about who David Reilly was. That's what he needed for his health."

It was 3:45 a.m. and time to get some sleep. Gretchen had to be up soon to take Billy to his service. Mike and I had been driving all evening, so we were eager to get some sleep.

Gretchen said good-night and left us to get ready on our own. We unrolled the sleeping bags on the bunk beds. I took the top, and Mike took the bottom.

After we brushed our teeth and got into our feety-pajamas—just kidding, but I do miss those!—I went into the den and sat on the couch that David used to sleep on. I shut off all the lights and talked to him out loud, but quietly enough so I wouldn't wake anyone else.

"I bet you never thought I would be here, staying in your apartment with your sister and nephew, without you here."

After I talked to him for a while, I went to bed and drifted off to sleep.

I was in David's old apartment waiting for Gretchen and Billy to finish getting ready for Billy's Reconciliation. The front door of the apartment opened, and I was slightly nervous about who was out there. I was by myself, so I would have to introduce myself without the help or comfort of Gretchen doing it for me.

The door closed, and David stood there in the living room. "Rocky! Why the hell are you here?"

"I need to see your grave. It's really important that we stick together, your family and me. I can't believe how sad I am all the time about you dying."

"Hey, me-han. You're being completely ridiculous, feeling that way," David said.

To hold back the tears, I focused on the sink. I couldn't keep the waterworks back, so I put my arms around his neck and cried. He pulled away and walked to the sink to wash his face for Billy's ceremony. When I looked in the mirror above the sink, I couldn't see his reflection. I darted my eyes from his body right in front of me to the mirror where he was elusive.

"David! You can't go! You can't leave!"

He just turned around so I could look at him. When I finally took my gaze off him, he disappeared.

Gretchen and I walked to Billy's Reconciliation ceremony alone.

There were no more dreams, or images, that I could recall that vividly during the rest of the night. When I awoke, the apartment was empty. Mike was still sleeping.

After I wrote down my dream in my notebook, Mike woke up, and we agreed that we should be showered and dressed by the time they came home from church.

We were both eager to meet David's nephew.

When they came home, Billy and I had a massive lightsaber battle in his bedroom while he was still in his suit. After that I told Gretchen about my dream in detail. I ended the description of us walking to the ceremony after David disappeared.

"How did you know that we had walked to church?" she inquired.

I paused. I hadn't known that they had walked there. We had walked in my dream though.

"Rocky!" Billy yelled. "Watch this move!"

He suddenly struck my stomach with a glowing lightsaber.

When he finally put down the weapon, he played some video games while he waited for us to leave to visit the grave. Gretchen had to change, so Mike and I watched Billy skateboard around the screen.

"Hey, Billy?" Gretchen called from the other room. "Do you know where the tape of Uncle David is when he played that show in Boston?"

"I don't know!" he yelled back, without missing a beat on his controllers.

"Do you think it was one of the tapes that you took to your dad's house?" Gretchen came into the living room dressed casually, no longer in her church clothes. "Billy, do you think it might be over there?"

"I don't know."

"We can call him later and see if Billy's dad has the tape at his place across the street," she said to us.

"It's no big deal. If it's here, I'd really like to see it," I said.

David would definitely disapprove of the tape being at the person's house who had stolen his Robot Teen America money.

"Are you ready to go?" she asked Billy as a cue to turn off the television. "Every time we visit David, we bring him something and leave it at the headstone. We have this sunflower for today."

The plush sunflower with a smiley face on it reminded me of something out of *Teletubbies*. I thought it would make David laugh.

It wasn't really raining outside, but it was drizzling enough for us to grab our raincoats. I sat in the passenger seat of Gretchen's car, and Mike and Billy rode in the back. We headed straight for the grave.

The cemetery was less than twenty minutes away. During the ride, we kept the conversation light and talked to Billy about the music he liked. He had an unusual obsession with the rap artist, Eminem. He also admitted to us that his least favorite lyric by Uncle David was in the Heavy song "Lost" when David sang, "*I did everything I could do. / I did what I could / And I would die for you.*"

Gretchen acted as our tour guide. She pointed out places with historical significance and gave us a brief history of the area. I still just didn't completely accept that we were actually traveling to see David's grave. I would be seeing his name printed on a piece of granite.

When we arrived at Holy Sepulchre Cemetery in Cheltenham, the drizzle became more of a nuisance than actual rain. Gretchen maneuvered the car through the streets of the cemetery, and, with every turn, I found myself holding my breath.

The car slowed down, and I knew this was it.

I oddly became very calm. The car came to a complete stop, and we got out. Gretchen grabbed the smiley-faced sunflower. There was a very distinct hush outside. The drizzle and the softness of the landscape made the air somber and comforting.

The tombstone, I noticed as we walked toward it, had REILLY written in the center at the top. *David F. "Deagle"* was inscribed on the left side of the stone with his birth and death dates, *1971–2005*.

Seeing David's name on a tombstone wasn't what sent shivers down my back, but the fact that they had yet to plant grass over where the casket was buried. In front of the tombstone was just dirt. David was under there.

Gretchen put the sunflower in front of his tombstone and took a step back.

"Did you see who I brought to visit you?" she asked as she looked at his grave. "I brought Rocky and Mike."

Although I kept my head down, I still watched the headstone while Gretchen said hello to her brother. She spoke to him out loud for a moment, and I listened to what she was saying. I stared at the letters of his name, and my brain traveled back through all the memories I had of him.

The cemetery we stood in was just rows upon rows of the same landscape with different names inscribed on different headstones. It just felt so impersonal. Every time I looked up, seeing David's name on one of those stones somehow managed to bring me right back to reality. Although I was close to his body, I was farther away from him than I ever had been since the day we had met.

Was he here listening to us? Was he here watching us? Did he know that we had come to visit him? Did he understand what it meant to us that we were here?

"What does the name 'Deagle' on his headstone mean?" I asked.

"When we were very young, David had a tiny beagle stuffed animal that I would always steal from him. He wrote a 'D' on it to mark it as his own. From that moment on I called the stuffed animal, 'Deagle's Beagle.' Don't know why, but it stuck."

Gretchen then told Billy to get in the car so Mike and I could have some alone time with David, and say what we wanted to say to him.

I approached the tombstone, put the palm of my hand on top of it, and felt its jagged topography. When I breathed in, the air was cold and sharp. Somehow my body felt warm as I stood there.

I was silent longer than Mike. I listened as Mike talked to David out loud. The wind wasn't blowing that hard, but it felt like Mike's words were still being taken away and delivered somewhere else. When Mike was finished, I asked him if I could have a moment alone with David. He went back to the car and closed the door.

I kept my eyes on the dirt where I knew David's body was as I approached the tombstone.

"Hey, me-han. So here we are," I spoke out loud as I said my formal good-byes to him.

After a few minutes of speaking to him, and a few minutes of reflecting quietly, I decided that it was enough. I had used up all my good-byes. It was time to turn away and return to the car.

When I got in the passenger side, Gretchen asked me hold on a second. She got out by herself and stood at the foot of the dirt rectangle. We could all see that she was saying something but we couldn't hear her words. We didn't even breathe as we watched Gretchen speak to David's tombstone.

It seemed like a full minute had gone by, but it was really just a few seconds. The smiley-faced sunflower that we had placed at David's headstone suddenly blew over on its side. It wasn't specifically the sunflower that gave me the chills, but more the way Gretchen turned her head and looked at us in the car. She had a look of disbelief on her face.

Gretchen walked around the dirt rectangle, picked up the sunflower, and put it upright again. She returned to the car. I could tell that she was anxious to tell us something. I could even see it in her eyes.

"Okay, that was freaky," she said as she got into the car. "Look, I'm shaking and have goose bumps."

"What? What happened?" I asked.

"I said the prayer that I always say when I come to visit

him. When I was done, I said out loud, 'Look, I brought your friends here to visit you. Please give me a sign that you're here, and know that Rocky and Mike are visiting you.' And no less than a second later was when the sunflower fell over. David knows you are here. I am sure of it."

I looked at Mike, and I could tell from his face what was going through his head. I got chills all over my body. We kept our gazes glued to the tombstone as Gretchen put the car in Drive, and we drove away.

Gretchen felt that it was important to take us on a tour of where David had lived, so we drove around Philadelphia and its surrounding suburbs. She took us to the house where the Reilly family had lived until she was two years old. Then we stopped at the house where they had lived until David was in the sixth grade. Mike and I snapped pictures at each of these landmarks of David's childhood. We also drove by the townhouse where David lived when he was with Monica, and the hospital he was taken to the night before he died, where he eventually succumbed to the infection and passed away.

Gretchen took us by Edgar Allen Poe's house, the William Bell Tower, the Liberty Bell, Penn Station, Penn University, and the Philadelphia Eagles' football stadium. While stopped at a red light, we even witnessed a drug deal go down right next to my passenger-side window. We got to see the beautiful and the ugly side of the city that day.

Gretchen took us to 813 North Third Street, the place where David was living with his fiancée, Rachel, the night he had died. Gretchen stopped the car outside the gates and pointed to his door. Mike and I took a few pictures.

It was past lunchtime, and we were famished. Mike and I mentioned that we had never eaten authentic Philly cheesesteaks before. Our tour of the area, and the trip down David's memory lane, ended with Gretchen taking us to Jim's Steaks.

Jim's Steaks supposedly was only one of two sub shops in Philadelphia who could boast that they invented the cheesesteak sub and get away with it. The line snaked from inside the store, out the front door, around the corner, and down a side street.

"It's like this every weekend," Gretchen said. "But it's worth the wait."

The wait looked like it would be at least an hour just to order our food. How many chances would I have to eat an authentic cheesesteak in Philadelphia? While we were waiting in line, Stephanie called me, and I told her about everything we had done and everything we had seen. When we finally got into the shop, we saw that they were selling Jim's Steaks T-shirts. There was no way we were going home without one.

Finally we got our Philly cheesesteaks and headed back to Gretchen's apartment. For some reason, I kept getting tongue-tied, and I called them chilly pheesesteaks. Billy thought this was incredibly funny. For the rest of the weekend, the term *chilly pheesesteaks* became an ongoing joke.

"Why don't you call your dad and ask him if he has the tape of Uncle David at his house?" Gretchen asked Billy on the ride home as she dialed the number on her cell phone and handed it to Billy in the backseat. "He's staying at his dad's tonight," she whispered to me.

"Dad?" Billy said into the phone. "Do you have that tape of Uncle David playing that show?" After a few minutes, he handed Gretchen back the phone and said, "He says he doesn't have it."

"Where could that tape be?"

We got back to the apartment and sat in the living room. We opened up our *chilly pheesesteaks* and watched television. Billy went back to the video game he had been playing earlier.

We talked about how I gave David a birthday gift every year. I was telling Gretchen how, when I worked at Suncoast, I bought David movies for his birthday and sent them to him at this address.

"Wait, don't tell me," she said. "You sent him *Billy Madison* and *Happy Gilmore* one year!"

"Wow! How do you even remember that?" I asked.

"I don't know. I just remember David telling me about it once. I don't think I saw those in his stuff though, when I went through everything after he died."

"That's okay. He said he used to bring them on the road to watch in the tour bus. I'm sure something happened to them along the way."

"Yeah. That's amazing that I even remember those two movies," she said. "It was like I just heard the names in my ears. It sparked a memory of David having a friend that would send him movies all the time."

After a while of hanging out in the living room, it was time for Billy to go over to his dad's house across the street.

Then all of a sudden, Mike got sick. He went into the bathroom and was in there for a long time. Long enough to worry Gretchen. I even thought that this trip might be over, and we would have to return home already. Mike apologized when he came out the bathroom and said that he needed to lie down. I think he was embarrassed too. He was dizzy, and he looked terrible.

Once he closed the door to Billy's bedroom to lie down,

I sat with Gretchen in the living room. The topic of the tape of the show from T.T. the Bear's Place came up again. It was really driving Gretchen nuts that she couldn't find it.

"You know, as great as it would be to see that show again, I do have a copy of it on CD," I told her, to make her feel better if she couldn't find it.

"Really? Well, if I give you a copy of the show on DVD, if I ever find it, would you mail me a copy of the show on CD?"

"Of course!" I replied.

"I really want to find it while you're here since you were the one who set up that show in the first place. The only thing left to do is ask David. I've torn this entire apartment apart since last night looking for that damn tape!" Then she said, "David, if you're here, please give us another sign. Don't make the cemetery a fluke."

There was nothing for a full minute, just silence. I secretly hoped that something would happen so the incident at the cemetery couldn't be blamed on just the wind. Another minute went by, and we stayed silent.

Right when I was about to change the subject to lessen the blow of disappointment, Gretchen stood up. "The tape is in my room!"

She practically sprinted down the hallway. She returned to the living room with a VHS tape in her hands.

"You have got to be kidding me," I said.

"It was in my desk drawer next to my bed. I thought I had checked there last night! I just got this overwhelming feeling to check those drawers again. Here it is."

It seemed that had David told his sister where the tape was when she asked him. She was holding the infamous show in her hands, after all these years. Gretchen asked if I wanted to watch it right away, but I suggested that we watch it later that night when Mike was awake. He would've killed me if we told him that Gretchen had found the tape and we watched it while he was sick in the other room.

Maybe we'd watch it with a drink, and we could really enjoy it. I really wasn't ready to see it in the daylight, or sober, especially this soon after visiting his grave.

The layout of Gretchen's apartment was such that, by entering the front door, there was a staircase to the left and a hallway straight ahead. The hallway went to her apartment and the staircase went to the space where David used to live. It was bigger than a studio apartment but smaller than a one-bedroom.

The weekend that Mike and I visited, the upstairs space was being rented to a French chemist who was doing research. His name was Marc, and he spoke enough English to carry on a conversation. While we were in the living room talking, Marc came home, and Gretchen called him in. She introduced me as David's friend, Rocky. We talked with Marc for a few minutes. Then he said he needed to go upstairs to shower and change, but he would come down afterward to hang out.

"Is it weird having someone you don't know living in David's old space?" I asked her.

"Sometimes. But he's a really nice guy. I was waiting for him to come home to ask if I could take you up there. That's really where David lived. Yeah, he used to crash and stay down here on that couch in the den, but upstairs was really his place."

After Marc went upstairs, Mike finally emerged from Billy's room looking sleepy, but a hundred times better.

"How are you feeling?" I asked.

"Great. Whatever it was passed, and I slept it off. How long was I asleep?"

"About two hours or so."

"Really? Oh, man. I'm so sorry!"

"Why are you apologizing?" Gretchen asked.

"I feel really bad. I don't know what happened. At one point there, I really thought we were going to have to leave. I feel great now though."

"Guess what Gretchen found while you were sleeping!"

"The tape of the T.T. the Bear's Place show?"

"Yep!"

"Where was it?"

"In my bedroom in a drawer. I asked David to help me find it, and it was like I just knew exactly where it was," Gretchen answered.

"No doubt he answered you," Mike said solemnly.

"Yeah. We wanted to wait and watch it with you tonight. You missed Marc. He's a French chemist who lives upstairs in David's old place," I said.

I knew this would be interesting to Mike since he had been a French major, spending a semester studying in France. Mike had even worked for Air France after he graduated college. Unfortunately he was laid off directly after the 9/11 attacks.

"He'll be back down shortly. He just went upstairs to shower. Does anyone want a drink?" Gretchen asked.

"I'd like to buy a bottle of David's favorite beer and toast to him tonight," Mike said.

Gretchen agreed. She knew exactly what beer Mike was talking about. It was the beer that I couldn't buy for David when he stayed with me because he didn't he have any identification on him. It was Raspberry Belgian Lambic Ale.

"I'll take a Captain and Coke," I said.

"I'll wait until we can get the Lambic ale," Mike said.

"When Marc comes back down, we'll go to the only place in the area that sells it and get some."

"You should really try it," Mike said.

"Nah. You know I don't drink beer. I can't stand the taste of it."

"It doesn't taste like real beer," Gretchen replied.

"You'd probably like it," Mike added.

I shrugged as Gretchen handed me my rum and Coke.

"While we're waiting for Marc to come back, can you tell me about David's death? I got the online version from websites and obituaries, and then I got the versions from the Rooster and Dave Sherman, some other friends, and people David was working with. I feel like I only have part of what actually happened."

"Okay. You know that he was living with his girlfriend, Rachel, when it happened. David went to bed Friday night around ten o'clock and said good-night to Rachel. She stayed up to watch TV or something. At two o'clock in the morning, she went to bed and slid under the covers next to him. She hadn't noticed that anything was really wrong yet. At four o'clock, she woke up and realized that he wasn't breathing or responding to her, so she called 9-1-1. She did what little CPR she knew on him until the ambulance got there, and then they rushed him to the hospital. He had shallow breathing and a very faint pulse. He was still alive, but they had no idea how long he had gone without oxygen. She called me from the hospital, and I rushed over there. I was with him until he died. They got a steady pulse back, but he could only breathe with the assistance of machines. He had slipped into a coma. He was completely unresponsive to any stimulation. His natural reflexes were gone, and he wasn't reacting to any of their tests. They told us that, even if he started breathing again on his own, they were very doubtful that he would be anything more than a vegetable for the rest of his life. They felt there was too much brain damage from the lack of oxygen. He would never be David again, even if he pulled through. He was hooked up to machines and unresponsive to any stimuli for twenty-four hours straight in the hospital. What had happened was the infection that he had in his tooth for so many years—and not getting it properly treated—finally started the domino effect. The infection entered his bloodstream and ruptured the ulcer that he had in his stomach from years of drug abuse."

I nodded. I knew that David had problems with his teeth almost the entire time that we were friends. I also knew of the ulcer. David used to joke that it was going to be the death of him. That was his way of dealing with his pain.

"After almost twenty-six hours of being in the hospital in a coma, at 5:50 Sunday morning, October 16, he passed away. If you want the technical reason for him slipping into the coma in his sleep on Friday night, this was what was explained to us. The infection in his tooth got into his bloodstream and ruptured the ulcer in his stomach. He bled out in his stomach, and the fluid backed up into his lungs as he slept. Then he suffocated and went into cardiac arrest. So it was a string of events that caused his death. Ultimately it was the ulcer bleeding out that caused the respiratory arrest."

Mike and I were speechless. I was trying to put myself there in the hospital, but I couldn't. It all seemed surreal. David would have been a vegetable for the rest of his life. No matter what, he was gone. It just seemed so unfair. It was like something from a nightmare.

Stephanie called me again, right before Marc came back. Since Stephanie also spoke French, after having spent a few months in Oxford, England, as an au pair for a French-speaking family, she was telling me things to say to Marc in French. He laughed at my pronunciation.

Gretchen asked Marc if he wanted to stay and hang out with me while they went to get the Lambic ale. Gretchen and Mike left, and Marc and I stayed and watched television. He asked me a ton of questions—in his best broken English—about American college and commented on how different it was in France.

After what felt like an eternity, Gretchen and Mike finally returned.

"What took you guys so long?"

"Well, we passed a local bar that I used to go to with David, so we stopped for a drink and lost track of time," Gretchen said.

"You guys were at a bar having a drink?" I asked.

"Did you guys get to know each other?" she asked Marc.

He said that we had a nice conversation.

Mike and Gretchen sat down and opened one of their Belgian Lambic Ales. They asked if I wanted to try some. Since it was David's favorite drink, and we were here to toast him, why not?

"To David," Mike said.

We all took a drink.

"Should we watch the T.T. the Bear's Place show?" I asked.

"Do you want to see one of my brother's shows?" Gretchen asked Marc.

"Sure!"

"This one was from about five years ago in Boston. Rocky was the one who set up this show and basically did everything for it."

Gretchen got up and approached the VCR. I realized that I was already holding my breath. Hearing an audio version of this show was one thing, but getting to actually see David again was another. Of his entire two-hundred-plus gigs in his career, this was the one that felt like it really was mine as much as it was David's.

Directly to the left of the television in the living room was David's old laptop that Gretchen had left open, but was turned off, on a small end table. Although it had been there all weekend, we hadn't yet paid it any attention. We were told, during our first tour of the apartment, that it was David's. Gretchen had retrieved it after he had died. She had set it up on the small table next to the television screen because sometimes she watched movies on it.

"This show was breathtaking," Mike said to Marc.

"You were there?" he asked.

"Yeah. I was there with my girlfriend at the time. It was one of the most emotional things I had ever seen."

Gretchen pushed the tape into the VCR and sat down with the remote. She pressed Play, and the television screen went black for a moment.

"I wonder if they started recording early enough to catch me on the stage doing David's soundcheck with his guitars," I said. I thought it would be weird to see myself when the tape started.

The tape began at the exact moment that my soundcheck of Yellow #1 riffs was over, and I was jumping off the small stage. I could see my baseball hat and my profile disappear off the side of screen.

"There you are!" Gretchen yelled. The shot of me was under half a second.

We could hear the crowd cheer as David came into view of the camera and sat down with a guitar. It was strange to see David again on television, especially in a setting so familiar to me. His hair was all messy, and he was in his pajamas. I had forgotten what he looked like back then, and how thin and frail he was. Nevertheless he definitely looked happy.

We watched him open the show with "Miss You More Than Anything" from *Up off the Floor*. Although the sound on the tape was an exact copy of the audio I had, adding in the visual of the show made it feel completely new.

The first song of the show came to an end. Even though David's old laptop was turned off, and the screen was completely black, we heard the whirling sound of the hard drive as it powered up by itself. It only took a moment for the screen to come to life as David was getting ready to go into "Can't Come Down" on the television.

There, on his laptop, was a picture of David pointing.

"What the fuck?!" Mike exclaimed.

"That was David's last wallpaper picture on his laptop," Gretchen explained hesitantly. "It's a picture of him in the studio working on *How Humans R(x)*."

The wallpaper image of him pointed to the television screen where he was still playing.

"How is that even possible?" I whispered.

"I have no idea."

"It looks like he's pointing at himself on the TV screen," Mike added.

"This is so fucked up!" I said.

"There's no way that this is a coincidence or that the laptop had a power surge," Gretchen started. "Think about it. All weekend we've been having signs from him that he knows you're here. I thought the sunflower at the grave was amazing, but this is just crazy!"

"It's like he really is saying hello. What else could it be? We're watching a tape of the show that you organized and the laptop, with a wallpaper of him that just so happens to be pointing at the TV, turns on all by itself after the first song finishes?" Mike said.

I think even Marc was getting freaked out, and he didn't even know David.

"Should we turn it off or leave it on?" I asked.

"Clearly he wants it on right now," Gretchen answered.

We finished watching the forty-five-minute show with David's laptop turned on, pointing at himself, from one screen to the next.

The concert ended, and Gretchen explained to Marc that David used to live in the apartment where Marc was staying upstairs. She asked if he would mind taking us up there, so Mike and I could see where David called home for so many years of our friendship. Marc agreed.

We climbed the staircase in the hallway between the front door and Gretchen's living room and entered the upstairs apartment. It was the perfect size for a single person. It was small but laid out perfectly. There was a kitchen, a bedroom, bathroom, and a small living room/sitting area. I could picture David here, happy, with a guitar and a keyboard.

David always had only a few personal items. All he really

needed was just a place to stay with his family and to be able to write music without being bothered.

On the floor there was a tag—which had obviously been attached to Marc's luggage at some point—that had a cartoon diagram of a man trying to lift something and hurting his back. The word *HEAVY* was printed across the top of the tag. Obviously the tag had been placed on the luggage to mark which bags were heavier than others, but there was something weird about the tag all by itself on the floor of David's old apartment, since David had those two Heavy songs.

We went to bed shortly after our trip upstairs. That night I didn't dream of David. He had probably exhausted all of his attempts of saying hello throughout the day while we were awake.

Sunday morning arrived, and Billy was already back from his dad's. He was in the living room playing video games when Mike and I woke up.

We had a lunch date with Suzanne around noon, and she lived almost an hour away. We also didn't want to overstay our welcome with Gretchen and Billy.

Gretchen made us a pot of coffee, and we sat in the living room.

"I have something that I want to give to both of you," she said. "But if they're not ready before you leave, then I will just mail them to you."

"Okay," I said. My interest was piqued.

"After David died, I was sent copies of tapes of David's

old bands that he was in before God Lives Underwater, even before he met Jeff. I'm burning them for you guys right now."

Mike and I were speechless. My eyes must have gotten really big.

"That's amazing!" Mike said.

I was in disbelief that we were going to be able to hear these songs. It was like being handed the Holy Grail.

What Gretchen was actually making for us were copies of the homemade demos of three old bands David was in, between 1988–1989: Kan Do Kill, which only had a two-song demo called *Wintertree*; A Sheet of Metal had only recorded an eight-song album called *Fine Trash Alloy*; and Killing the Barrowbird was only a five-song album called *Sunflowers*.

"I remember the night A Sheet of Metal recorded *Fine Trash Alloy*," Gretchen said, reminiscing. "It was in David's bedroom when he was in high school. Neil, the singer, was over for the night, and all I wanted to do was go to sleep. I heard the songs over and over through the wall. I was so pissed off at him. I just wanted them to stop the noise and to go to bed. Little did I know how important it would become so many years later." She paused. "Also I'm going to let you guys go through his personal stuff in the corner and pick out whatever you want to have as a keepsake. I'd rather have his personal stuff go to friends than be given away to strangers or destroyed."

"You really don't have to do that," Mike said.

I agreed. There was something weird about leaving here with David's shoes or cologne or whatever. But then I thought that, if we came across the pajamas that he wore at the show at T.T. the Bear's Place, I might just be inclined to take those for sentimental reasons.

We rummaged through the crates of his stuff and came upon a small toiletry bag. Gretchen opened it and inside were a bunch of blue tattered guitar picks.

"These are the picks that he used when he was writing the *Inside* album," she said. "He sat right there on that couch and pretty much wrote the entire album, finishing a song a night. Do you guys want these?"

I felt better taking David's guitar picks that he used to write and record an album than some other more personal items. Mike and I agreed, and Gretchen dropped them in our hands. I put mine safely in my wallet.

She went back to the crates and commented that she really hadn't gone through everything yet. It was still too hard to look through his stuff.

Then she came upon a large case of CDs. She flipped through it. Some were burned; others were blank, and some were bought from the store. Suddenly there was a disc with my handwriting on it: Cat Stevens's *Tea for the Tillerman*.

"Stop! Go back!" I yelled. "That's the copy I burned for David when he stayed with me back in 2001, the weekend of the T.T. the Bear's Place show!"

"Do you want it back?" she asked.

"No. I still have the original. It was a gift for David. I'd rather just leave it."

She closed the case.

"You know, I keep feeling like David is trying to tell us something right now," Gretchen said. "I'm not hearing his voice, but I keep getting the feeling to 'look behind the TV.' I don't know what that means."

Mike and I shook our heads. That didn't have any significance for us either.

"For some reason, there seems to be some urgency to it too," she said.

Gretchen stepped toward her big television in the living room. David's laptop was turned off and black again. She even asked Billy to pause his video game, and she pulled out her television to investigate what was behind it. She found an old photograph that had fallen behind there, which didn't include David, but nothing else. She slid the television back.

"That's weird. I keep getting this feeling to look behind the TV, and I don't know why."

She let it drop, and we shrugged it off.

Mike and I took turns showering and getting dressed. After we packed, we knew we only had a few minutes left with Gretchen and Billy. My heart suddenly felt heavy, not knowing when I would ever see them again. I felt like we had bonded so much in just thirty-six hours.

"Your discs aren't done yet, so I'll just mail them to you," she said. "I'm also going to put the T.T. the Bear's Place show onto DVD for you and mail that out as well."

"That would be awesome!" I replied. "I can burn you the audio version of it."

"That would be great."

Mike and I gave Billy a hug, and Gretchen walked us to the front door past the stairs that led up to David's old apartment. At the door I hugged Gretchen good-bye and thanked her for everything.

"No, thank you! I feel like I had more contact with David this weekend while you were here than any time since he passed. I should be thanking you. I really feel like he knew you guys were here and he just kept popping up. I just wish I knew what 'look behind the TV' meant."

"Maybe we'll never know," Mike said.

We walked to my car and pulled out of the driveway.

I called Suzanne and told her that we were on our way. After the hour long drive, we arrived at the spot where we were going to meet her.

Once Suzanne showed up, we drove to a Ruby Tuesday's and ordered lunch. We shared David stories, and I realized that Suzanne actually had the most contact with David during the few years (2002–2004) where I had the least contact. It was interesting to hear her fill in some of the gaps for me.

While we were waiting for our food, my cell phone rang, and it was Gretchen.

"I have good news and bad news. What do you want to hear first?"

"The good news," I said.

"I found out what 'look behind the TV' means."

"What?"

"That's the 'bad news' part. You left your glasses here in the bathroom."

I understood how that was bad news. We were already an hour closer to home, so to go back and get my glasses would be an hour back to Gretchen's, and then another hour just to get back to this point on our return. It was already later in the afternoon than we wanted it to be.

What I didn't understand was what 'look behind the TV' had to do with me leaving my glasses there in the bathroom.

"Okay. Going back would add another two hours to our ride home."

"Well, I can just wrap them up really good and overnight them to you."

I decided that was probably a bad idea. "Nah. We'll just shoot back as fast as we can."

We finished our lunch with Suzanne and made our way back to Gretchen's apartment. When we arrived, she was waiting at the front door for us.

Mike and I both got out of the car and went back inside.

"The other good news is that I finished both your discs!"

That alone was worth the trip back to her apartment! She handed us the discs with *David's Teen Years* written in Sharpie on them.

"Let me show you what 'look behind the TV' meant," she said as she brought us back into the den with all of David's stuff. "See where David's old TV is against the wall?"

David's small television was piled on top of a bunch of boxes and was leaned against a wall.

"Come and see what's on the other side of that wall where the TV is."

I looked, and then it all made sense. David's old television leaned against the wall that separated the bathroom from the den, and the television rested just a few inches above the sink on the other side of that wall in the den.

"Look what's on the top of the sink," she said.

My glasses! "Holy fucking shit!"

"I know. I still have goose bumps from it. When I found your glasses, I was like, wow! David was trying to tell me to look behind his TV, not mine, and that's why we didn't find anything. He was trying to catch you to tell you that you had forgotten your glasses before you left."

"Unbelievable," Mike replied.

"Well," I said, "we really should end our visit on that note."

Gretchen walked us to the door again. This time I had my glasses in my hand and the *David's Teen Years* disc. I immediately put it in the disc changer, once we got back in the car.

"Do you want to stop by the funeral home that held David's funeral to take some pictures, since we're back here anyway?" Mike asked.

I remembered that we had passed it on the way in, so I agreed. I only had three pictures left in my camera, so we pulled over and shot the last pictures of the outside of the Emil J. Ciavarelli Funeral Home.

When that was done, we headed back home to Massachusetts with the music of David's old high school bands filling up the inside of my car. One of the demos of David's old bands was titled *Sunflowers*. There seemed to be an uncanny sunflower theme that surrounded our visit.

A week later, when we got the pictures back from the trip, we realized David knocking over the sunflower at the grave wasn't the only way he had made his presence known while we were there. One of the photographs of the tombstone and the sunflower also contained an orange mist in the photo about six inches off the dirt where his body lay.

It looked like it traveled through the sunflower and stopped at the base of the tombstone.

Back in December 2005, I had seen From Autumn to Ashes play an amazing show at Axis. They were touring on the *Abandon Your Friends* album. The drive and passion to be in a band again suddenly came out of nowhere. It was so powerful that it was almost crippling.

The very next day after the show, I jumped online and searched for bands looking for singers. A band out of Beverly was looking for a singer, and their influences matched up with mine. Although I had never actually sung that style of music before, I shot them an email anyway. After my audition, I got the job, and we wrote songs almost immediately. Once again I was back in my element.

We had six songs written when Stephanie and I confirmed that I was going to move to Georgia to be with her. It was only fair that I told my new band that I would be leaving. I made the announcement at the next practice. I figured it wouldn't be that big of a problem for them to find a new singer, as we hadn't even played a show yet and had only been together for three months.

The guitarist, Josh, surprised me when he told me that he wanted to move to Georgia with me to keep the band going. He wanted to get a fresh start on a lot of things in his life. I couldn't believe it.

In May 2006, two months after Mike and I had visited David's grave, Josh and I moved the band to Georgia together. He moved in with me and Stephanie in our apartment.

Josh and I immediately scouted for a bass player and a drummer to finish the new lineup after we got settled in. Stephanie was friends with the drummer of a local band called Ashes of Osiris. After she introduced us to Jason, we asked him to keep an eye out for anyone looking to join a prog-metal band. None of us expected what happened next.

Ashes of Osiris broke up less than a month later. Jason and their bass player, Tim, tried out for our new band. We clicked immediately. Our new lineup was now in place. I was back in my first real band again after a full year of being removed from the music world when The Grave Machine had broken up.

Josh and I still had the six songs that we had written in Massachusetts in our back pocket. We used those as a springboard to get the new band off the ground. We named the band Transpose.

We recorded our debut album, *A Delicate Impact*, in 2007. While we were in the studio recording the album, we covered God Lives Underwater's "Miss You More Than Anything" from *Up off the Floor*, as a bonus track.

We sampled David talking to the audience during the T.T. the Bear's Place show in the song to add more of his spirit into our version.

Luckily Gretchen was going to Disney World with Billy for a week. Stephanie and I made plans to drive to Orlando and spend the day with them at Universal Studios. It was great to spend the whole day with them. Stephanie and Gretchen bonded right away. Gretchen told me that Billy was so excited to see me again.

Stephanie and I took Billy on rides, and Gretchen became less of David's sister to us and more like family. After riding the rides and spending all day with them, Stephanie and I made the drive back up to Georgia.

Gretchen informed us she and Billy were making one more trip to Disney World later that year. We all agreed we should meet up again for the day. This time we would visit Epcot Center.

Just prior to that second trip, Billy surprised me and called me all by himself without Gretchen even knowing it. He just wanted say hello and to thank me for some Star Wars stuff I sent him in the mail.

When I told Gretchen, she said, "I had no idea he did that! You know what he has started calling you?"

"No. What?"

"He's been calling you Uncle Rocky."

"Does that mean that Stephanie will have to be called Auntie Rocky when we see you later this year at Epcot?" I joked.

I thought how funny it was that even David's nephew was calling me Uncle Rocky, all because of a hat I wore to a concert back in June 1995. It was amazing how strong a bond and a positive friendship came from such a great loss.

During the summer of 2006, there was a buzz again from the God Lives Underwater online community.

Jeff Turzo had finally started a new band with the rest of the guys in God Lives Underwater, and Matt Mahaffey, who was the singer of the band Self, on vocals. This new band, called Wired All Wrong, was essentially God Lives Underwater with a new singer under a different name.

There was much debate and stipulation amongst the God Lives Underwater fan community. Would Wired All Wrong sound like God Lives Underwater? If they did, which album would they resemble the most? Would they play old God Lives Underwater songs live?

Wired All Wrong's debut album, *Break out the Battle Tapes*, was released on September 12, 2006. They sounded more like the singer's old band, Self, rather than God Lives Underwater with a new singer.

As much as *Break out the Battle Tapes* was a fantastic album, Wired All Wrong was proof that only one band had the ability to truly home in that unique sound. Wired All Wrong fell short of what made God Lives Underwater songs magical.

October 21, 2006, was my wedding day.

Both Josh and Jason from Transpose were groomsmen in my wedding and we all flew to Massachusetts together. Dann and Mike were also groomsmen. Gretchen was sent an invitation but unfortunately had to decline due to a previous commitment.

The head table at the reception had an empty chair set up next to Stephanie's bridesmaids, prepared just as if someone would be sitting there. The only difference was that there were two beautiful yellow roses lying across the plate.

One rose was for Stephanie's cousin who had passed away four months earlier. The other yellow rose was for David. We felt that it was important they sat up there with us at the head table, so they would know that there was still a spot for them at our wedding.

During the dancing part of the reception, Mike asked me to go with him to David's chair. As we approached the head table, he pulled out an unopened bottle of Raspberry Belgium Lambic Ale from a brown bag and set it in front of the yellow roses. He also produced a champagne glass with a gold rim at the top. The glass had *Lindemans Kriek/Peche/Pomme/Framboise Merchant du Vin* printed around it. Mike placed the glass next to the bottle and the yellow roses.

We didn't say anything to each other when he did that. We just took a moment and stared at the unopened bottle of

David's favorite beverage. Although this was the happiest day of my life, Mike and still I took those few moments to speak to David. We knew when it was time to return to the blaring music and the festivities happening around us.

I joined my wife on the dance floor with the image of David sitting in his chair at the head table, reaching over the yellow roses and grabbing the ale.

"Thanks, me-han!"

EPILOGUE

"You've gone and left me lost. / Will I ever see you again?"
Heavy: "Lost"

A few months after our wedding, Stephanie became pregnant with our first child. Bizarrely her due date was on the second anniversary of David's death, October 16, 2007! It was actually Stephanie's suggestion to honor David's memory forever through our child's name. Analise Reilly Paone arrived a bit early on September 26, 2007.

In 2008 Gretchen was awarded legal Power of Attorney for the Estate of David Reilly. This meant that she was David's voice in all decisions regarding his music and finances. Any future God Lives Underwater business, and all of the business with his other bands and solo career, was handed to her.

Once this happened, I immediately contacted her about the possibility of getting *How Humans R(x)* a commercial release. Gretchen explained to me that she wasn't prepared emotionally yet to take on such a task, but she did agree that David's final album should be released to the fans at some point. Another roadblock that I was facing was that the songs, although completed, weren't exactly mastered for a proper release.

The album had been finished since 2005. However, Chris Swartz, the owner of the record label, who had paid for the recording of the album, had signed over complete control of the masters to David's producer, Walt Bass, as payment for working on the album. Legally owning the album was sort of Walt's paycheck, because David died before Walt was ever paid. Since the masters were under Walt's control, he wasn't doing anything with them.

Gretchen and I came to an agreement. She would lobby to receive the rights of the recordings from Walt in order to get me the songs. It was then up to me to find an engineer who would master the album. Once the album was finished, it would be sent to her for approval. If she didn't like the way it sounded, it would be shelved forever. If she liked it, then I would be in charge of the official release.

All of Gretchen's requests for the tapes were denied by Walt.

I contacted Jeff Cavanaugh again, who was still running Creative Armada. He was the most appropriate logical starting point for *How Humans R(x)*.

Since I couldn't obtain copies of the masters from Walt, Jeff agreed to listen to the versions of the songs that David had emailed to me before David died, to see if Jeff could piece the songs together himself. Our goal was to bring the album as close to the industry standard as we could, using the earlier versions of the songs that David himself had liked enough to send to people. I mailed Jeff the songs, and he spent his spare time working on finishing *How Humans R(x)*.

When Jeff finished the album in 2009, he sent it back to me for approval. I told Gretchen that I had a finished version of *How Humans R(x)* that I thought she would be very happy with. I told her that we were going to keep Jeff's original artwork that David had approved back in 2005. She asked me to send her a copy of the album.

I mailed her two copies and held my breath. It took her almost a month to get back to me. I didn't want to hound her about it, but I was impatient and a bit nervous that she might hate the way it came out. She finally emailed me and asked me to give her a call.

I was so scared that she was going to nix the whole thing. This was the last album by David, the album that so many God Lives Underwater fans, and fans of his solo material, were waiting to hear. The entire release of this album now rested on our shoulders.

Gretchen said that she loved it, except for one detail. The album originally had eleven songs on it. She requested that "Love Will Complicate," the duet between David and Brittany Garrison, be removed from the official release of the album. Gretchen said that there was some bad blood between her and Brittany, ever since David's death. There were some disputes between them over the legal rights to the songs that David had helped write on her album. Since Gretchen didn't want Brittany's presence on David's album, "Love Will Complicate" was removed.

Jeff, Gretchen, and I had a phone meeting about the release. Since we were putting it out ourselves without any label attachment, we decided that I would be in charge of getting the album printed. Gretchen also felt that only die-hard fans should be able to have a copy. She wanted it to be a very limited run. They would be numbered just as David had done with his Robot Teen America album.

We decided that there would just be one hundred physical copies of *How Humans R(x)* printed, and only ninety of them would be for sale. The other ten were to be split between Gretchen, Jeff, and myself.

We weren't legally allowed to make any money on the album, since the rights still belonged to David's producer, and he denied both Gretchen's and David's mother's many high-priced offers to buy the songs from him. No matter how much money they offered him, Walt just wouldn't sell the album. I was told that an offer even went as a high as ten thousand dollars, and he still wouldn't budge.

In order to prevent any violations, I decided to sell the available ninety copies for the exact amount that they cost me per unit to duplicate. Not only did I purposely fail to make any money on *How Humans R(x)*, but, in the end, I even lost a few hundred dollars.

I made an announcement about the official release of *How Humans R(x)* on the God Lives Underwater website. The first ninety people who contacted me would have a copy reserved for them. Although I received hundreds of emails within the first few days, only the first ninety were answered. I had to rely on each time stamp, since so many flooded my in-box at once.

How Humans R(x) was physically released in December 2009. The response was so overwhelming from fans who weren't able to buy a copy that Gretchen and I had a follow-up meeting about it. I suggested printing another hundred copies, but she vetoed that idea. That would diminish the limited run and the specialness of anyone who had a copy of the album.

At this point Gretchen made me her unofficial advisor for David's estate. This meant that she had full confidence in me to make decisions on anything dealing with David's music in David's best interest. I couldn't help but think back to when I was just an eighteen-year-old fan hanging outside one of his concerts, and how far I had come as a friend and as a business partner, even after his death.

Right after Gretchen awarded me with decision-making abilities, I was contacted by a fan who wanted to release a tribute album to God Lives Underwater. After much deliberation back and forth, I green-lighted *Drowning in Air: A Tribute to God Lives Underwater*. The compilation consisted of bands from all over the country contributing their covers of songs from all four of God Lives Underwater's albums. Transpose even submitted our cover of "Miss You More Than Anything" that we recorded during the *A Delicate Impact* sessions. *Drowning in Air* was released in the summer of 2010.

In 2011 Transpose released our second album, *Retribution*. We played locally and went on multiple regional tours to promote our new album. After *Retribution* was released, we added our cover of "Miss You More Than Anything" into our set list. It had become a fan-favorite. Ironically a large percentage of our audience had no idea it was even a cover of a God Lives Underwater song.

Our version of the song became a staple of our encore and gained so much popularity online that we made a video to the song. We incorporated a lot of the pictures that I took during my trip to Ambler in 2006 when I visited David's grave.

After I initially published this book in 2007, and throughout the unofficial release of *How Humans R(x)* in 2009, I received numerous emails from fans all over the world. People asked about how to get a copy of the Fluzee album, the Robot Teen America album, the Heavy songs, and the two solo albums. All of them were either off the market or limitedly released.

Since I wasn't legally allowed to touch or make money from any God Lives Underwater songs or any songs from David's two solo albums, I focused on everything else. I compiled a digital-only anthology called *Life After the So-Called God Lives Underwater Age* which included the two Heavy songs, Fluzee's *7*, Robot Teen America's *Living In Syn*, the entire T.T. the Bear's Place show from 2001, Killing the Barrowbird's *Sunflowers*, Kan Do Kill's *Wintertree*, and A Sheet of Metal's *Fine Trash Alloy*. The compilation was released on the eighth anniversary of David's death, October 16, 2013. It was also the very first official release from Scout Media, the company that Stephanie and I created together.

On a sad note, Wilma, the turtle, finally died on January 13, 2014. To my best guesstimate, she was around eighteen years old.

At the end of 2011, Kerrie acquired a copy of this book and read it. I hadn't spoken to Kerrie since the last time I had seen her back in 1998 with David. I received an email from her, asking if she could chat with me on the phone about the book. I was terrified because I knew that I didn't paint her in the best light throughout this book. I was very honest with my attitude toward her in the narrative. I prepared myself to be berated over the phone.

I called her, and it was actually just the opposite. By the end of our conversation, we switched between laughing and crying while we reminisced. We buried the hatchet for good, and we both had the opportunity to explain how we had felt toward each other during those years. Since Kerrie had this book, she was finally able to see everything through my eyes. It was only after she told me her side of the story that I was able to see the same situations through her eyes. It all boiled down to a matter of perception. She refused to accept an apology from me about the way I portrayed her in this book.

Kerrie described it best when she said, "Everything in this book was written as a snapshot in time, at the time you were experiencing it. Your emotions are honest. You should never apologize for them. As hard as it was to read about how you felt about me, I knew that it came from how much you cared about David. And that's where your real integrity with this book comes from."

With a smile on my face, I hung up the phone and wiped the last few tears from my eyes.

THE DAVID REILLY SONGOGRAPHY

Officially released material

GOD LIVES UNDERWATER
GLU (1993/1995)*
　1. Drag Me Down
　2. No More Love
　3. Lonely Again
　4. Nothing
　5. Try
　6. Waste of Time

Empty (1995)
　1. Still
　2. All Wrong
　3. Fool
　4. Empty
　5. Don't Know How to Be
　6. No More Love*
　7. 23
　8. We Were Wrong
　9. Weaken
　10. Tortoise
　11. Scared

Life in the So-Called Space Age (1998)
1. Intro
2. Rearrange
3. From Your Mouth
4. Can't Come Down
5. Alone Again
6. Behavior Modification
7. The Rush Is Loud
8. Dress Rehearsal for Reproduction
9. Happy?
10. Vapors
11. Medicated to the One I Love (Outro)*

Up off the Floor (2000/2004)*
1. White Noise
2. Tricked
3. 1% (The Long Way Down)
4. Whatever You've Got
5. No Way (You Must Understand)
6. Slip to Fall
7. History
8. 72 Hour Hold
9. Miss You More Than Anything
10. Positivity

non-album tracks
1. Weight (from the *Mortal Kombat: More Kombat* Soundtrack 1996)
2. Stripped (from the *Morning Becomes Eclectic* broadcast 1998)
3. Hush That Noise (B-side from the "Rearrange" single 1998)
4. Fly on the Windscreen (from the *For the Masses* compilation 1998)

5. Choir Boy (outtake from *Up off the Floor* 2000)
6. Fame (from the *15 Minutes* Soundtrack 2001)

> David Reilly – vocals, keyboards, synthesizer, programming, guitar
> Jeff Turzo – vocals, keyboards, synthesizer, programming, guitar
> Andrew McGee – guitar
> Adam Kary – drums (1993 – 1996)
> Scott Garrett – drums (1997 – 2000)
>
> Sean Beavan – bass, programming, extra guitar on *Up off the Floor*
> Pinky Turzo – back-up vocals on "Positivity"
> Dave Alverado – live bass (1996)
> Kevin Agunas – live bass (2000)

* *GLU* was recorded in 1993, but released in 1995.
* "No More Love" – The version on *Empty* is identical to the version on *GLU*.
* "(Outro)" – This is not a separate track number on *Life in the So-Called Space Age*, however, there is a distinct pause of silence after "Medicated to the One I Love" before this untitled lengthy outro starts. I have listed it as "Outro" purely because it is very similar to the "Intro" track that starts the album.
* *Up off the Floor* was recorded in 2000, but released in 2004.

HEAVY (1995)

1. Lost
2. Someone Else

> David Reilly – vocals, guitar, keyboards, drums
> Jeff Turzo – keyboards, synthesizer, drums

ROBOT TEEN AMERICA

Living in Syn (2001)
1. Track 1
2. Track 2
3. Track 3
4. Track 4

    David Reilly - Windows-based music program

FLUZEE

7 (2002)
1. Far from Home
2. Blaming the Truth
3. Take Good Care
4. Situation
5. Final Frontier
6. My Famous Lie
7. December 7th

non-album track
1. R5

    David Reilly – vocals, guitar, bass, keyboards
    Adam Kary – bass, drums, live guitar
    Patrick Haslup – drums

    Jeff Turzo – keyboards & programming on "Blaming the Truth"

    Missy Zahnweh – live bass
    Brett Simonsen – live drums

DAVID REILLY
Inside (2004)*
1. Keep Dreaming
2. 1 Ft. in the Grave
3. Stay
4. Spinning
5. Blaming the Truth*
6. Far from Home*

>David Reilly – vocals, guitar, bass, keyboards, synthesizer, programming, drums
>Jeff Turzo – keyboards & programming on "Blaming the Truth"
>
>Dave Trusso – live guitar
>Benjamin Juul – live drums

* "Blaming the Truth" & "Far from Home" originally appeared on the Fluzee album *7*.

Untrained Minds (2005)
1. Track One
2. Track Two
3. Track Three
4. Track Four

How Humans R(x) (2005/2009)*
1. My 'Til Tomorrow
2. Brokenhearted
3. Just a Clear Mind
4. Crazier Than Me
5. Here We Go Now
6. Final Frontier*
7. Please Come Back
8. Love My Way
9. Take Good Care*
10. Saying Goodbye

non-album track
1. Love Will Complicate

    David Reilly – vocals, guitar, bass, keyboards, synthesizer, programming, drums
    Walt Bass – bass, samples
    Lauren McGinley – violin on "Brokenhearted"
    Dave Sherman – shaker on "Saying Goodbye"
    Brittany Garrison – vocals on "Love Will Complicate"

* "Final Frontier" & "Take Good Care" originally appeared on the Fluzee album *7*.
* *How Humans R(x)* was recorded in 2005, but unofficially released in 2009.

Life After the So-Called God Lives Underwater Age (2013)
(from Heavy):
1. Lost
2. Someone Else

(from Fluzee *7*):
3. Take Good Care
4. Final Frontier
5. Situation
6. My Famous Lie
7. December 7th
8. R5

(from Robot Teen America *Living in Syn*):
9. Living in Syn (Part 1)
10. Living in Syn (Part 2)
11. Living in Syn (Part 3)
11. Living in Syn (Part 4)

(from *Solo Live at T.T. the Bear's Place*):
13. (David explains The Show)

14. Miss You More Than Anything
15. (David talks about tuning his guitar)
16. Can't Come Down
17. Happy?
18. 23
19. (David talks about Tom & Jerry)
20. Lonely Again
21. Medicated to the I Love
22. No More Love
23. (David talks about Monica)
24. Ordinary Man*
25. Whatever You've Got
26. Scared
27. Stripped

(from Killing the Barrowbird *Sunflowers**):
28. Sunflowers (Part 1)
29. Eyebrain, Sightrain
30. Pain
31. Juice
32. Sunflowers (Part 2)

(from Kan Do Kill *Wintertree**):
33. Wintertree
34. Untitled Instrumental

(from A Sheet of *Fine Metal Trash Alloy**):
35. Skaters, You Suck!
36. Mucous
37. Dead Groupies (So Sorry That I Killed You)
38. Pennies from Hell (Escalator to Purgatory)
39. 2much Phlegm!
40. Vomit or Die! (Upchuck)
41. Cruelty to Animals
42. Gum!!!!

* "Ordinary Man" was written when David was sixteen years old in 1987.
* Killing the Barrowbird *Sunflowers* was a demo recoded in 1991.
    David Reilly – vocals, guitar, keyboards, drum machine, samples, synthesizer
* Kan Do Kill *Wintertree* was a demo recorded in 1988.
    Linda LaRosa – vocals
    David Reilly – guitar, bass, keyboards, drum machine
    Dan Francis – live bass
    Bill Eggleton – live drums
* A Sheet of Metal *Fine Trash Alloy* was a demo recorded in 1988.
    Neil "Crazy Man" Harkins – vocals
    David "The Executioner" Reilly – guitar, bass, drum machine

ACKNOWLEDGEMENTS

I would like to thank the following people, all of whom contributed their time and energy to this book:

My wife, Stephanie, who took on the daunting task of proofreading the initial draft and who also stayed on my back during the times that I just didn't feel like writing.

David's sister, Gretchen, who opened her home and her heart to me. The bond that Stephanie and I have with Gretchen is eternal.

Dann Pacuilan, for being my historian. He was always available to discuss, correct, or confirm dates and places of the events written in this book, no matter what time of day or night.

Michael Stewart, for validating any other facts that my memory was fuzzy on.

Jeff Cavanaugh, for donating his time and talents. He recreated the spirit of the narrative as the front cover art.

Hilary Hebert, for transcribing the Armada Sound System's podcast interview in a timely fashion so it could be included in the book.

Dan Golden, for accepting the task of editing and revising the book for its second edition printing.

Katrina KinCannon, for being the primary proofreader for the second edition.

Teresa Evans, for being the concluding proofreader for the second edition.

Denise Barker, for being the copy editor for the second edition.

I would also like to thank all the people who were close to David and who reached out to me to offer any assistance, blessings, or confidence: Jeff Turzo, Andrew McGee, Adam Kary, the late Tim Turzo, Brett Simonsen, Dave Sherman, Brittany Garrison, Dave Trusso, Benjamin Juul, and Lauren McGinley.

www.ingramcontent.com/pod-product-compliance
Lightning Source LLC
Chambersburg PA
CBHW032024290426
44110CB00012B/659